Nariman Skakov is Assistant Professor of Slavic Languages and Literatures at Stanford University.

Published and forthcoming in *KINO: The Russian and Soviet Cinema* Series

Series Editor: Richard Taylor

Advisory Board: Birgit Beumers, Julian Graffy, Denise Youngblood

Alexander Medvedkin: kinofile Filmmakers' Companion
Emma Widdis

Central Asian Cinema: A Complete Companion
Edited by Michael Rouland and Gulnara Abikeyeva

Cinema and Soviet Society: From the Revolution to the Death of Stalin
Peter Kenez

The Cinema of Alexander Sokurov
Edited by Birgit Beumers and Nancy Condee

The Cinema of Tarkovsky: Labyrinths of Space and Time
Nariman Skakov

The Cinema of the New Russia
Birgit Beumers

Dziga Vertov: Defining Documentary Film
Jeremy Hicks

Eisenstein on the Audiovisual: The Montage of Music, Image
Robert Robertson

Film Propaganda: Soviet Russia and Nazi Germany (second, revised edition)
Richard Taylor

Forward Soviet!: History and Non-Fiction Film in the USSR
Graham Roberts

Real Images: Soviet Cinema and the Thaw
Josephine Woll

Russia on Reels: The Russian Idea in Post-Soviet Cinema
Edited by Birgit Beumers

Savage Junctures: Sergei Eisenstein and the Shape of Thinking
Anne Nesbet

Soviet Cinema: Politics and Persuasion under Stalin
Jamie Miller

The Stalinist Musical: Mass Entertainment and Soviet Cinema
Richard Taylor

Vsevolod Pudovkin: Classic Films of the Soviet Avant-Garde
Amy Sargeant

Queries, ideas and submissions to:
Series Editor, Professor Richard Taylor: rtkino@hotmail.co.uk
Cinema Editor at I.B.Tauris, Philippa Brewster: philippabrewster@gmail.com

THE CINEMA OF TARKOVSKY

Labyrinths of Space and Time

Nariman Skakov

Published in 2012 by I.B.Tauris & Co Ltd
6 Salem Road, London W2 4BU
175 Fifth Avenue, New York NY 10010
www.ibtauris.com

Copyright © 2012 Nariman Skakov

The right of Nariman Skakov to be identified as the author of this work has been asserted by him in accordance with the Copyright, Designs and Patent Act 1988.

All rights reserved. Except for brief quotations in a review, this book, or any part thereof, may not be reproduced, stored in or introduced into a retrieval system, or transmitted, in any form or by any means, electronic, mechanical, photocopying, recording or otherwise, without the prior written permission of the publisher.

ISBN   978 1 84885 629 5 (hb)
ISBN   978 1 84885 630 1 (pb)
eISBN 978 0 85773 079 4
ePDF 978 0 85772 119 8

A full CIP record for this book is available from the British Library
A full CIP record is available from the Library of Congress

Library of Congress Catalog Card Number: available

To my mother

KINO: THE RUSSIAN CINEMA

GENERAL EDITOR'S PREFACE

Cinema has been the predominant art form of the first half of the twentieth century, at least in Europe and North America. Nowhere was this more apparent than in the former Soviet Union, where Lenin's remark that 'of all the arts, cinema is the most important' became a cliché and where cinema attendances were until recently still among the highest in the world. In the age of mass politics Soviet cinema developed from a fragile but effective tool to gain support among the overwhelmingly illiterate peasant masses in the civil war that followed the October 1917 Revolution, through a welter of experimentation, into a mass weapon of propaganda through entertainment that shaped the public image of the Soviet Union – both at home and abroad and for both elite and mass audiences – and latterly into an instrument to expose the weaknesses of the past and present in the twin processes of *glasnost* and *perestroika*. Now the national cinemas of the successor republics to the old USSR are encountering the same bewildering array of problems, from the trivial to the terminal, as are all the other ex-Soviet institutions.

Cinema's central position in Russian and Soviet cultural history, and its unique combination of mass medium, art form and entertainment industry, have made it a continuing battlefield for conflicts of broader ideological and artistic significance, not only for Russia and the Soviet Union, but also for the world outside. The debates that raged in the 1920s about the relative merits of documentary as opposed to fiction film, of cinema as opposed to theatre or painting, or of the proper role of cinema in the forging of post-Revolutionary Soviet culture and the shaping of the new Soviet man, have their echoes in current discussions about the role of cinema *vis-à-vis* other art forms in effecting the cultural and psychological revolution in human consciousness necessitated by the processes of economic and political transformation of the former Soviet Union into modern democratic and industrial societies and states governed by the rule of law. Cinema's central position has also made it a vital instrument for scrutinising the blank pages of Russian and Soviet history and enabling the present generation to come to terms with its own past.

This series of books intends to examine Russian, Soviet and ex-Soviet films in the context of Russian, Soviet and ex-Soviet cinemas, and Russian, Soviet and ex-Soviet cinemas in the context of the political history of Russia, the Soviet Union, the post-Soviet 'space' and the world at large. Within that framework the series, drawing its authors from both East and West, aims to cover a wide variety of topics and to employ a broad range of methodological approaches and presentational formats. Inevitably this will involve ploughing once again over old ground in order to re-examine received opinions, but it principally means increasing the breadth and depth of our knowledge, finding new answers to old questions and, above all, raising new questions for further enquiry and new areas for further research.

The continuing aim of this series is to situate Russian, Soviet and ex-Soviet cinema in its proper historical and aesthetic context, both as a major cultural force and as a crucible for experimentation that is of central significance to the development of world cinema culture. Books in the series strive to combine the best of scholarship – past, present and future – with a style of writing that is accessible to a broad readership, whether that readership's primary interest lies in cinema or in political history.

Richard Taylor
Swansea, Wales

CONTENTS

x	List of Illustrations
xi	Acknowledgements
xii	Note on Transliteration
1	On Space(s) and Time(s)
15	Chapter 1 Dreams of *Ivan's Childhood*
42	Chapter 2 Visions of *Andrei Rublev*
74	Chapter 3 Phantasies of *Solaris*
100	Chapter 4 Memories of *Mirror*
140	Chapter 5 Revelations of *Stalker*
167	Chapter 6 Recollections of *Nostalghia*
193	Chapter 7 Illusions of *Sacrifice*
217	Postscript
222	Notes
241	Filmography and Credits
249	Bibliography
260	Index

ILLUSTRATIONS

Pages		Chapter 1
18	[1.1]	*Ivan's Childhood*: the beginning
23	[1.2]	*Ivan's Childhood*: the well scene
33	[1.3]	*Ivan's Childhood*: the negative scene
38	[1.4]	*Ivan's Childhood*: the end

Pages		Chapter 2
43	[2.1]	*Andrei Rublev*: the beginning
52	[2.2]	*Andrei Rublev*: the Russian Crucifixion
58	[2.3]	*Andrei Rublev*: the 'Hymn to Love' sequence
64	[2.4]	*Andrei Rublev*: the iconostasis
72	[2.5]	*Andrei Rublev*: the end

Pages		Chapter 3
76	[3.1]	*Solaris*: the beginning
79	[3.2]	*Solaris*: the tin box with soil
87	[3.3]	*Solaris*: the library scene
97	[3.4]	*Solaris*: the end

Pages		Chapter 4
106	[4.1]	*Mirror*: reflections
116	[4.2]	*Mirror*: the dream
127	[4.3]	*Mirror*: the 'Life, Life' sequence
131	[4.4]	*Mirror*: the house surrounded by the wood
138	[4.5]	*Mirror*: the end

Pages		Chapter 5
145	[5.1]	*Stalker*: the beginning
150	[5.2]	*Stalker*: the Revelation scene
158	[5.3]	*Stalker*: the Emmaus scene
165	[5.4]	*Stalker*: the end

Pages		Chapter 6
170	[6.1]	*Nostalghia*: the beginning
179	[6.2]	*Nostalghia*: doubling
187	[6.3]	*Nostalghia*: flawed buildings
191	[6.4]	*Nostalghia*: the end

Pages		Chapter 7
196	[7.1]	*Sacrifice*: the first apocalyptic vision
208	[7.2]	*Sacrifice*: the encounter with Maria and reflections
211	[7.3]	*Sacrifice*: the final apocalyptic vision
214	[7.4]	*Sacrifice*: the beginning and the end

ACKNOWLEDGEMENTS

I would like to express my sincere gratitude to Julian Graffy, who has been my inspiring mentor and patient reader for the last eight years. This book could not have been written without his guidance.

Nancy Ruttenburg provided scrupulous, imaginative and sympathetic commentary on the manuscript – a dream for any author. Julie Draskoczy, Kiersten Jakobsen, Folahan Olowoyeye, Tom Roberts, Natasha Synessios and Richard Taylor shared with me their illuminating insights and set productive challenges. My editors at I.B.Tauris, Philippa Brewster and Cecile Rault, have provided a great deal of support and encouragement. I am also grateful to Anna Lordan for her patient proofreading. Any mistakes that remain are my responsibility.

I wish to offer heartfelt thanks to my Oxford mentors, friends and colleagues for their everlasting intellectual presence in my life: Philip Ross Bullock, Reidar Due, Catriona Kelly, Martin Kemp, Alexander Morrison, Michael Nicholson, George Pattison, Thomas Welsford, Andrei Zorin and the bartenders at the Lamb & Flag.

I am also indebted to my Stanford colleagues and friends who generously shared their ideas with me and created such a stimulating environment for work and research: Adrian Daub, Gregory Freidin, Marisa Galvez, Monika Greenleaf, Hans Ülrich Gumbrecht, Héctor Hoyos, Pavle Levi, Gabriella Safran and Laura Wittman.

Finally, I would like to thank Aleksei Danilov, Veta Kravchenko, Alibek Mergenov, Rachel van Mitten Wedgwood Michael and Zhanara Nauruzbayeva for their inspiring friendship, which keeps me sane. I would also like to express my gratitude to Moshe Feldstein – Nimrod of rare rhymes – for keeping me company at the gym and for blissful poetic moments.

NOTE ON TRANSLITERATION

The transliteration system used for proper names in the text of this study is that of the Library of Congress, without diacritics, with the following emendations:

1) When a Russian name has a clear English version, such as Eisenstein, Dostoevsky, that is preferred.
2) When a Russian surname ends in -ii or -yi, this is replaced by a single -y, e.g. Tarkovsky.
3) When a Russian given name ends in -ii, this is replaced by a single -i, e.g. Arseni.

The standard Library of Congress system is used in the Notes, the Filmography and the Bibliography.

ON SPACE(S) AND TIME(S)

If the flow is slow enough and you have a good bicycle, or a horse, it is possible to bathe twice (or even three times, should your personal hygiene so require) in the same river.

Augusto Monterroso

On 15 February 1971 the Russian film-maker Andrei Tarkovsky noted in his diary: 'For many years I have been tormented by the certainty that the most extraordinary discoveries await us in the sphere of Time. We know less about time than about anything else.'[1] The phenomenon of 'Time', not just mere 'time', was a central preoccupation of the director throughout his career. Tarkovsky's enigmatic and occasionally disjointed remarks were supplemented by repeated references to ideas about time from Heraclitus, Montaigne and Schopenhauer. However, while one does not find a comprehensive and uniform philosophical treatment of time in the director's texts and notes, his cinema reveals a highly original and consistent *vision* of time. The unhurried and elongated nature of Tarkovsky's films makes time an almost palpable, yet elusive and fragile 'entity'. It was probably this kind of time that the Russian poet Osip Mandelstam compared with a 'shy chrysalis, [a] cabbage butterfly sprinkled with flour'.[2]

Mandelstam's metaphor makes us think of inconspicuous change, slow movement and permanent evanescence – qualities which are strongly associated with the image of time encountered in each of the seven feature films by the Russian master. However, the vividness of the given metaphors is achieved by virtue of their physicality: the muffled chrysalis and the butterfly wings sprinkled with flour are palpable, spatial images. Time is spread out in space, and it evolves into the notion of plastic temporality. Cinema, which organizes spatially localizable visual elements in time, testifies to this evolution. Tarkovsky appeared to ignore the apparent fact that extraordinary discoveries await us also in the sphere of 'Space'.

Time

Time as such lies at the core of Tarkovsky's aesthetic framework, which he discusses intricately in numerous texts. The two English-language publications of his writings – his diary and his book on film art – both have the word *time* in their titles: *Time Within Time* and *Sculpting in Time* constitute a quest to comprehend and to locate the fourth dimension. But, more importantly, the director's thoughts about various temporally bound components of the cinematic image, such as the colour and texture of filmed objects, his trademark long take and, lastly, his major aesthetic formula – cinema as 'sculpting in time' or 'imprinted time' – celebrate the temporal qualities of cinema. These strategies reveal time respectively as an agent of change, as duration and as an all-encompassing reservoir of being and creativity.

In *Sculpting in Time*, Tarkovsky claims that 'even though the world is coloured, the black-and-white image comes closer to the psychological, naturalistic truth of art'.[3] However, if the cinematographer is to use colour, he or she should do it with the utmost care, since colour reveals the condition of physical matter over time, its change and its endurance. Thus, leaves changing colour or rust on an old gate are ideal filmic images revealing a natural process – nature immersed in duration. Physical matter faces the unpalatable fact of impermanence and decays with the passage of time. Tarkovsky's sensitivity to colour partially explains the use of variable types and gradations of colouration in every single film with the exception of *Ivan's Childhood*, which is shot entirely in black and white. Each time there is a transition from monochrome into colour photography, usually accomplished through images of nature, the viewer is made aware of the temporal motion – the textures of objects reveal the passage of time.

The same passage of time is a key feature of the *long take* – the embodiment of Tarkovsky's vision of cinema. It is undoubtedly the director's most celebrated stylistic device, the abundant use of which was justified as an attempt to represent 'real time' within a single shot. The long take can be defined as an uninterrupted – and in Tarkovsky's case usually slow-paced – cinematic shot which lasts longer than the conventional editing pace of the film. The long take remains open and refuses to be closed (edited), striving towards continuous presence. It invites the viewer to put aside the narrative framework and to contemplate time in its pure form – to locate 'TIME within TIME'.[4]

However, the centrepiece of Tarkovsky's preoccupation with the notion of time remains his vision of cinema as a process of 'sculpting in time'. The formula emerges in the third chapter of his book:

> What is the essence of the director's work? We could define it as sculpting in time... the film-maker, from a 'lump of time' made up of an enormous, solid cluster of living facts, cuts off and discards whatever he does not need, leaving only what is to be an element of the finished film, what will prove to be integral to the cinematic image.[5]

Time captured, imprinted, and preserved in its natural forms and manifestations, is the ultimate foundation of film art for Tarkovsky. Reality, as living facts plunged into the flow of time, is turned into its impression – a cinematic image – by means of temporal cuts. Thus, an ability to detect the passage of time becomes a necessary cinematic tool: a film-maker should observe mundane and simple events through the prism of time in order to reveal cinema's essential ambition 'to convey a sense of fact and of texture [*fakta i faktury*], dwelling and changing in time.'[6] In this light, it becomes clear why Tarkovsky sees documentary chronicle as 'the ultimate cinema':[7] the genre stands for the process of observation and reconstruction of reality per se, where fact regains its texture.

The 'sculpting in time' formula, together with his penchant for the abundant use of long takes, naturally places Tarkovsky in opposition to the intellectual montage advanced by Sergei Eisenstein. For the early Soviet film-maker, cinema provides a largely figurative reference to reality, and its essence lies in the director's ability to assemble disparate and usually short shots to form a coherent and assertive discourse. Montage is thus generally perceived to be a process in which reality is fragmented and then reorganized into a dialectical framework, where new ideas emerge from the collision of disparate visual elements. It strives to deliver an unambiguous emotional or political message. As André Bazin notes, this type of montage does not show the viewer an event, it merely alludes to it.[8] For Tarkovsky, on the other hand, cinema reveals reality in its full objective glory. Montage should always remain hidden, since its obtrusive presence disrupts the passage of time.[9] Its mission is to juxtapose shots filled with time and not with meanings.[10] Moreover, 'time flows in a film not by virtue but *in defiance* of montage-cuts'.[11] Consequently, the switch from the linear, semantic plane of the montage of representations to the temporal domain presents an abstract image of 'captured' time – the 'sculpture' of time.

The film-maker's fixation with the notion of time has been noted by many commentators,[12] among whom Gilles Deleuze occupies a special place. Some of the most illuminating pages of Tarkovsky criticism are connected with the discussion of the influential film theory concept of *time-image*, and its derivative, *crystal-image*. Deleuze's famous dichotomy – the pragmatic, character-bound *movement-image* of so-called classical cinema vs. the abstract *time-image* of post-war cinema – can be read as a clash of subordination between two fundamental concepts: space and time. Movement-image is a bearer of narrative, and comprises a linear progression of spaces and characters organized by means of montage. Time-image, in contrast, presents an abstract situation with loose narrative ends – it 'creates paradoxical movements'.[13] Deleuze also suggests that one of the ways for the direct time-image to come into existence is through the crystal-image – a convergence of an actual present and a virtual past image, to the extent that they cannot be distinguished.[14] The cinema of Tarkovsky, for Deleuze, is an embodiment of the latter:

> There are crystallized spaces, when the landscapes become hallucinatory in a setting which now retains only crystalline seeds and crystallizable materials. Now what characterizes these spaces is that their nature cannot be explained in a simply spatial way. They imply non-localizable relations. These are direct presentations of time. We no longer have an indirect image of time which derives from movement, but a direct time-image from which movement derives. We no longer have a chronological time which can be overturned by movements which are contingently abnormal; we have a chronic non-chronological time which produces movements necessarily 'abnormal', essentially 'false'.[15]

This 'chronic non-chronological time' helps to reveal cinema's potential to organize time in a non-empirical way. Time in *time-image* seems to liberate itself from the burden of the three spatial dimensions – setting or character relations no longer represent a linear progression of narrative in time, but are presented in a completely disjointed state. Space is no longer a location of action and a site of interaction. Indeed, many of Tarkovsky's characters inhabit hallucinatory landscapes, completely lose the sense of spatial orientation, and, consequently, dwell in the 'chronic non-chronological time'.

However, there is a striking difference between Deleuze's theory and Tarkovsky's praxis. While the former's metaphysics of time is based on the mathematical-structuralist concept of controlled variation and presents the image of time devoid of any moral or theological 'burden', the latter's temporal 'sculptures' are overwhelmingly anthropocentric, and they strive towards a certain divine ideal. Time for both, though differently conceived, is an essential category, and discussions of it almost stagnate into a fixation of habit. Deleuze's time-argument in his two-volume study and Tarkovsky's reflections on cinema are supplemented by a recurring reference to Hamlet's perception of the universe, where 'time is out of joint' – this assertion about temporality reveals the dramatic essence of the discourse at stake.

Space and Time

However, the argument of this book is that space is also out of place, and this displaced place is an intrinsic part of the 'out of joint' time, for *joint* refers to a junction at which two entities (that is, space and time) are joined or fitted together.[16] The topographical curve of the river of time is too prominent to be ignored. *Space* does matter, and the notion still shapes Tarkovsky's and his commentators' temporally 'obsessed' discourses. At some points space emerges as an idea-trace in the process of complete erasure and at times as a concept that endures drastic reformulation. The persistent attempts to underrate or even suppress the spatial constituent of cinematic experience by elevating its temporal qualities, so vigorous in the second half of the twentieth century, expose themselves in their full glory in the cases of Tarkovsky and Deleuze. However, space evades the underrating and suppression – as Michel Foucault puts it, 'it is not possible to disregard the fatal intersection of time with space.'[17] Time is an event which takes place.

The situation is akin to Borges' story 'The Garden of Forking Paths', which presents an artefact – a combination of book and maze – invented and written by the former governor of Yunnan, Ts'ui Pên.[18] In the story, the labyrinth-text comprises an attempt to rethink the category of time; it describes a world in which all possible outcomes of an event occur simultaneously, and this leads to a further proliferation of possibilities – the forking takes place in time, not in space, though the metaphor used ('forking') is inherently spatial. What is striking is that while time is the sole point of concern for the fictional author, he does not use the word that signifies time in the narrative. As Borges writes: '*The Garden of Forking Paths* is an enormous riddle, or parable, whose theme is time; this recondite cause prohibits its mention. To omit a word always, to resort to inept metaphors and obvious periphrases, is perhaps the most emphatic way of stressing'.[19] Borges' apophatic narratives create a sense of mystifying presence by advancing a blatant absence. In a way, the cinema of Tarkovsky and critical discourses around it follow this path, with one exception: the victim of suppression, and hence the subject of expression, is the notion of space. To follow the metaphor further, forking paths regain the three spatial dimensions and evolve into a spatio-temporal labyrinth.

Space as such emanates from Tarkovsky's three time-sensitive concepts mentioned above. The colour photography reveals the progression of time by exclusively spatial means: time manifests itself on the surfaces of objects such as a rusting gate or changing leaves – texture expresses the specific state of matter in the film. The long take, in its turn, is an elongated dwelling in a single (though extended) space, while sculpting in time is literally a process of the spatialization of time. A vision of time is always accomplished through the spatial prism. The two entities are interrelated and, as Éric Rohmer suggests, 'spatial forms of expression must correspond to a film's general method of expressing time'.[20] Moreover, film is divided into static frames which are then projected or spatialized to produce an illusion of continuity. Indeed, spatialization of time lies at the heart of cinematic experience, for cinema organizes spatial elements in time, and Tarkovsky's art is no exception.

In a diary entry of 11 January 1981, omitted in the English edition, Tarkovsky entertains the idea of making a film which would consist only of ten episodes, with time or temporal progression as their sole foundation.[21] Time in these episodes would function as the main aesthetic feature and would be imprinted through varying emotional, atmospheric and optical states. The director chooses transitional, unstable and difficult-to-capture natural phenomena – twilight, dispersing fog, air without a breeze, intermittent rain – as states conveying temporal qualities. However, as is the case with colour, time manifests itself through space – natural topoi allow temporal progression to be perceptible. If this project were executed, the viewer would be presented with an abstract image of time located in a concrete spatial framework.

The spatio-temporal dynamics are even more intricate in the renowned Tarkovskian long take, with which the director created some of the most memorable images of temporal flow. The single continuum of the long take purposely stretches a monotonous, mundane experience and provides an alternative mode of perceiving reality.[22] Once external spatial markers are removed, time is exposed as a fleeting phenomenon. Action or movement, as agents of space, cease to have a purely narrative end – the very fact of their continuous presence in time becomes more significant. In Deleuze's words, the real plane is 'no longer represented or reproduced but "aimed at".'[23] The importance and uniqueness of each moment is thus underlined and temporal markers are glossed over, so that the viewer can experience an instant of life in its singularity, which reveals 'the dominant note of every moment of existence'.[24] This shift of accent from narrative to duration culminates in the semblance of a semantic crisis – the meaning is not imposed on the viewer, but is hidden away or scattered in time. The constant expectation that semantic implications will reveal themselves in the single continuum of the long take tends to exhaust the viewer. No quick-and-easy resolution is available – hence Tarkovsky's notoriety as a challenging or even 'boring' director.

The elevation of the temporal plane, taking place in the long take, is achieved through spatial manipulation – the way space is perceived by the viewer undergoes a qualitative change. The camera movement in the long take reveals a single vision of an event, instead of providing a multiplicity of views of it. The physicality of space becomes manifest because of identification with the camera. This feature is underlined in the early writings of Béla Balázs, who describes an experience of a long take in the following way: 'Spatial *continuity* is not disrupted. We feel the space, not merely as a container, a frame for the objects, but *the space itself*, independently of the individual objects it contains.'[25] Moreover, in addition to the sense of embodiment, the long take can be described as a temporal continuity where every moment is a memento of a transcendental quality, since the viewer tracks a sweeping movement without any motor effort on his or her own part. As some critics suggest, the viewer's glance occupies a privileged, unique space, which is also 'the place of God, or the all-perceiving subject, gifted with ubiquity'.[26]

The extreme examples of the long take in Tarkovsky's cinema are those sequences in which time becomes an almost palpable, that is, spatial, entity. Of this temporal materiality Walter Benjamin writes with respect to Baudelaire's poetry: 'time is reified: the minutes cover a man like snowflakes'.[27] The panning circular sequence in a peasant's hut in *Andrei Rublev*, the shots of nature in *Solaris*, the recurring forest images in *Mirror*, the threshold of the wish-room sequence in *Stalker*, Gorchakov carrying a candle in the pool in Bagno Vignoni in *Nostalghia* and Alexander's apocalyptic vision in *Sacrifice* are all expressions of the long take in its pure form: the viewer is enveloped in time. Moreover, the apparent absence of action, and hence the monotony, in these instances creates a narrative emptiness that generates an urge to fill it with some kind of meaning or metaphysical presence.

Finally, the 'sculpting in time' formula also contains in itself traces of space. The terms of cartography (the science of registering space) and chronology (the science of registering time) make one think that space is usually associated with writing (*graphia*) and time with speech (*logos*). The term 'cinematography' thus consists of two spatial terms: in addition to *graphia* there is *kinēma* ('movement') and the combination of the two makes 'inscribing motion'. 'Sculpting in time', as an alternative to cinematography, preserves the *graphia* part, for 'sculpting' is synonymous with 'inscribing'. However, movement is sacrificed for the sake of time: *chrónos* takes over *kinēma*. The director's formula becomes a spatio-temporal entity.[28] It should be noted, however, that this rhetorical move does not constitute a ground-breaking concept, since Bazin as early as the late 1950s, claims in his discussion of the ontology of photography that 'the image of things is likewise the image of their duration, change mummified as it were'.[29] Cinema's characteristic feature, for the French critic, is an ability to remove art from the state of 'catalepsy' and to present an image of duration.

What makes Bazin's and Tarkovsky's metaphors unique is their inherent ambiguity: 'change mummified' and 'sculpting in time' are impossible amalgams, which are bound to remain mere figures of speech. The cinematographic objective 'merely' to record motion is replaced by an ambition to capture temporal flow. Time, however, is not a palpable substance and is never static. Even in its recorded form, as an edited cinematic sequence with 'the actuality of time'[30] being printed on celluloid, or more abstractly as 'a matrix of *actual time*',[31] time still resists that occupation of a certain spatial point that is a prerequisite for sculptural material (physical matter). Time cannot be conceived of using the three spatial dimensions because it itself constitutes a fourth, qualitatively different dimension. Thus, Tarkovsky defines his art in impossibly possible terms – his definition is based on the constant striving towards the unachievable.

The given confusion is a relatively common problem, for time is often thought of as space-like (for instance, in the concept of temporal topology), and some philosophers suggest that instead of two separate empirical realities, space and time, there is but one entity, an extensive continuum called *space-time*.³² Physicists also believe that time is not independent of space, and the theory of relativity posits that there is no categorical distinction between the space and time coordinates, just as any two spatial coordinates belong to the same empirical category. Moreover, it is commonplace to claim that the human awareness of time is spatially bound: the progression of externally localized events (causal relations) makes temporal relations manifest themselves.

Space and time are indeed fundamentally interrelated – neither taken by itself can exist without the other. Points and moments are interconnected – time is intrinsically spatial, while space is intrinsically temporal. The Russian critic Mikhail Bakhtin follows this presupposition and unites the two categories in the influential concept of the *chronotope* (literally 'time-place'). The chronotope is the matrix governing all narratives, and the concept derives from the stance that 'time is *profoundly spatial and concrete*. It is not separated from the earth or from nature. It, as well as the entire life of the human being, is all on the surface.'³³

The essential interdependence between space and time is reflected in the ways in which their meanings are negotiated in dictionaries. 'Time' is traditionally defined as a 'limited stretch or space of continued existence, as the interval between two successive events or acts, or the period through which an action, condition, or state continues' (*Oxford English Dictionary*, henceforth *OED*). This standard definition situates time in the chronological or narrative domains, and spatial *marking*, as it has been known since the time of Aristotle, is crucial to this understanding of temporal flow (seconds of the clock, tree-rings, pendulums, the sun and stars, actions – all serve as indicators). To complicate the matter further, the *OED*'s definition of 'space' is also an intricate 'confusion' between space and time. The first entry defines space as '[d]enoting time or duration' and is followed by a definition which construes the same term as '[d]enoting area or extension'.

The confusion dates back to the most famous attempt to spatialize time in the history of philosophy – Zeno's paradox. It comprises a thought experiment which posits that Achilles can never overtake the slow tortoise once he has allowed it a head start because whenever the speedy warrior reaches a point where the tortoise has been, he still has farther to go because his contender has moved on slightly. This physically improbable but mathematically plausible condition results from the fact that Achilles must reach an infinite number of points in space – an endless series of tasks – before overtaking the moving reptile, whatever its speed. This infinite spatial progression means that it is impossible for the race to end in time: temporal eternity emerges from this spatial infinity.

According to Henri-Louis Bergson,[34] this paradox is a mere illusion because Zeno of Elea represents time by spatial means; that is, time and movement coincide with the line that underlines them – the path of Achilles and the tortoise. Movement, however, is indivisible and not 'made of immobilities'.[35] Nor can time be represented by static instants. The *OED* definitions thus fall into a trap by applying spatial markers to represent time. They seem to ignore the fact that the essence of time – duration – lies beyond the stasis of space. The confusion results from the fact that language always 'translates movement and duration in terms of space',[36] and that is why *experience*, for the French philosopher, should become the gateway to the domain of time. The discontinuity of physical life seems to be an issue for Bergson, and he suggests as an alternative the concept of *durée* – an endless continuity perceived not by some kind of abstract analytic skills but by first-person intuition.

Bergson clearly tries to make the notion of time assume a role of dominance over space: he suggests that '[q]uestions relating to subject and object, to their distinction and their union, should be put in terms of time rather than of space'.[37] At the same time, his definitions of *durée* are permeated with spatial sentiments: duration is 'the continuous progress of the past which gnaws into the future and which *swells* as it advances'; it is also 'a stream against which we cannot go' or, finally, '[w]herever anything lives, there is [...] a register in which time is being *inscribed*'.[38] Swelling, stream and inscription are manifestly spatial terms. Deleuze, the author of *Bergsonism*[39] – a text that attempts to foster 'a return of Bergson' and extension of his project – occupies a similar antinomic stance. The critic dedicates three chapters to Bergson in his two-volume cinema study and puts forward the concept of aberrant movement, as illustrated in the cinema of time-image. While movement-image comprises the subordination of time to movement in space, time-image is liberated from space by the deconstruction of the spatial coordinates. Time, which evades empirical, spatial rigidity, is Deleuze's alternative to Zeno's linearity of spatialized time.

In the passage cited above on Tarkovsky's crystal-image and chronic non-chronological time, Deleuze refers to spatial concepts undergoing a process of self-deconstruction: crystallized topoi, hallucinatory landscapes, abnormal and aberrant movements constitute a set of non-localizable relations. These 'spaces' avoid centring, resist being placed on the Cartesian system of coordinates, and become emptied and disconnected 'any-space-whatever',[40] which replaces qualified, extended space. 'Any-space-whatever' is a domain characterized in purely optical or sonic terms, and has clear affinities with Tarkovsky's imagined film project about time where scenes from nature, as opposed to dramatic action, comprise the sole filmed matter. The resulting disembodied view of the world lacks an acting subject. Instead, it presents a 'mere' seer. Deleuze's intellectual project resulted in a substantial shift in theories of cinema. However, this resolute attempt to liberate time from the dictatorship of space on the cinematic screen is still infiltrated by spatial categories. 'Any-space-whatever', though reconceptualized, remains a space.

Spaces and Times

Space and time, once withdrawn from the theoretical domain and put into the realm of cinematic praxis, cease to be conceived of as forming a homogenous entity and evolve into discontinuous spatio-temporal threads. Diverse takes, made at different times, are woven together by film-makers to create what appears to be a continuous cinematic image. Thus the evident continuity of film, as Robert Stam suggests, 'consists of a perpetual discontinuity'.[41] Tarkovsky's cinematic project is remarkable not only because it does not hide the discontinuous nature of cinema; its distinctive essence lies in the fact that it amplifies the discontinuity of the filmic experience. The director's films, from *Ivan's Childhood* to *Sacrifice*, create non-linear relationships between separate times, places and people. By exploring the ephemeral qualities of cinema – its imaginary, oneiric and hallucinatory potential – Tarkovsky implies that homogenous, 'real' reality is also an artificial construct.

The status of the cinematographic apparatus, as 'a realist guarantee for the unreal',[42] has led a number of film theorists to find inspiration in the revealing/concealing space of Plato's cave from *The Republic*. Chained people watching shadows on the wall in the allegory of the Cave – that is, immobile viewers in a movie theatre – offer a powerful metaphor for how reality manifests itself in a ghostly fashion. However, René Descartes' 'dream argument' from *Meditations on First Philosophy* may be related more plausibly to the spatio-temporal discontinuity of Tarkovsky's cinema. The argument posits that the act of dreaming functions as evidence that the senses we trust to distinguish reality from illusion deceive us from time to time. The Cartesian postulate that there are 'never any sure signs by means of which being awake can be distinguished from being asleep'[43] tells us that imaginary spatio-temporal frameworks do infiltrate the objective domain of the real. A dream, a phantasy or an illusion of the senses is an experience that fails to fit into the unitary spatio-temporal scheme. The same concerns caused the Russian poet Joseph Brodsky to claim: 'For, on the scales of truth, intensity of imagination counterbalances and at times outweighs reality.'[44]

The British idealist philosopher Francis Herbert Bradley[45] continues the Cartesian line of scepticism, and suggests that there is no single all-embracing space-time but a plurality of spaces and times. Bradley wonders: why should we take time as one succession and not as a multitude of series? In support of this challenge, he draws attention to the relation between events in dreams and those in fictional stories. In these imaginary narratives, events are indisputably temporal entities, since they are temporally related to other events in the same imaginary narratives. Yet these events cannot be located in the framework of objective historical time. In addition, the temporal span of a fictional story or dream is usually much greater than its actual duration, and events are not always arranged in a linear manner – memories from childhood or flashbacks can easily interfuse with current events. Bradley underlines differences between physical (objective, vast and systematic) and experiential (subjective, minute and fragmented) space and time.

Unlike these philosophers, Tarkovsky does not *represent* various spaces and times through coherent argument, but rather *enacts* relationships between them on the cinema screen. Thus the viewer experiences the argument. While the phenomenological nature of space and time is tackled by thinkers by exclusively verbal means (for instance, as a reflection on the ontological status of objects, or on certain grammatical phenomena such as the reality or unreality of tensed sentences), the director's films present *visions* of space and time. Spatio-temporal discontinuity and disconnectedness are characteristic features of Tarkovsky's cinema: it lacks the homogenously stretched four-dimensional continuum. The director displaces topographical coordinates and imposes temporal leaps: he enters the cinematic labyrinth at times by means of a spatial aberration and at times through a temporal anomaly. These displacements and leaps create narrative digressions, which consequently disorientate the viewer.

While storyline in conventional cinema functions as a spatio-temporal regulator, the loose narratives of Tarkovsky's films do not create a linear progression in space and time (these are not the clear waters of the Heraclitean river) but constitute a multiplicity of muddled (muddy) streams – they accomplish a move 'from established absolutes to unstable conditionals'.[46] Tarkovsky contrasts the latter with the linear logic of the former when describing his aesthetic strategy: 'I am seeking a principle of montage, which would permit me to show the subjective logic – the thought, the dream, the memory – instead of the logic of the subject. [I try to] show things which are not necessarily linked logically.'[47] Spatio-temporal discontinuity and disconnectedness indeed mark the processes of thinking, dreaming and remembering.

* * *

The theory and praxis of Tarkovsky's cinema in many ways follow the forking path of Deleuze's time-image discourse. Space undergoes a conceptual modification while time emerges as a renewed phenomenon with great force. The Russian verb the film-maker uses in his key aesthetic formula for 'to sculpt' is *vaiat'*, which is connected with *vit'* – 'to weave', that is, to form a continuous web of interlacing yarns. 'Weaving in time' strengthens the spatial aura of the formula: 'sculpture in time' becomes 'texture of time'. Tarkovsky's films, one may suggest, have a certain complex texture, a textile labyrinth, where the relationship between individual temporal threads (past–present–future) is not immediately apparent. The result is a consistent re-enactment of non-linear relationships between various spatio-temporal frameworks. Every point in space 'remembers' events at different dates, while every instant of time is 'filled' with events at different places. Both space and time always already contain spatio-temporal multiplicity, and the director simply amplifies this quality.

The absence of a linear continuum is one of the key features of the seven films that will be discussed in the present book.[48] Dreams, visions, phantasies, memories, revelations, recollections and illusions are phenomena which present alternative spatio-temporal patterns; they disrupt the linear progression of events and create narrative discontinuity. Within each chapter, dedicated to the discussion of one of Tarkovsky's seven feature films, one of these phenomena will function as a refrain. The films' characters constantly re-enter atemporal zones where rigid frontiers between present and past are removed, where the past is revisited by the present and vice versa. Their quests, which are usually spiritual in nature, are not connected with a place governed by a single temporal pattern. Memories from the past, visions of the future and mere 'irrelevant' hallucinations all displace them both temporally and spatially. A number of stylistic traits and recurring motifs of Tarkovsky's visual universe function as spatio-temporal destabilizers. Irrational cuts, filters, and the use of varied film stock (monochrome, black and white, colour) disturb linear narrative. The Tarkovskian soundtrack, or rather soundscape, does not transparently cue emotions or moods, but adds to spatio-temporal disorientation. The director employs cinematographic means to deliver a commentary on the human condition, which for him constitutes an experience of reality as a subjective layering of inextricable snippets of various times and spaces.

1

DREAMS OF *IVAN'S CHILDHOOD*

The production history of *Ivan's Childhood* (*Ivanovo detstvo*, 1962), Tarkovsky's debut feature film, is a story of drudgery and labour in vain, but with a triumphant ending. The Mosfilm studio initially commissioned Eduard Abalov to adapt a novella by Vladimir Bogomolov for the screen, but then stopped the production due to the unsatisfactory quality of the rushes. A year later, in June 1961, a new artistic team was appointed, with Andrei Tarkovsky as its director. The script, which was based on a typical Soviet war-hero text, subsequently underwent drastic changes and the previously filmed material was discarded in its entirety. The resurrected film features key elements of Tarkovsky's aesthetics and launches his intricate cinematic journey in space and time. In spite of being rooted in the socialist-realist tradition, however, *Ivan's Childhood* transcends the rigid boundaries of the genre. The film still traces the fate of Ivan: it shows how the wandering child becomes a war hero by joining reconnaissance troops and providing crucial information for the Soviet army at the cost of his life, but the heroic war narrative is transformed into a drama of lost childhood. Ivan's military achievements are overshadowed by his castaway, orphaned condition – the boy is stripped of heroism and glory.

This transformation in some way explains why Abalov's film project and the novella, both succinctly titled *Ivan* (a simple personal name), became the film *Ivan's Childhood* (the noun 'childhood' paired with the possessive adjective of 'Ivan' in the original Russian). The chronotope of childhood is non-existent in the text, while it shapes the cinematic adaptation. A vision of real and at the same time abstract childhood, not the figure of Ivan with his military exploits, is the sole concern of the film. First lieutenant Galtsev, the conventional first-person narrator of the text, gives way to Ivan – the visionary narrator within the film. The child-protagonist, however, does not direct or oversee the progression of events – there are no internal monologues or off-screen commentaries: he is merely a seer who longs for his childhood.

The difference between the literary precursor (the novella *Ivan*) and the cinematic successor is striking, and already manifests itself in the way the two works begin their narratives. 'I intended to check the battle outposts that night, and, giving orders to wake me at 4.00, I turned in a little after eight'[1] is the straightforward and somewhat uninspiring opening sentence of Bogomolov's novella. It announces the military setting and provides precise and factual information. The writer, who himself joined the Soviet army in his teens and served in military intelligence, offers competent knowledge of warfare, and the reader gets a sense of what lies ahead from the very first sentence – a tragic but life-affirming heroic narrative, which unambiguously presents the heroism of the Soviet people in their struggle against the ruthless enemy. More importantly, the novella begins with the pronoun 'I' – a definite grammatical construction. The reader is not yet aware who this 'I' is, but its presence is already established. The beginning of the film, on the other hand, is characteristically Tarkovskian – it disorientates the viewer from the very start. *Ivan's Childhood* begins with a dream, while the dreaming subject is not yet introduced. The socialist-realist artefact is transformed into a product of 'socialist surrealism'.[2]

The very first shot shows Ivan, curious and carefree, looking through an improbably massive spider's web. The boy listens attentively to a cuckoo, as if observing the Russian belief that the bird can predict how many more years a person will live. His face seems to be an image of innocent, happy childhood, but his countdown to death has indeed already begun. The boy then explores the peaceful Central Russian landscape until he encounters a butterfly. The image of the flying insect is followed by Ivan's own flight – a crane shot lifts him right off the ground. The implausible elevation of the hero signals that the filmic reality encountered by the viewer has an improbable character. A rejoicing Ivan is raised above the surrounding trees and then gradually approaches the land as if sliding down a hill. The lightness of the flight is consequently balanced by the heaviness of gravity; the boy carefully observes tree roots interweaving in the clay earth. A cuckoo is once again heard, and the sound is followed by Ivan's encounter with his mother, who carries a bucket of water, maternal milk, from which Ivan drinks. Air, earth and water – three out of four natural elements – manifest themselves in full glory. The fourth – fire – comes in the form of sudden machine-gun fire, which kills the mother (Figure 1.1). This dense journey from a state of utter happiness to one of devastation and loss is interrupted, and the boy wakes up; the transformation is accompanied by music, which, unlike the music or soundscape of Tarkovsky's subsequent films, transparently cues the viewer's emotions.

Pavel Florensky's dictum that 'art is materialized dream'[3] seems to have caught the director's attention, since he wrote down the saying in his diary.[4] The category of dream as an alternative reality is essential to Tarkovsky's aesthetic strategy and manifests itself in his very first film. The oneiric qualities of *Ivan's Childhood* are difficult to overlook. The cinematic journey, which is supposed to depict the cruel realities of warfare, begins with an unreal event: the dream. This antagonistic interplay between alternative realities, such as dream-hallucination and 'real' reality, is at the core of the film's overall compositional strategy. Indeed, the director claims that he clearly saw the structure of the film when he conceived the idea of dreams and 'extraordinary effects involved in dreams, memories and fantasies'.[5] The dreams punctuate the film's narrative, and the protagonist is the dreaming subject, who differs from everyone else and who is probably on the brink of experiencing something which Eugenio Montale calls 'the constant contempt of those who think reality / is what one sees':[6] for his father-figures and mentors fail to recognize his inability to distinguish between the real and the imaginary.

The boy is traumatized by the brutality of warfare. He confronts the past by re-experiencing the most memorable scenes and events of his life. It appears that the trauma manifests itself in a Freudian manner – through dreams based on certain memories of childhood. Indeed, the classic phenomenology of dreams posits that nightmares allow the brain to learn how to gain control over emotions resulting from distressing experiences. To seek meaning in dreams is a natural human impulse, and this epistemological quest is expected to deliver therapeutic effects. But Ivan's dreams are neither curative nor redemptive; they do not provide either guidance or divine inspiration. Instead, they tend to disorientate both the protagonist and the viewer. The dreams challenge the representational order of ordinary experience. They constitute repetitive patterns, which enclose the character and distort his perception of reality.

Jean-Paul Sartre, in an open letter to Mario Alicata, the editor of *L'Unità*, fiercely defended *Ivan's Childhood* from attacks in the Italian

Figure 1.1

press. The philosopher illuminates the conceptual kernel of the film when he states that Ivan's condition is a drama of the inability to differentiate between the imaginary domain of hallucination and the cruel reality of the war:

> We continue to see Ivan from the outside, just as in the 'realistic' scenes; the truth is that the whole world is a hallucination for this child, and that this very child, monster and martyr, is in this universe a *hallucination for the others*. This is why the first sequence cleverly introduces us to the true and false world of a child of the war, in describing everything from the child's actual flight through the woods to the false death of his mother... Madness? Reality? Both: in war, all soldiers are mad; this monstrous child is an objective witness to their madness because he is the maddest one of all.[7]

A state where a hallucination confronts or experiences another hallucination is the aesthetic condition of the film. The displaced boy finds himself in a spatio-temporal labyrinth where one is unable to make distinctions between inside and outside, war and peace, dream and reality, or madness and reason. Sartre continues: 'for this child gravitating toward suicide, there is no difference between day and night. In any case, he does not live among us. Actions and hallucinations are in close correspondence.'[8] Ivan's place of dwelling is somewhere else – it is real and unreal at the same time.

To some extent, Sartre replicates Arthur Schopenhauer's argument about dreaming, which Tarkovsky quotes in his own diary. The German philosopher's line of reasoning is delivered through the prism of time: 'The fact that time flows the same way in all heads proves more conclusively than anything else that we are all dreaming the same dream; more than that: all who dream that dream are one and the same being.'[9] Schopenhauer also deconstructs the overbearing presence of the singular plane of reality and undermines the safe distance and stable boundary between the observer and the observed – they both merge into one dreaming entity. The latter point is literally realized towards the end of the film, when Galtsev appears to be dreaming Ivan's dream: the act of dreaming is accomplished posthumously by another person, when the boy, the original dreaming subject, is dead.

The cinematographic apparatus is an almost perfect means for a director if he or she attempts to create an artistic universe with unstable boundaries between dream and reality, for the screen knows only one homogenous plane – a flow of images at twenty-four frames per second. Moreover, cinema in general can be perceived as a duplicate of the real plane and at the same time as an equivalent of dream. On the one hand it records real or staged events, which indeed have taken place, and on the other, as several critics have pointed out, the cinematic experience in a dark theatre is comparable to the process of dreaming. Tarkovsky's film inhabits this liminal dream–reality zone, and thus fully exploits the key features of the cinematic apparatus: Ivan, other characters and the viewers all experience the unreality of the real, and they all dream dreams.

However, since the protagonist's nightmares are not mere manifestations of the unconscious domain, the dream–reality binary is not a fully satisfactory conceptual framework for *Ivan's Childhood*. One could consider Ivan's illusionary experiences, since they indeed represent a visually distinct spatio-temporal plane, to be akin to a 'vision quest' as practised by Native American tribes. A vision quest takes place before puberty and constitutes a turning-point in life, for its purpose is to find spiritual and secular guidance. A child sets off on a personal spiritual quest alone in the wilderness for several days, usually goes through a delirious experience, and acquires the spiritual knowledge necessary for adulthood. Ivan, who is no longer a child but has not yet reached adulthood, sets off on his vision quest into the wilderness of the other bank of the Dniester-Styx, but ultimately fails to reach his goal. He never returns.

Oneiric Waters

But before the final ill-fated quest to the land of the dead is accomplished, Ivan enters the domain of Morpheus several times. After capturing the boy on the front line, a sentry guard escorts him to Galtsev's quarters, where he challenges the authority of the commanding officer. The misapprehension is resolved and Ivan is given paper and a pencil to record his secret information, and then offered a washtub with hot water. Water transfigures the boy; he emerges as a blond, pale, skinny youngster. He listlessly takes a couple of spoonfuls of gruel, and then falls asleep on the table, exhausted. Water again emerges in the foreground: the sound of dripping water starts haunting the scene, and Ivan begins dreaming of a well.

Though a drastic temporal change is imposed (a vision of the real or distorted past), no spatial cut is introduced in the sequence. A close-up of burning logs is followed by a shot of an iron bowl collecting dripping water and Ivan's arm hanging over the side of the bed. Water, which is apparently falling from a hole in the roof, drips over the boy's hand. The two antipathetic elements – water and fire – share the same space in this scene. This antagonistic fusion constitutes a conceptual move which signifies a transition from the real to the visionary realm; it frames the dream sequence: the episode begins with the image of water and its opposite, fire (burning logs and dripping water), and concludes with the same combination (a gunshot combined with splashes of water). After the close-up of the wet hand, the camera tracks aside and unexpectedly reveals that Ivan's bed is placed inside a deep well.

The transition from Galtsev's hut to the well, accompanied by eerie music, is startling. The two incompatible places are joined together into a single spatial extension. What is crucial here is the fact that the continuous temporal stretch is not disrupted either; there is no montage-cut and the sweeping-tracking camera ensures temporal continuity. This momentary cinematic trick, which lasts for about two or three seconds, has immense aesthetic consequences. The temporal transition (from the present to Ivan's past experience) is accomplished through space. Space and time intersect and form a complex spatio-temporal web. Tarkovsky refines this artistic device throughout his career, and perfects it in later works such as *Mirror*, *Nostalghia* and *Sacrifice*.

The spatial incongruity, the confluence of the hut and the bottom of the well, is followed by the fallacy of spatial-bodily 'identity' when the camera 'looks up', for it catches a glimpse of a second Ivan, who drops a feather down the well. The singularity of the protagonist is undermined: Ivan is sleeping at the bottom of the well and at the same time peeking inside from above. The boy's identity splits and the paths of his two alter egos converge in a single space, the well. It is striking that dissociative identity disorder, a medical condition, includes symptoms that seem to be manifest in Ivan: distortion or loss of subjective time, auditory hallucinations, and recurrent flashbacks of abuse or trauma. The viewer is tempted to psychoanalyse Ivan, for his dreams seem to be an open book even for an amateur psychoanalyst. However, Ivan's dreams exceed the grief–happiness binary pair; the oneiric visions constitute a more subtle interplay.

A rather sentimental conversation is taking place at the top of the well. The mother tells her son that even on a bright sunlit day one can see stars at the bottom of a very deep well. Ivan is puzzled: how is it possible to see a star during daytime? 'For you it is day, for the star it is night', is the answer he receives. Day and night, black and white, illusion and reality once again intermingle in the film. The explanation, though apparently improbable and scientifically false, excites the boy; he reaches down and tries to catch the light beneath the surface of water. The virtuoso camera shot, as if from beneath water, is followed by another split-identity image: Ivan is again inside the well trying to catch the star – the same feeble and glimmering light, but this time the image is accompanied by ominous German voices. The well in this sequence functions as a mirror, and it fails to distinguish between the real plane (Ivan) and the virtual plane (his reflection). Tarkovsky uses the well's rectangular shape as a framing device, and water is a natural reflecting surface. Ivan merges with his own reflection-double and enters another domain. But unlike Alice he does not enter Wonderland; his province is a ruinous Wasteland: Soviet Russia at the height of the Second World War.

The interplay between the top and bottom levels, accomplished by means of close-ups and distant shots, leads to a dramatic culmination: life and death, another binary pair, make their way on to the cinematic screen. The mother lifts the bucket up (a life-affirming gesture) but, once a sudden gunshot is heard, it plunges back down the well and hits the water's surface (an image of death). Water splashes out over the murdered woman, and once again the boy returns to his dying mother. In the first two dreams there is no gradual transition between waking and sleeping, and instead the director introduces hard cuts, accompanied by sharp sounds such as screams or gunfire, which contrast the serene unreality of dream and the harsh reality of war (Figure 1.2). The dreams end in high delirium.

On a symbolic level the sequence is highly illuminating: Ivan, as an innocent child, is unable to help his mother – he is deep inside the well trying to catch a star (a juvenile delusion). He can only passively observe the drama that is taking place at the top. Ivan subsequently climbs out of the well of childhood and launches his merciless revenge. The boy ceases to believe in human kindness and the possibility of happiness in general. He leaves his illusions at the bottom of the well. The well as such is an important artefact in *Ivan's Childhood*, and the second dream is not the only episode in the film where the viewer encounters it. The opening dream sequence contains an image of the mother carrying a bucket of water on her way from a well, which is visible in the corner of the shot when Ivan and the camera are sliding down a hill; a well appears several times in the sequence with a mad man in his ruined hut, and Ivan subsequently leaves a loaf of bread and a tin of food for the man on the well's rim; finally, at the end of the film, the viewer sees Ivan's mother, presumably on her way from the same well of the first dream, with the same bucket of water.

The well, as a trope, traditionally stands for a boundary between the mundane world and the underworld. Because of this liminal

Figure 1.2

essence a wish can be made in it, and some sources have healing properties. As if aware of this, Ivan drinks water from the well which is symbolically provided by his mother. The woman carries a bucket full of water, and her son drinks from it at the very beginning and at the very end of the film, in his first and last dreams. However, this proves not to be living water – the well in Ivan's dream has mainly deathly connotations: its subterranean waters can be seen as taking their source from the rivers of Hades. Indeed, the river is another important water-source in the film, and it is difficult to overestimate the semantic implications of its recurring presence. The very first 'real' episode of the film shows Ivan making his way through the swamp; the water is stagnant and heavy, as if burdened with evil. The same dead water dominates the episode of crossing at the end of the film, when Ivan sets out on his last mission. After the boy bids farewell to Kholin and Galtsev, the camera performs a slow tracking movement over the surface of water – the only use of the quintessentially Tarkovskian long take in the film – as if it is seeing Ivan off. The world the tracking shot reveals is upside down, and crowns of leafless trees are reflected in stagnant water covered with aquatic plants.

The deathly water is also in the vicinity of the corpses of the two hanged partisans with a sinister 'Welcome' sign. The corpses transform the banks of the Dnieper into the unwelcoming banks of the Styx. Indeed, when Ivan is transported across the river – to the other bank – he enters the domain of death and never comes back; the Ukrainian river interflows with the River of the Dead, and the reconnaissance mission becomes a funeral crossing. Unlike Achilles, who was dipped in the Styx in his childhood, Ivan does not acquire invulnerability: he falls victim to the Nazis.

A recording of the folk song 'Masha May Not Cross the River', by the legendary Russian bass Fedor Chaliapin, functions as another water-related omen in the film. Galtsev and Kholin listen silently to the song at a table immediately after they have made the journey to the other bank, when Ivan has already crossed the river. Katasonych and Galtsev had previously tried to play the record, but their attempts were always interrupted (in Galtsev's case it was Kholin who interfered with irritation: 'Have you gone out of your mind?'). The lyric song about a failed romantic encounter is transformed into a funeral march.[10] Kholin himself puts the record on, and the two men listen to it as if mourning the departed child.

Thus, water in *Ivan's Childhood* seems to have strong deathly connotations. The sound of water dripping is prominently heard in the bunker before the boy sets on his last mission – the close-up of his head is followed by a shot of the death-inscription on the wall, and both are wrapped in the sound of dripping water. Water is already aware of Ivan's tragic end. In his discussion of the so-called Ophelia complex, Gaston Bachelard lays out a theoretical ground for the water-death case by stating that 'water is an invitation to die'.[11] The philosopher offers poetic praise for the substance of water, and compares it with the other natural elements:

> [W]ater is also a *type of destiny* that is no longer simply the vain destiny of fleeting images and a never ending dream but an essential destiny that endlessly changes the substance of the being. [...T]he Heraclitean flux is a *concrete* philosophy, a *complete* philosophy. One cannot bathe twice in the same river because already, in his inmost recesses, the human being shares the destiny of flowing water. Water is truly the transitory element. [...] A being dedicated to water is a being in flux. He dies every minute; something of his substance is constantly falling away. Daily death is not fire's exuberant form of death, piercing heaven with its arrows; daily death is the death of water. Water always flows, always falls, always ends in horizontal death. [...] death associated with water is more dream-like than death associated with earth: the pain of water is infinite.[12]

For Bachelard, water is a transitory entity and there is only one type of transition possible – from life to death; and the passage of time is a passage of death. The flow of waterly images in *Ivan's Childhood* resonates with Bachelard's argument. This water, sourced from wells, buckets and rivers, comprises Ivan's essential destiny and envelops the hero. It does not provide a Narcissistic image, it is never still. On the contrary, it flows, vibrates, and splashes. The boy drinks it, swims and washes in it. He readily fulfils his fateful lot and immerses himself in the deathly water: he is moving towards death from the very first dream of the film, when he carelessly drinks water from his mother's bucket. Water is a dense image in Tarkovsky's aesthetic universe, and the life–death interplay in *Ivan's Childhood* is the first instance of the director's lifelong preoccupation with this element.

Ruinous Landscape

The image of a dilapidated building – an occupied ruin – is another Tarkovskian trademark aesthetic element, which prominently emerges in each of the seven feature films. A decrepit and semi-destroyed edifice is a spatial manifestation of the passage of time. Matter endures the process of decaying, and the outcome is a clear image of time imprinting itself in space. All of Tarkovsky's films contain a trope of dilapidated construction of sorts, from ruined churches to littered space stations. The story of *Ivan's Childhood*, unlike the subsequent films, provides a natural excuse for the director to introduce this element: the devastation of war manifests itself first and foremost in images of obliteration. The landscape in the film is littered with crashed aeroplanes, broken agricultural equipment and burned wheat fields. This evidence of devastation is intensified by images of various edifices, such as peasant huts, ruined windmills, churches, and German military and political offices, in decrepit, burnt and shattered states.

The trope of the dilapidated building emerges most prominently in the episode with the mentally deranged old man. The sequence, due to its eccentric character, evolves into a visionary interlude that provides a meta-commentary on the evils of warfare. Ivan encounters the ragged man during his attempt to run away from the command headquarters in order to avoid being sent back to the rear and forced to enter a military school. The boy passes by a devastated village and decides to rest in what seems to be an empty cattle shed. He enters it not through a door, for there are no more walls, but through a gaping breach. Some remaining planks guard the 'entrance', and their sharp edges are pointed towards Ivan as if threatening him. The camera angle and the overall composition are uncharacteristic for Tarkovsky, since the geometry of space, not the character's human presence, dominates the screen. The sound of a creaking wooden door, which is not yet visible, underlines the emptiness of the devastated construction.

Ivan looks at the grey autumn sky through a breach in the ceiling and gazes at the passing clouds. Suddenly he hears a rooster crow; the bird, with bound legs, hops off towards a chimney but is immediately caught and brought down by the elderly peasant. The apprehensive boy gets up and notices the man, who has apparently lost his mind, through a door frame. The damaged passage between the inside and outside informs the whole composition of the consequent subjective shot, while the creaking and dangling door intermittently conceals and reveals the scene. The man, humming a song with a picture frame in his hands, looks for something in the ruins of the house. Before noticing Ivan he notes to himself, 'This stove's always – it'll stand just as it always has.' The Russian stone stove, as opposed to the wooden hut, has a longer lifespan, and its durability transforms it into an image of the nation's future recovery.

The bewildered and slightly frightened boy realizes that the madman is looking for a nail. The man invites Ivan 'in' and asks the boy to help him find it. They also exchange a few remarks: 'Have you got far to go?' asks the peasant. Ivan's indefinite answer – 'Far' – invites an almost metaphysical, and yet more indefinite, commentary: 'That's it...everyone has far to go. And why? Who knows?' The two confused and disorientated people, in spite of the age difference between them, find themselves in a similar situation when they have been bereaved by the war: one has lost his wife and the other his mother. Finally, Ivan finds a nail, but it turns out to be the 'wrong' one. This is followed by a rather impatient and grammatically deformed speech: 'Where did I put it? I had it just now...he was so tall, wore glasses and had hair like this [shoulder length].' The madness manifests itself in the incoherent speech: the nail, the initial subject, evolves into the Nazi soldier who killed the old man's wife. The deranged peasant continues wandering around the site of devastation, and tries to transfigure his hut, make it habitable, before his wife 'comes back'. The futility of his efforts is underlined by a nonsensical gesture: he wipes and then hangs with great care a certificate of merit – a Soviet 'icon' – on one of the remaining intact walls.

Though the discursive constituent of the episode is relatively straightforward, the interplay between the dehiscent apertures provides a more subtle visual commentary. The decrepit edifices are unable to protect their inhabitants from the natural elements, and instead function as a poetic refrain which erases conventional spatial frontiers, such as that between inside and outside, and creates an image of improbable atemporal space without any stable markers. This space becomes the Deleuzian any-space-whatever: the postwar period has greatly increased the situations which we no longer know how to react to, in spaces which we no longer know how to describe. These were 'any space whatever', deserted but inhabited, disused warehouses, waste ground, cities in the course of demolition or reconstruction.[13] The resulting spatial disorientation has temporal consequences: the past–present–future division is no longer applicable. Ivan and the old man both try to escape the present spatial desolation through leaps to another time – the improbable time of dream and hallucination which overcomes the forms of the outer world.

The cellar of a ruined church, which is transformed into the command headquarters and bunker, is another significant any-space-whatever in *Ivan's Childhood*. It is difficult to overestimate the role of this literally transfigured, formerly spiritual and currently military space. It functions as one of the centres of resistance, with icons and crosses still hanging on the walls: before, the building used to guard the souls of the Russian people, and now it protects their bodies. The boy is brought to the bunker-church at the beginning of the film, and he uses it as his base before setting off on his final mission at the end. More importantly, Ivan uses the building as a gateway to his visions: he dreams two of his four dreams here.

The headquarters are not completely undamaged. The interior is ascetic and its roof is leaking, as the viewer knows from the second dream, but it is still habitable. This is a deformed shelter, which still protects its dwellers from atmospheric precipitation. The intermediary nature of the edifice allows extraordinary phenomena to take place. In addition to dreaming dreams here, Ivan transforms the bunker into a hallucinatory site. A message scrawled on the wall ('There are eight of us. All under 19. In an hour from now they'll shoot us. Avenge us') helps him to call up phantoms of the past – the executed adolescents – and to imagine and re-enact events which have already happened.

In the course of the film, in his dreams and recollections, Ivan hears the voices of Nazi soldiers and of people who perished, and repeatedly 'interacts' with them. Off-screen 'characters' – disembodied ghosts of the past – invade the cinematic space. The fantasy of war, which takes place in the bunker, is the most prominent and narratively significant of these invasions. It begins with a symbolic gesture of the boy raising a bell (a much bigger bell, with similar symbolic connotations, will be cast and raised by the same actor, Nikolai Burliaev, in Tarkovsky's next film, *Andrei Rublev*). The viewer hears Ivan's off-screen voice ('Steady, steady') while he is crawling on the floor with a knife in his hand. Suddenly the boy throws a bottle and breaks a lamp; darkness envelops the room. German voices, children's sobs, atonal music and partial illumination create a sense of anxiety. Ivan's torch catches fragments of the inscription by the murdered adolescents.

This is followed by an unexpected change in the point of view: a spot of light from the electric torch, which has been in Ivan's hands, now illuminates the protagonist, who looks straight into the camera. The ordinary game is transformed into an extraordinary vision. The camera slides left and discovers another boy, who is lying on the floor and whose appearance strongly resembles that of Ivan. It slides back to reveal Ivan himself with the knife, and then again to the left, but this time it catches a glimpse of a woman who looks very similar to Ivan's own mother – she wears a headscarf and looks frightened. The next leap of the camera shows Ivan standing by a large mirror, which duplicates the character. The camera lingers on the boy and his reflection, then quickly turns towards the apparition of the mother and finally comes back to Ivan. These vertiginous, chaotic movements undermine the reality–illusion dichotomy. Ivan faces the dead people and witnesses apparitions not in his dream but in 'reality'. The improbable ghostly presence of illusion is superimposed on the space of reality by means of contingently abnormal movements and a shifting point of view. Identities are split and time is muddled.

The back-and-forth, almost hysterical movement of the camera disorientates the viewer. The pace of editing, together with the mode of superimposition of images, is purely Eisensteinian, while tilts and distortions dominate the camerawork. These stylistic devices constitute an exception in Tarkovsky's oeuvre. High-pace montage tends to disappear in favour of long tracking shots in the subsequent films. The director's style seems to be unfurling in *Ivan's Childhood*: the techniques he employs belong to the past tradition of analytical montage, but he already reveals clear intentions to break from them. Tarkovsky's major achievement in this first feature is precisely the introduction of the alternative plane of reality by means of the exposure of a non-empirical relationship between space and time.

The linearity of time and its division into past, present and future are absolutely crucial to conventional narrative films. The viewer agrees to follow conventions and accepts violations of the linearity of time when he sees a clearly marked past event or a dream. Dreams, hallucinations and visions in *Ivan's Childhood*, however, belong to another plane. The viewer no longer observes them from the outside; he or she joins the boy in his spatio-temporal delirium. There is no longer any delineation between the subjective and objective planes. Tarkovsky's camera repeatedly introduces excessively unrealistic points of view, while the soundtrack and set illumination frequently alternate between diegetic and extra-diegetic. This, together with the overall spatio-temporal discontinuity, the constant leaps to other spaces and times, results in a state where illusionary reality is meticulously intertwined with real events without clear-cut divisions. Ivan's hallucinatory game is a great illustration of this tendency.

The game reaches its climax when the boy starts ringing the bell. What seems to be a diegetic element turns out to be an off-screen intrusion, since the bell continues to ring even when Ivan stops moving the clapper. The roar of attacking soldiers is heard, and the hallucinating child 'joins' them. The attack gradually evolves into a chase after an arch-enemy, who must be captured alive. Ivan's imagination transforms a military coat on a hook into the hiding enemy. The boy threatens the captive – he claims that he remembers him and will try him in court. The imaginary victory reaches its final culmination, and Ivan bursts into tears. Suddenly the unreality of the vision is 'balanced' by the reality of war: the Germans start bombing the Russian bank. A missile strikes somewhere nearby and the explosion that follows hits an icon inside the bunker-church. A worried Galtsev rushes back to the place to see if the attack has frightened the boy. He finds Ivan in a very calm, almost indifferent state: the reality of war does not provoke fear, since all of his traumas – the only sources of dread and anxiety – are located in the past.

Time, for the protagonist, as it follows from the hallucinatory play, is a reversible category. Ivan's past is the only reality for him. He does not live in the present, and refuses to think about the future (this partially explains his reluctance to join a prestigious military school). He constantly returns to his own traumatic past: he is haunted by dreams about it and consciously re-enacts certain events, which may or may not have taken place. Even when the boy encounters a woodcut in an art book he projects his own past experience on the artistic image. In Albrecht Dürer's *The Four Horsemen of the Apocalypse* he recognizes Nazi soldiers he once saw. Dürer's universal Apocalypse becomes the Apocalypse of Ivan's life. This vision, together with the dreams and the bunker episode, constitutes a leap to a phantasmic space and an attempt to reverse the category of time. In this light, Tarkovsky's extensive commentary on the supposed (ir)reversibility of time is highly informative:

> Time is said to be irreversible. And this is true enough in the sense that 'you can't bring back the past', as they say. But what exactly is this 'past'? Is it what has passed? And what does 'passed' mean for a person when for each of us the past is the bearer of all that is constant in the reality of the present, of each current moment? In a certain sense the past is far more real, or at any rate more stable, more resilient than the present. The present slips and vanishes like sand between the fingers, acquiring material weight only in its recollection. King Solomon's ring bore the inscription, 'All will pass'; by contrast, I want to draw attention to how time in its moral implication is in fact turned back. Time can vanish without trace in our material world for it is a subjective, spiritual category.

> The time we have lived settles in our soul as an experience placed within time.[14]

Tarkovsky's observations on the ephemeral quality of the present moment do not constitute a unique contribution to the philosophy of time, for it has been highlighted before by many thinkers. However, the director's elegant rhetorical move – the implied formula-statement 'All has passed', a reversal of King Solomon's dictum 'All will pass' – has interesting theoretical consequences. The leap from Solomon's domain of the future ('will pass') to the realm of the past ('has passed') extracts the category of time from its futurity. Instead, time enters the physical territory of the past and becomes petrified, mummified or imprinted. The shift is accompanied by a material transformation: time turns into sand slipping between the fingers, it gains 'material weight' and 'settles in our soul'. The director's vision of the category of time and its space-related consequences justifies Ivan's wanderings in the spatio-temporal labyrinth of his childhood.

Oneiric Negative

The temporal flow again gains flesh in the third dream. This time it transforms itself into a heap of apples carried by a lorry. The oneiric landscape is considerably transfigured: the boy's mother and the Russian countryside no longer shape the vision. The dream, which takes place during Ivan's nap before he sets forth on the last mission, begins in a rather conventional manner. The boy-dreamer lies down, and his eyes track the ceiling and move towards the revenge-inspiring inscription, which now appears on the ceiling, instead of the wall as in the hallucination sequence. The sound of dripping water and the dream-like music again invade the cinematic space. Ivan closes his eyes and dreams the third dream. The rigid boundary between illusion and reality is established and there is no abnormal transition as in the second vision, where the spaces of the two domains are conflated. Dripping water turns into heavy rain, and Ivan finds himself sitting next to a girl on a heap of apples carried by a lorry on a warm summer day. A sudden flash of lightning changes the background of the scene – the panorama of moving trees – into negative. This sudden and explicitly improbable change in illumination accompanies the encounter between the two children in the cart.

Ivan offers the girl an apple from the heap, but she smiles and shakes her head in refusal. He stretches out for another but it still does not appeal to her. The third attempt also fails, but this time

Ivan's companion laughs happily, completely soaked by the rain. The girl is subsequently seen two more times in rapid succession and in one continuous camera movement: once again, the unity of a character's identity in *Ivan's Childhood* is undermined. Each time, her appearance and facial expression change drastically: the girl 'quietly' smiles and her hair is soaking wet, while her face is relatively dry in its second appearance on the screen. The final time she appears completely dry, for the rain suddenly stops, and the girl has a rather gloomy stare. The awkwardly bouncing negative background shapes all three of the 'apparitions' (Figure 1.3).

The scene in the cart is followed by a lyrical interlude – probably the most peaceful and life-affirming scene in the film. The lorry emerges from the tunnel of trees in negative to the open and sunny space of a river bank. Its cart is open and apples fall out of it. A few horses enter the camera's field of vision and start eating the scattered fruit. The transformation from the heavy rain and the negative background to the sunny dry day is striking. Light as such is another aesthetically loaded element of the film. Light flares shoot up and illuminate the devastated landscape, while sunlight is present almost exclusively in the dream sequences. The sunlit space of childhood is contrasted with the gloomy realm of war.

The negative–positive interplay is the key aesthetic device in the episode. The director recollects at some length how he conceived the idea of introducing the negative plane while making the film:

> [I] glimpsed black sunlight sparkling through snowy trees and a downpour of gleaming rain. Flashes of lightning came in to make it technically feasible to cut from positive to negative. But all this merely created an atmosphere of unreality. What about the content? What about the logic of the dream? That came from memories. I remembered seeing the wet grass, the lorry load of apples, the horses, wet with rain, steaming in the sunshine.[...] Looking for simple solutions to the problem of conveying the unreality of the dream we hit on the panorama of moving trees in negative, and, against that background, the face of the little girl passing in front of the camera three times, her expression changed with each appearance. We wanted to capture in that scene the child's foreboding of imminent tragedy.[15]

The upturned dark background envelops the naturally lit day scene, which depicts Ivan's encounter with a little girl. The logical relationship between light and darkness in their function of representing

Figure 1.3

objects is undermined. The two meet in the dream and their antagonism is neutralized, since they are made to share a single space. Their spectral coexistence creates a sense of elevated joy infiltrated by a sinister premonition: the past happiness of childhood is mixed with the future fateful end. Only the improbable dream-topos can accommodate two disparate realms and states, such as day and night or happiness and sorrow.

'Black sunlight' and 'snowy trees' in summer constitute the abnormal spatial setting of the sequence. Their improbable, inverted nature is a result of light reversal, from positive to negative. This artistic device clearly belongs to the domain of photography, for the negative is a piece of film constituting the original from which a photograph is then developed. It records a scene in front of the lens at the moment of exposure. In the resulting image, light and dark areas appear the opposite way round to the way in which they emerge in the printed photograph. The negative has strong photographic connotations, while its opposite – reversal film – is more associated with the cinematic process, since it yields a positive image without an intervening negative, and can be projected onto a screen.

By using the negative, Tarkovsky appeals, as it were, to the first level of truth, for the negative reflects the various amounts of light received during exposure, and comprises the first surface to interact with reality as such. Photography, in this sense, has more claims to veracity than cinema. The essence of the negative is its potential to deliver a truthful, undistorted image of reality, and the director exploits this purely photographic effect. However, his obsession with photography is not confined to this sequence. A photograph plays a crucial narrative role towards the end of the film.

The photograph is a witness to a particular moment in time which has already passed. It is a herald of the past. It is exactly this feature that is employed by Galtsev when he looks at Ivan's image from the Nazi archive: the photograph calls up the past. As an archetypal photographic image, it restores something which is no longer there. Together with perished voices it generates an image of Ivan – it resurrects him for a brief moment in order to let Galtsev and the viewer learn the boy's fate.

The photograph and the archival file are real and factual documents of the war. They are equated with the veracity of the documentary chronicle used in the film. Both are witnesses to the atrocities committed by the Nazis. Indeed, the scene in the archive is preceded by horrifying images of violence inflicted by fascist generals and officers upon their families and their own selves. The footage showing the partly burned bodies of Joseph and Magda Goebbels, surrounded by the corpses of their six children, is followed by a documentary chronicle capturing the moment when the surrender documents were signed, and footage showing the bodies of a high-ranking officer and his family. The destructive urge proved to be fatal to those who were possessed by it. These manifestations of the *real* plane no longer stand out, but rather become integrated into a certain co-inhabited real–fictional contemporaneity. The images depicting the grand fate of the villains are succeeded by a story of one of their (fictional) victims.

Ivan's file emerges strikingly in the film. A soldier browses through various files scattered on the floor of a German office and monotonously reads aloud the verdicts written on them. There are only two types of verdict: death by firing squad or by hanging. One of the files attracts Galtsev's attention, but it falls down through the breach in the floor and the officer has to jump down in order to retrieve it. The deficiency of the building again emerges as a poetic motif. This time its dilapidated state contains not a single trace of hope, as in the case with the peasant's hut with the preserved stove or the church-bunker with icons still decorating its walls. These are destroyed or damaged, but they are open to the sky (through breaches in the ceiling or the absence of ceiling altogether): they look upward, as it were. In contrast, the wrecked German building is a site of evil: instead of the purifying rainfall it has dark ashes flying in the air, and the breach it contains is in the floor: it looks downward, to torture cells.

The camera follows Galtsev down and moves into the death chambers. The officer 'sees' the horrifying site, which is actually presented by means of documentary material: hooks attached to the ceiling, a bloodstained guillotine, pieces of barbed wire. For Susan Sontag, a photograph is a reminder of death, for it highlights the passage of time, which is always directed towards death: 'All photographs are memento mori. To take a photograph is to participate in another person's (or thing's) mortality, vulnerability, mutability. Precisely by slicing out this moment and freezing it, all photographs testify to time's relentless melt.'[16] The German soldiers indeed participated in Ivan's mortality by taking his photograph and then executing him. The photograph brings along the pain of death. Suddenly, the head and shoulders of Ivan appear on the screen, as if he were hanging upside down. The boy's head – as if cut by the guillotine – rolls over the floor, and he stares right into the camera without blinking. Ivan, however, appears to be neither dead nor alive.

For Roland Barthes, the photograph is a manifestation of intense immobility: 'A trick of vocabulary: we say "to develop a photograph"; but what the chemical action develops is undevelopable, an essence (of a wound), what cannot be transformed but only repeated under the instances of insistence (of the insistent gaze).'[17] The very essence of photography denies the possibility of rhetorical expansion and, for Barthes, this fact connects it with the Haiku, in which everything is already given: 'neither the Haiku nor the Photograph makes us "dream".'[18] By contrast, the photograph of Ivan, in the case of Tarkovsky's film, is not limited to what is given in it. The intense immobility of Ivan's face allows a flow of memories and visions to take place. Finally, this very photograph makes Galtsev and the viewer dream a posthumous dream, as if on behalf of the dead boy.

Immortal Hide-and-Seek

The dreaming subject of the sequence at the end of the film is not Ivan, for the hero is already dead. The concluding episode comprises an abstract vision, which is introduced by means of the Nazi archival file. The figure of the boy is resurrected from the pages of carefully preserved official memory and presented for the last time as an emblematic image of innocent suffering. An imaginary lyrical scene from Ivan's childhood brings the feature to a close.

The director uses a shot/reverse-shot technique after the body of Ivan is rolled over the floor of the death chamber, as a means to enter the imaginary realm. The viewer looks straight into the boy's eyes, but the intended off-screen addressee of Ivan's gaze is his mother. The woman, who stands on the bank of a river, lovingly looks 'back' at her son. The camera then moves down and finds a smiling and shirtless Ivan drinking water from a bucket, which has been carried by his mother. The two people, dear to each other and now dead, thus 'meet'. Shot/reverse-shot is a feature of the classical Hollywood style of continuity editing, and it undergoes a dramatic modification in this sequence. Traditionally, the technique de-emphasizes transitions between shots and ensures that the audience perceives a sequence of images as one continuous action that develops linearly and logically. However, the interplay of gazes at the end of *Ivan's Childhood* (Ivan, an apparition on the floor in the Nazi death chamber, looking up; the mother on the river bank looking down; Ivan, drinking water from the bucket, looking up) introduces spatio-temporal discontinuity or false continuity. The ghostly, improbable apparition of Ivan in the ruined Nazi building, which is a displacement in space and time in its own right, is followed by a further dislocation: the whole scene is moved to the river bank. The gazes do not provide a continuous narrative line; instead they constitute a densely layered intertwinement.

The mother, who cannot stop looking at her son, picks the bucket up and walks away along the bank of the river. This is followed by an establishing shot depicting Ivan and other children playing hide-and-seek. Ivan is 'it' – the chosen one – and he recites a counting rhyme, after which the children disperse. A withered tree appears in the sequence as a base from which the boy sets to seek his playmates. The camera finds the girl from Ivan's third dream hiding under a fragment of a tree trunk, and she remains unnoticed by 'it'. The withered tree again enters the camera's field of vision – the trunk of this tree and the seeking Ivan form the only two vertical 'lines' in the empty horizon of the river bank.

Ivan finally notices the girl and starts chasing her. The rejoicing children run barefoot on sand along the riverbank. A shot of the tree again appears for a brief moment, and then the camera finds the children running through shallow waters, on a strip of sand along the edge of the river. Ivan overtakes the girl, but instead of tagging her he continues running towards the open horizon. The ordinary children's game is transformed into an extraordinary vision: the boy runs on the water's surface. Finally, the last shot of the film returns Ivan to the bank; he stretches out his arm to try to touch the base of the tree, to win the game (Figure 1.4). This is followed by a close-up of the tree, and the approaching darkness of the trunk concludes the film.

The image of the conifer tree at the beginning of the film finds its double – the withered tree on the riverbank – at the end of *Ivan's Childhood*. The two trees have a certain proximity to the boy: he examines the spider's web scattered among the branches of the former, and uses the latter as the base for the hide-and-seek game. Both trees belong to the domain of dream, but the one at the beginning is alive while the second one is dead. This rather straightforward progression can be explained by the fact that Tarkovsky was still in the process of developing his filmic style, though some traces of his mature aesthetics are already in place. For instance, the fact that the illusionary realm occupies a prominent place in the structure of the film relates to his later obsession with alternative modes of perception of reality. An ordinary and in many ways clichéd space of warfare is transformed into a dream-topos with vague temporal coordinates but with concrete artefacts and natural elements. This topos is a space where the character can fly above a hill, catch a star in the well, or be surrounded by trees in negative.

Figure 1.4

Foucault, drawing inspiration from Bachelard, suggests that we do not live in a homogeneous and empty space, but instead inhabit heterogeneously phantasmic space. In his description of this replete topos, the thinker does not differentiate between ordinary and imaginary realms:

> The space of our primary perception, the space of our dreams and that of our passions hold within themselves qualities that seem intrinsic: there is a light, ethereal, transparent space, or again a dark, rough, encumbered space; a space from above, of summits, or on the contrary a space from below, of mud; or again a space that can be flowing like sparkling water, or a space that is fixed, congealed, like stone or crystal.[19]

The same can be said of Ivan's dreams and his reality: these adjacent topoi are dominated by various natural elements such as water and earth, and filled with light of various gradations. The to-and-fro between dream and reality is accomplished by drastic changes in illumination, while water functions as a connecting point between the two. Arseni Tarkovsky's poem 'The Willow of Ivan', written in 1958, a few years before the film was made, amalgamates the tropes discussed here in an uncanny manner: nature here plays a key role in the process of longing and of mourning. In the poem, the ghost of a dead soldier called Ivan returns to the landscape of childhood:

Before the war Ivan would walk by a stream,
Where a willow-tree grew – no one knew whose.

Nobody knew why it leaned over the stream,
But that was the willow of Ivan.

In his cape-tent, butchered in battle,
Ivan returned to the foot of his willow.

The willow of Ivan [*Ivanova iva*],
The willow of Ivan,

Like a white ship, is floating downstream.[20]

* * *

The words of Michel de Montaigne – 'Our waking is blinder than our sleeping. Our wisdom less wise than our madness. Our fantasies are worth more than our judgements' – which can be found in Tarkovsky's diary,[21] in a way perfectly summarize the situation depicted in *Ivan's Childhood*: the tragic story of the avenging child-soldier is a convergence of madness and sanity, of grief and happiness, and of dream and reality. The concluding, and in many ways emblematic, episode of the film combines all of these contradictory trends. The manifest parable-like abstraction of the ending marks the beginning of Tarkovsky's filmic style, which defies a linear progression of events and is more concerned with polyphonic clashes of different spatio-temporal planes. These collisions are accompanied by other trademark aspects of the director's aesthetic method which enhance the feeling of spatio-temporal disorientation: dilapidated buildings, the use of documentary chronicle, scenes of levitation and contemplative shots of nature are already part of the artistic texture of the debut feature.

Ivan's dreams shape the narrative of the film; they are placed at the beginning and at the end. Even more importantly, they take place during, right after or just before reconnaissance missions. The trips to the other shore are liminal, transcendental events, and are confined to margins. The boy has the first dream during his first mission, at the very beginning of the film, and his second vision takes place in Galtsev's quarters immediately after he accomplishes it. The narrative body, which includes the attempts to send Ivan to the military academy and preparations for another mission, and depicts the love triangle involving Masha and the two officers, occupies the centre of the film. These episodes, quite conventional for the socialist-realist war-film genre, stand for reality as such – they are common events. The hallucinatory play and the third dream announce the irreversible transition to the marginal domain. The play and the dream are placed just before the boy's final assignment, which culminates in fatal failure. The crossing of the river – a long, suspenseful journey to the other bank – clearly evolves into an otherworldly experience. Death enters the scene when Ivan's seat in the boat is taken by the two corpses of the Soviet soldiers from the German bank. The boy's death is announced in Galtsev's vision in the German archive, and the last dream, the posthumous vision, concludes the film. The framing function of the dreams and hallucinations is apparent, and their liminal, marginal essence is clearly emphasized.

From its very beginnings, Tarkovsky's cinema evolves as a form of art which continually alternates between real and imaginary realms. The fusion of realistic and fantastical elements shapes *Ivan's Childhood*; it becomes its core structuring tactic. The dreams, in a similar fashion to the chronotope of chivalric romance discussed by Bakhtin, 'no longer function merely as an element of the content, but begin to acquire a form-generating function'.[22] The dreams, in opposition to the 'real' scenes in *Ivan's Childhood*, constitute layers of alternative spatio-temporal frameworks – a rather common aesthetic strategy. What is remarkable is the way in which they enter the screen; the transition in most cases is accomplished without any clear borderlines between dream and reality being established. Reality already accommodates illusion. For instance, the sound of dripping water haunts the viewer frequently in the course of the film, and through this sound the director 'escapes' the unbearable cruelty of wartime reality into the joyful domain of dream. The protagonist himself is unable to differentiate reality from dream, memory or imagination. In the scene where Ivan looks at Dürer's woodcut, he sees contemporary Germans in the atemporal artwork. He also has the ability to hear the voices of dead people, and resurrects them when he plays. Ivan himself is resurrected at the end of the film as a carefully preserved fact – an archival file kept to admonish future generations.

The disruption of the swiftly flowing narrative *now* by an alternative plane of reality, such as a dream or hallucination, occurs prominently in *Ivan's Childhood*, and develops into one of the director's trademark devices. The linearity and rigidity of past–present–future progression is already undermined in Tarkovsky's very first feature film. The director challenges the unidirectional nature of time. His films provide an image of a conventional linear progression of events which gradually, and without any forewarning, evolves into a spatio-temporal maze with characteristic twists and turns. The patchwork of discrete spatio-temporal frameworks reigns supreme. Tarkovsky develops the device and reaches a state of perfection in his late films, where not only dreams but also such phenomena as visions, phantasies, memories, revelations, recollections and illusions start to infiltrate the domain of the real.

2

VISIONS OF *ANDREI RUBLEV*

While *Ivan's Childhood* was 'inherited' by Tarkovsky, *Andrei Rublev*, initially called *The Passion According to Andrei*, was the director's first independently conceived film project. The film, co-written with Andron Konchalovsky and completed in 1966, still remains unique in its scope and ambition, which were unparalleled for a production of this type. It deals with the life of the fifteenth-century Russian monk and icon painter. The 'biography' of the medieval artist was Tarkovsky's first and last attempt to work in the epic genre. With a substantial budget, a duration of more than three hours,[1] and several thousand extras, the film-maker delves into the world of medieval Russia.

It should be noted that Andrei Rublev was a relatively obscure figure at the time of the making of the film and had only just begun to emerge from oblivion. The artist had a mythic presence in Russian culture until the twentieth century, and was regarded as the definitive creator of only one icon – *The Trinity*. Ironically, the Soviet authorities are given credit for his cultural resurrection.[2] The subsequent Soviet efforts at ideological appropriation culminated in a major retrospective of Rublev's icons in 1960, which was almost certainly attended by Tarkovsky and probably inspired him to make the film.

The beginning of *Andrei Rublev* is arguably the most elevated and poetic of all of Tarkovsky's film openings. The film launches itself with a flight sequence. A character called Efim, who will not reappear in the film, prepares to take off from a belfry on his homemade hot-air balloon. The desired physical elevation is considered to be blasphemous by Efim's compatriots, and they chase the man in an attempt to prevent the experiment. The peasant-inventor manages to escape the pursuit while his helpers fall victim to the crowd. Efim soars in the sky and contemplates the hilly Russian landscape – punctuated with the curves of a river, marshes and dispersed herds of horses – until he plunges into a riverbank.

The fatal crash is followed by a very unusual element for Tarkovsky's cinema: a freeze-frame shot of the ground. The freeze-frame is an illusion of a photograph, and its motionlessness is manifestly non-cinematic. The shot of the ground reveals the irreversible finality of the inventor's apparent death. The viewer sees his unconscious body and the slowly deflating primitive hot-air balloon, which gives the impression of a dying animal: the cinema screen is gradually released from the state of immobility. A slow-motion shot of a stallion concludes the prologue: the camera captures a rare moment during which the graceful animal wallows in mud, then gets up and leaves the camera's field of vision (Figure 2.1). The cyclic composition

Figure 2.1

of the sequence (take off – flight – crash – wallow – leaving) delivers an affirmative message: life, with its ascents and downfalls, goes on.

The first part of the film's prologue takes place in a building that is somewhat defective – a walk-through belfry which functions as a point of departure for the Russian medieval inventor. All of its doorways are open, and there is no secluded or integral space inside. Efim and a team of helpers use multiple exits, and the aura of disorientation is intensified by the camera following the characters in constant motion. The edifice ceases to be an enclosed religious site, like the church-bunker in *Ivan's Childhood*. Its practical function – to announce religious gatherings commemorating celestial feats – is undermined, and it is used as a platform to declare man's ability to take flight and to overcome the terrestrial realm. The opening episode depicts a situation in which a human being elevates himself into the sky, which was unthinkable at the time. This abstract poetic sequence reveals the desire of a grimy medieval man to escape his dismal and coarse milieu. In many ways it envisages the fate of Andrei Rublev – a character who tries to flee from the harsh cruelties of medieval Russia and who constantly has visions about the celestial realm. These affirmative and benevolent visions inspire his art and become the subject-matter of his icons.

The film's narrative begins with three monks (Andrei, Daniil and Kirill) who are arguing about the amount of time they have spent at their home monastery, Andronikov. This minor fact immediately reveals the ambiguous role of time and chronology in the film. The characters appear to exist and act within an atemporal reality where past, present and future are not clearly divided. Though every subsequent chapter has a precise temporal indication (the film is divided into eight parts: 1. 'Buffoon', 1400; 2. 'Theophanes the Greek', 1405[–06][3]; 3. 'The Passion According to Andrei', 1406; 4. 'Holiday', 1408; 5. 'The Last Judgement', 1408; 6. 'Raid', 1408; 7. 'Silence [Love]', 1412; 8. 'Bell', 1423[–24]), and though the narrative stretches over the course of twenty-three years in a chronologically linear manner, that sense of linear flow is deceptive.[4]

The chronology of *Andrei Rublev* is displaced – space transforms the linearity of time into a maze. The division of the film into 'novellas', as it were, has a crucial impact on the viewer's often floundering attempt to orientate him- or herself in the medieval world presented on the screen. However, these temporal markers fail to help. The individual sections, in the guise of clearly divided temporal segments, constitute a chronology that is at best superficial, and do not provide a straightforward narrative progression. The linear straightness of the storyline is constantly violated by unheralded fantasy and lapses into recollection. Time in the film is utterly subjective, and the director himself claims that his ambition was to introduce a mode of montage that would reveal not narrative logic, but the logic of subjective experiences such as fantasy, dream or memory.[5]

Moreover, the epic narrative lacks a definitive centre. Rublev, like a genuine medieval artist, remains 'anonymous'; his presence is relatively obscure, and he often disappears from the camera's sight. Action as such is almost completely absent from *Andrei Rublev*. The action-based virtuosic battle scenes and the suspense-driven 'Bell' episode are not directly related to the protagonist(s): Rublev remains a mere observer of these events, while Daniil (the lifelong collaborator and friend of the real Rublev) and Kirill (a purely fictional character) appear and disappear from the stage without rhyme or reason. The film presents its characters in a state of non-action: Rublev's silence and doubt prevent him from carrying on his artistic pursuits, Kirill's envy disallows him from collaborating with other icon painters, and Daniil's unmotivated absence from the second part of the film rules out any possibility of his acting at all.[6]

In general, the aesthetic strategy of *Andrei Rublev* does not constitute an attempt to determine and present a coherent story of how this greatest of icon painters lived his life, but rather it endeavours to define his spatial coordinates and to imagine the conditions of his material and spiritual existence. In a comprehensive manner, Tarkovsky suggests that the novellas which constitute the film

> are not connected by a traditional chronological line, but by the poetic logic of the need for Rublev to paint his celebrated 'Trinity'. The episodes, each with its own particular plot and theme, draw their unity from that logic. They develop in interaction with each other, through the inner conflict inherent in the poetic logic of their sequence in the screenplay: a kind of visual manifestation of the contradictions and complexities of life and of artistic creativity...[7]

What is remarkable in the director's remark about 'novellas' is the inherent tension or even conflict between *word* and *image*. Storytelling appears to give way to visualization. Novella, as a short literary fictional narrative, is transformed into a visual panel, which together with other panels relates a story. The film as a whole, like a specific genre of icon painting (*polyptych*) which consists of multiple panels and lacks a definitive centre, becomes a visual representation or manifestation of Rublev's life and art. Word and image are interwoven.

Biblical texts unobtrusively enter the film, which provides a site for the dynamic co-existence of text (the quotations and lines of dialogue in general) and image (particular instances of Rublev's iconography and filmic material in general), since both are necessary constituents of a truthful depiction of Christian reality. As the Orthodox art historians Leonid Ouspensky and Vladimir Lossky suggest, iconography and biblical exegesis are inseparable due to the fact that 'the preaching of Christianity to the world was from the beginning carried out by the Church through *word* and *image*.'[8] The critics develop their argument further by referring to one of the Christian dogmatic postulates: 'Through His Incarnation [Christ], God the *Word* "being the brightness of His glory, and the express image of His person" (Heb. I, 3), reveals to the world in His Divinity, the *image* of the Father.'[9] It would thus appear to be natural that a film about a Christian icon painter – a producer of holy images – should be shaped by holy texts.

Texts inspire visions, and *Andrei Rublev* accomplishes the transformation from the textual to the visual. Lengthy biblical quotations are used to enter the domain of fantasy or memory. Moreover, the biography of the icon painter is a filmic vision per se, and the concept of *vision* is crucial to the film. Rublev is the sole character in Tarkovsky's cinema whose trade is to produce visual artefacts. However, the icon painter does not paint at all in the course of the film: only once is he depicted scratching soot from an icon of St George, which is not even his own creation. Instead he has visions: visual perception, a skill necessary for any pictorial representation, merges into an ability to have a visionary experience – a spiritual category.

The *OED* defines 'vision' as something 'which is apparently seen otherwise than by ordinary sight; esp. an appearance of a prophetic or mystical character, or having the nature of a revelation, supernaturally presented to the mind either in sleep or in an abnormal state'. The main character of *Andrei Rublev* does indeed have extraordinary sight, and is prone to enter abnormal states. The medieval monk and artist sees the world differently from his mentors: in his style he exceeds Daniil the Black, and differs dramatically from Theophanes the Greek. Rublev's ability to have a vision makes him a visionary – someone who is able 'or accustomed to see visions' (*OED*). His art cannot be mimetic; it derives from visions, fuelled by sacred words, and recreates events seen by his spiritual sight.

Historical facts and biblical texts serve as a basis for Rublev's visionary experiences and are crucial to the complex narrative pattern of *Andrei Rublev*. Indeed, lengthy quotations and clearly articulated world-views play a key role in the film, and constitute the most coherent and integral set of quotations in Tarkovsky's oeuvre. They all have biblical origins, and are presented as historically organic material in its natural habitat. Quotations from the Old Testament Ecclesiastes and Isaiah, and the New Testament First Corinthians and Matthew are not mere disposable supplements; they reflect discursive themes and significantly influence the narrative progression of the film. The textual allusions appear to help the director to set forth a purely fictional justification for Rublev's individual style of iconography, which has been perceived by art historians as distinctively Russian. Fine, unruffled lines and a warm colour palette generate the tranquil and compassionate iconographic images for which Rublev is famous and held in reverence by the Orthodox Church. These peaceful manifestations of the divine are set in contrast to Theophanes the Greek's iconography, based on the ideas of threat and punishment.

Moreover, some narrative moments in the film are clearly inspired by scholarly texts: the descriptions of the conflict between Vasili of Moscow and Iuri of Zvenigorod (sons of Dmitri Donskoi) and the Patriarch's attempts to reconcile the brothers can be found in Lazarev.[10] Even Rublev's hesitation about painting the frescoes of the Last Judgement in the Dormition Cathedral in Vladimir, which presumably results in two summers of work (1408–09), and his period of 'inactivity' from the completion of the frescoes until the mid-1420s, though purely fictional fantasies on the part of the script-writers, derive from their effort to interpret gaps in historical knowledge.[11]

Thus, the importance of the textual material in *Andrei Rublev* cannot be overestimated. Texts shape the director's visualization of Rublev's life: the icon painter was a great translator of sacred words into visual signs, and Tarkovsky attempts to follow his approach. The interplay between image and text can already be noted in the first seconds of the film, before the narrative begins. The opening credits appear on a white background, which is not just a random surface but a plastered wall. Its emptiness is artificial, and it yearns for an image to be laid over it. The glaringly white plaster is presented to the viewer as if it is ready to receive a fresco, which would reveal in all its glory the days and deeds of a certain saintly person (Rublev, incidentally, was declared a saint by the Russian Orthodox Church in 1988). The blank space of the wall and of the cinema screen is then, gradually and unhurriedly, filled with scenes from and events surrounding the life of Andrei Rublev.

There are also several purely visual points of derivation for certain of the film's *mises-en-scène*, in the same manner as there are real sources for the textual allusions. In *Sculpting in Time*, Tarkovsky made clear reference to Vittore Carpaccio's visual techniques. The great Venetian painter is renowned for his complex crowd-dominated compositions, which frequently have no main characters:

> The point is that *each* of the characters in Carpaccio's crowded composition is a centre. If you concentrate on any one figure you begin to see with unmistakable clarity that everything else is mere context, background, built up like a kind of pedestal for this 'incidental' character. The circle closes, and as you gaze at Carpaccio's canvas your will follows, meekly and unwittingly, the logical channel of feeling intended by the artist, wandering first to one figure apparently lost in the crowd, and then on to the next.[12]

The viewer does indeed lose Rublev from his spectrum of vision as the 'main' protagonist is consumed by the crowd and spatially dislocated. The icon painter cannot, for example, be distinguished from the secondary characters in the 'Buffoon' and 'Theophanes the Greek' episodes; he is also a face in the crowd during a substantial part of the 'Raid' novella; finally, he becomes a pure spectator in the 'Bell' sequence, during which Boriska emerges at the centre of the storyline. Tarkovsky's method of obscuring the central figure does indeed correspond with Carpaccio's approach to composition.

But Carpaccio's low-relief vistas appear to be a less pertinent source of inspiration and reference to *Andrei Rublev* than do the perspectival pictures of Pieter Bruegel the Elder, with their blurred or completely absent central subjects. Though a product of the Renaissance, Bruegel did not share the anthropocentric conviction prevailing at the time, and his canvases' 'vividness frequently conceals a puzzling center of meaning'.[13] The painter often used the genre of landscape to accommodate several narrative scenes (placed both in the foreground and background) in a single panoramic space, whereas the scope of Carpaccio's paintings is often less ambitious, and, in addition, several of the Italian master's representative works depict interior scenes in which only one or two characters are present (for instance, *St Ursula's Dream* or *St Augustine in His Study*). More crucially, Bruegel is literally quoted in the film.

The Passion According to Andrei

The 'Passion According to Andrei' episode, which contains the first and key vision in *Andrei Rublev*, includes the crucifixion scene clearly inspired by Bruegel's composition of winter scenes (for instance, *Hunters in the Snow* or *Winter Landscape with a Bird Trap*).[14] It also corresponds to *Jesus Carrying the Cross (The Way to Calvary)*, in which the figure of Christ is situated in the centre but obscured by dozens of surrounding scenes – the painter does not dramatize the event, as if intending to conceal its holy and at the same time disconcerting nature. In addition, the literal dislocation of the famous biblical scene (a Russian snowy landscape with actors in traditional Russian garb instead of the desert Golgotha) has affinities with Bruegel's *Adoration of the Kings in the Snow*, which also situates the canonical story within a setting that is authentic to the painter (a snowy Flemish village instead of desert-like Bethlehem). The artists displace the topography of the biblical narrative.

The Russian Christ wears bast-shoes, and has Slavic facial features and possibly habits – he eats snow to quench his thirst. Moreover, the script indicates that the cross he carries is made of birch wood[15] – a stereotypically symbolic Russian tree. The whole scene is permeated with a melancholic mood intensified by stylized Russian choral music. Close-ups of exhausted faces and of dragging feet are mixed with almost flat long takes of the whole procession, which accompanies the Russian Christ to the site of his crucifixion. The visual treatment of the scene certainly evokes Bruegel's canvases, which usually depict scenes of epic scale but through small visual 'windows'; the grand collective action always consists of smaller individual sub-actions.

The 'Passion According to Andrei' episode opens with an exchange between Andrei and his pupil Foma wandering in a small wood. The former reproaches the latter for his incessant lies and lack of diligence while contemplating their natural surroundings – a brook, a small snake and various vegetation and roots. The spiritually mature and gentle master stands out in the presence of the somewhat infantile pupil. The discursive centre of the episode, however, is a meeting between Rublev and Theophanes. The encounter on the riverbank is preceded by a vision of flight, available only in the 205-minute extended version.

Foma, on his way to take glue off the bonfire, notices something lying on the ground. It turns out to be a dead swan, and the apprentice carefully observes the decaying carcass: he chases a carrion beetle with a stick and then carefully lifts the bird's wing. This gesture is further developed in a somewhat literal manner: the image of the lifted wing is followed by a flight sequence.[16] The flight functions as a memory of the dead bird. The abstractness of this given memory is achieved by alternating landscapes: in a few seconds the swan flies over spring water-meadows, a river with banks covered in snow, and a summer field. The continuous space during the flight is counterbalanced by the discontinuous time, which manifests itself through alternating seasons. This short, unmotivated vision is in fact a trace of the 'Hunt' episode, which was never filmed but can still be found in the script. However, this brief flight prepares the viewer for an extended leap to a radically other space and time: the most crucial vision in the film. The presence of the flight sequence serves as a connecting bridge between Foma's curious examination of the dead bird and Rublev's vision, the ultimate flight of imagination: the Russian Passion.

It should be noted that Foma's role in the sequence is ambiguous. He may be the one who visualizes Rublev's narrative and experiences the Russian Passion vision, though this is not narratively justified, due to his immaturity. At the same time, he is about to become an icon painter, and in the longest version he proudly states to Rublev: 'All the same I can see better than any of them.' When the sound of the conversation between Rublev and Theophanes emerges, the camera finds only the figure of Foma in its field of vision – the adolescent washes brushes in the river and listens attentively to the exchange between his masters. Moreover, the apprentice reappears off-focus in the background when the camera stares at Rublev's back, just a few seconds before the vision commences. Finally, the ending of the crucifixion sequence is followed by a close-up of an attentive Foma sitting by the same river, washing brushes and listening to Rublev and Theophanes.

Whether it is Foma who experiences the vision or not, one cannot overestimate the role of the river in the sequence. The categories of space and time are amalgamated by this flow of time through river bends scattered in space. The river, as a spatial entity which is usually taken as a major metaphor of time, accomplishes a temporal or even atemporal leap: it connects the given real topos of Rublev and Theophanes (a small forest by a river in summer – the narrative present) and the imaginary topos of the Russian Christ (a hilly terrain with a river in winter – narrative timelessness). In addition, the preceding swan's-flight sequence can be seen as uniting the summer and winter scenes: the bird indeed flies over different seasons. Spatial continuity is blended with (a)temporal displacement. The comparison can be even further extended; perhaps Rublev oversees the two distinct spatio-temporal frameworks – the narrative now and the atemporal vision – from the height of the flight of his imagination? The river over which the swan flies is transformed into the summer river where Foma washes his brushes, and then into the winter river from which the Russian Christ drinks.

The discursive kernel of the episode remains the exchange between Theophanes and Andrei. In the course of a highly agitated argument, Theophanes recalls how Christ's passion was marked by the unfaithfulness and weakness of his pupils. Towards the end of his speech, he makes explicit reference to the Last Judgement – the concept which will soon drive Rublev into an artistic cul-de-sac: 'The Last Judgement will be upon us soon, and we shall all be burning like candles. And you mark my words, when it comes . . . They'll all be blaming their sins on each other, and panicking, and trying to barricade themselves from the Almighty...' To this Andrei replies: 'I don't understand how you can paint with ideas like that in your head', and this bewilderment betokens his artistic doubts.

The original script of the film contains a more conventional visualization of the Passion episode in which climatic conditions and topography seem to correspond to historical reality. Theophanes the Greek imagines the Passion to be in its traditional location, and Christ to be surrounded by a highly adversarial crowd:

> In the stifling white dust a vast mob was walking up the sun-baked, stony road leading to the top of the hill; they were shouting, their mouths gaping and crooked, and throwing stones at a man who walked, his head held high, surrounded by soldiers who were keeping him away from a crowd excited to fever-pitch by the prospect of an execution; amongst them were horsemen, and a huge flock of bleating sheep, terrified by this mass of frenzied people; and in the midst of the monstrous whirlpool of human hatred and betrayal was the Nazareen[sic], stumbling and falling to his knees, his face bloody; and the heavy oak cross, which was passed along on upstretched hands by people blinded by their thirst for blood, dripping with sweat, their faces grimy with the dust of the road; the cross glided over the crowd to a pit; there they laid him down on the wooden beam, fell on him, stretched out his exhausted arms along the branches of the cross, and drove black, forged nails into his palms with blows from the back of an axe.[17]

The Greek master's alien and fearsome vision of Christianity is based on the concept of punishment. The Passion according to Theophanes is manifestly violent, with heat and dust intensifying the brutality of the scene. The people here are certainly not Russian; they do not have a specific nationality – the craving for Christ's blood unites them. This verbal vision takes place before Andrei's winter crucifixion. The two visions, one verbal and hidden and one visual and explicit, clearly represent two distinct discourses shaping *Andrei Rublev*. The notions of punishment and threat are alien to the Russian icon painter, and to counter Theophanes' idea of interminable, all-encompassing evil, Andrei puts forward his own view, which develops into a visionary picture of the meekly suffering Russian people voluntarily ascending Golgotha. Submissiveness and the capacity for suffering, the *kenotic* ideals of Christianity, are highlighted in the Russian crucifixion scene (Figure 2.2). The leap to another space and time is accomplished through Rublev's

Figure 2.2

voice-over, which unites the two spaces; the uninterrupted soundtrack provides a sense of continuity.

Tarkovsky's visual interpretation of the Passion draws on some of the basic aesthetic premises of iconographic art, which postulates that 'the action is not enclosed in or limited to a particular place, just as, while being manifested in time, it is not limited to a certain time'.[18] Besides, according to the Christian doctrine, the coming of Christ is perceived as a *kairotic* event which transcended the ordinary notion of time; the event can be repeated in the soul of every Christian until the end of time (the Last Judgement). By displacing the event spatially (to Russia) and re-enacting it temporally (in the fifteenth century), or even atemporally, Rublev reflects the essence of his belief in a universal, active Christianity based on love and forgiveness. He allows abstract categories to emerge in all their glory in earthly time.

The meekness of Rublev's vision is not a mere flight of the filmmaker's imagination. Russian scholars frequently describe Rublev's oeuvre as serene, peaceful, unruffled, or meek.[19] They usually compare his iconography with the Byzantine tradition represented by Theophanes the Greek in order to highlight the Russian icon painter's individual style. These contrasts tend at times to be overly speculative, and are not usually rooted in reflective art-historical analysis. For instance, critics are disinclined to take into account those most essential functions of iconography – to transmit tradition, to strip the icon of personal whims, and for the icon painter to remain anonymous.

Nevertheless, the basic binary pair – darkness vs. light – is a common starting point for scholars writing about Russian iconography, and it seems reasonable that Tarkovsky, who was informed by recent studies of the subject, built his narrative line with this antagonistic interrelationship at its core.[20] Theophanes and Rublev do not share a common world-view, and this fact allows the Russian artist to develop his own distinctive style. In the course of his passionate speech, Theophanes makes a reference to Chapter 1, Verse 6 of the Book of Ecclesiastes: 'The wind goeth toward the south, and turneth about unto the north; it whirleth about continually, and the wind returneth again according to his circuits.' For Theophanes, the condition in which humanity finds itself is devoid of a sense of progress and culmination. The result is a world shaped by human malevolence of a cyclical nature, and the only way out of this vicious circle of human existence is to be found in the complete surrender of oneself to God, which is accomplished through fear of divine judgement. For Rublev, on the other hand, Christ's Passion is a *kairotic* event – and voluntary spiritual re-enactment is its essential element. The two versions of Christ's Passion (one of which – Theophanes' – is confined to the script, and materializes only in fragments in the Greek icon painter's speech) embody two divergent interpretations of the doctrine, and are set to collide. Rublev's vision, however, since the artist himself is the main protagonist – or rather, the main subject of the film's artistic enquiry – is given noticeable priority: it enters the screen.

At the same time, the function of the winter crucifixion scene is not purely cerebral or textual in nature. While the discourse it attempts to deliver is vital, its fundamentally visual qualities should not be underestimated. Christ's Passion in the Russian winter landscape can be treated as a cinematic icon, which the director models on Rublev's art. The board nailed to the cross contains an orthographically corrupted version of the Greek inscription – 'Jesus Christ, the God of Suffering' – which can be found on Orthodox icons of the crucifixion. The inscription immediately withdraws the scene from the realm of *mimesis*: the winter crucifixion is not an attempt to imitate a certain historical event, it rather presents an *image* of that event. Rublev's vision, inspired by a story of Christ's Passion, evolves into an icon: Tarkovsky's visual cinematic presentation.

In this light, Slavoj Žižek's criticism of the sequence for its allegedly 'bad actors playing it with ridiculous pathos, with tears flowing'[21] should be reconsidered. The aesthetics of Orthodox iconography are based on the notion of stylization: the multiplicity of vanishing points or the absence of shadows are its key features, which can be considered as aesthetically awkward or even 'ridiculous'. However, this 'ineptness' establishes a visible borderline between the terrestrial and celestial realms: an icon does not belong to everyday reality and does not follow the optic conventions which regulate it. In the same manner, the 'bad', stylized acting, together with the incongruous doubling (the Virgin and Mary Magdalene are depicted at the bottom of the hill in the distance when the Russian Christ falls down, and then the two women appear right beside Christ when he gets up), deliberately highlights the otherworldliness of the event. Christ's Passion is not a mundane event, and it indeed stands out in terms of the acting style, which is usually impeccable in Tarkovsky.

This corresponds to the very essence of iconography. It does not try to *imitate* nature at a particular moment of time, since imitation is the domain of classical art, which usually accommodates a 'vision' in a framed canvas, emphasizing its artificial character. On the contrary, it tries to *present* active and eternal spiritual 'archetypes' and a 'vision' is usually housed in an unframed wooden surface or a wall, which underlines its corporality. As the authors of one of the classical studies of Russian icons put it: 'The icon is regarded as one of the ways by means of which it is possible and necessary to strive to achieve the task set before mankind, to achieve likeness to the prototype, to embody in life what was manifested and transmitted by God-Man.'[22] The possibility for spiritual ideals to be re-enacted in the here-and-now is crucial, and Tarkovsky seems deliberately to follow the tradition.

The Last Judgement

The narrative line of the film posits that Rublev was able to paint the Old Testament Trinity, which is itself a complex concept – the oneness of three – but struggled to give a pictorial rendering of the Last Judgement – a less 'complicated' idea in doctrinal terms. The icon painter is appalled by the presumed violence of the latter notion, and dares to challenge the established canon. His doubts manifest themselves in a masterfully orchestrated *mise-en-scène* in a blooming summer field, when he faces his mentor and friend Daniil the Black. What makes this scene interesting is the fact that Andrei does not really face Daniil; on the contrary, the two characters repeatedly look in different directions. Their world-views literally do not coincide. This is an abnormal form of interaction, since the two men share the same space but strive towards different directions and reject the possibility of ideological confluence. Like discontinuous time, which lacks the linearity of one singular temporal thread, these spatial encounters are 'damaged' and aberrant; they are heralds of further spatial dislocations.

In the blooming field, Andrei confronts his mentor and friend Daniil. An inability to justify his artistic block renders Rublev's speech fragmented and highly disturbed: he is disgusted by the idea that his art would intimidate people. Daniil, in his turn, is unable to appreciate Andrei's anxieties since, for him, the Last Judgement is an accepted concept within Christian doctrine. The role of the icon painter is simply to follow the established tradition of pictorial representation. The film script contains Daniil's extended, bewildered speech: 'I didn't invent this! The old masters painted like this and Theophanes also taught us to paint in this way! Look at Byzantine manuscripts and manuals!'[23] The references to Theophanes and the Byzantine School in general are important, since these are aesthetic prototypes which shaped early Russian iconography and which Rublev allegedly rendered obsolete. Moreover, the 205-minute version of the film contains an additional scene which precedes Foma's departure:

[Andrei:] – Even if you kill me, I shouldn't know what to paint.

[Foma:] – What d'you mean, you don't know? We've been told to paint the Last Judgement.

[Andrei:] – The thing is, I think it would be better not to paint the Last Judgement at all.

[Daniil:] – What do you mean?

[Andrei:] – I want... There is nothing I want, nothing... That's it...

For Foma, it is also clear how the scenes of divine punishment should be depicted. Now a senior apprentice, he does not interrogate accepted standards, nor does he challenge the doctrine. The period of idleness nevertheless provokes Foma to leave his master and accept an invitation to decorate a village church. It is notable that the commission is for the Last Judgement.

Unable to visualize the doctrine, Rublev wanders about inside the cathedral, surrounded by dazzlingly white walls. The icon painter tries to overcome his artistic block by escaping to another space and time. The wall is a spatial marker which merges the church where Rublev cannot start working on the Last Judgement frescos with the Grand Duke's apartment. The whiteness of the wall inside the cathedral is not even a metaphor for Rublev's artistic silence, so obvious is its function. The wall's serenity encloses the icon painter's desperate cry. It also serves as a visual refrain, transferring the narrative from the present time to the realm of Rublev's memory: his encounter with the Grand Duke, his family, and the stonemasons working for him.

The whiteness of the wall is echoed in the whiteness of milk which is splashed over Andrei by a playful infant duchess, and in the white stone of the duke's new apartments. The whiteness is further emphasized in the contrast between a charred black log and hovering white poplar fluff – a shot which immediately follows the close-up of Andrei against the white background. The return to the present which follows is accomplished by Rublev smearing dirt or dark paint over the same white wall, as if he refuses to 'soil' the virgin surface with frightening images of the Last Judgement. Literally, white and dark forces, and by extension two versions of Christianity which are based respectively on love and punishment, clash in this very resonant episode.

Before the wall is soiled, however, it functions as a means of spatio-temporal displacement. Andrei starts reading a passage from Chapter 13 of First Corinthians with the dazzlingly white colour as background. His voice is somewhat poignant at the beginning of the quotation, and then develops an elevated and joyous tone once he enters another space and time and the little girl enters the scene, now located in the Grand Duke's apartment. Rublev addresses the uncomprehending child with the highly complex text and gently reproaches her for splashing milk:

> Though I speak with the tongues of men and of angels, and have not charity, I am become as sounding brass, or a tinkling cymbal. And though I have the gift of prophecy, and understand all mysteries, and all knowledge; and though I have all faith, so that I could remove mountains, and have not charity, I am nothing. And though I bestow all my goods to feed the poor, and though I give my body to be burned, and have not charity, it profiteth me nothing. Charity suffereth long, and is kind; charity envieth not; charity vaunteth not itself, is not puffed up, doth not behave itself unseemly, seeketh not her own, is not easily provoked, thinketh no evil; rejoiceth not in iniquity, but rejoiceth in the truth; beareth all things, believeth all things, hopeth all things, endureth all things. Charity never faileth: but whether there be prophecies, they shall fail; whether there be tongues, they shall cease; whether there be knowledge, it shall vanish away. For we know in part... (First Corinthians 13: 1–9)

The text, which is also quoted in full in Tarkovsky's book,[24] is known as the 'Hymn to Love'. It is one of the richest poetic passages of the New Testament, though it is written in prose. The form in which it is composed is based on the notion of contrast and consists of thirteen simple verbs, arranged in the order positive-negative-positive. Paul contrasts love with other religious actions, virtues and perishable things, or describes it in negative terms. The visual sequence of Rublev's recollection is based on striking contrasts in the same manner: the burnt wooden carcass of the Grand Duke's former palace is contrasted with the new white stone chambers; Rublev's meek appreciation of the work done by the masons with the stern disapproval of the Grand Duke's second-in-command Stepan; the childish innocence of the duchess either with the naughtiness of her brother or with the vicious ambition of her father who, 'blinded' by his own rivalry with his brother, decides to blind the masons; Andrei's inability to paint frescoes in Vladimir with his role as a restorer of burnt icons; or the whiteness of milk dripping into a brook towards the end of the episode with the dark, yawning eye-sockets of the blinded men (Figure 2.3).

Figure 2.3

Moreover, in the 205-minute version of the film, the ending of Chapter 13 of First Corinthians is read out by Rublev before the rest of the text. The icon painter starts reciting the Hymn immediately after Foma leaves. This is a significant addition, since the prolonged presence of the voice-over establishes a more rigid bridge between the two divergent places – the church and the Grand Duke's apartments. The content of the quote itself is also vital:

> When I was a child, I spake as a child, I understood as a child, I thought as a child: but when I became a man, I put away childish things. For now we see through a glass, darkly; but then face to face: now I know in part; but then shall I know even as also I am known. And now abideth faith, hope, charity, these three; but the greatest of these is charity. (First Corinthians 13: 11–13)

The beginning clearly refers to a child whose knowledge is not yet complete, who in turn becomes 'a man' whose knowledge becomes absolute from the perspective of the final revelation. It is possible that these very sentences served as a narrative pretext for the little duchess to enter the scene; the words remind Rublev of the encounter. Furthermore, the additional passage is a celebrated reference to two modes of seeing: 'through a glass, darkly' and 'face to face', in which, once again, clarity and darkness are contrasted. The very last sentence constitutes the ultimate glorification of love, which is conceived by Paul as the only characteristic of the present which is final and complete, unlike other Christian gifts and qualities, which are always provisional and imperfect.

The vision-memory, which starts with the elevation of love as the greatest virtue, culminates in one of the most brutal scenes of the film – the blinding of the masons. The whiteness of milk meets the darkness of blood. The ruthless competition between the dukes finds its victims in the simple working peasants. The slaughter scene is visually connected with Rublev's inability to paint; poplar fluff, present both in the church and in the forest where the murders take place, creates an aura of surreal calm. Dreamily flying fluff enwraps the tormented characters. The very last image in the blinding scene is milk splashed into a small pond. The image of the white substance, which announced the leap to another space and time with the little duchess splashing milk at Rublev, also concludes the vision. The whiteness of milk is consumed by the dark waters of the pond, and this is immediately followed by the abrupt return to the cathedral where Rublev soils the white surface of the wall – here again, dark matter is violently imposed on a white plane.

The elevated hymn to love, the ruthless murder of the stonemasons and the desecration of the wall are followed by another extensive quotation from First Corinthians. According to some theologians, Paul's epistle is notorious for 'somewhat disappointing descent[s] to the practicalities',[25] and the following passage from Chapter 11 is one of them. After Andrei violently soils the surface of the cathedral's white wall and, emotionally devastated, begins to cry, Daniil asks Sergei, a junior apprentice, to read aloud a random passage from the Scriptures. The boy, who was found by Rublev after the stonemasons were blinded and who actually opens the 'Last Judgement' episode by pitifully asking Foma for permission to swim, reads from Chapter 11 of First Corinthians.

His uninspired and awkward reading is in sharp contrast with the preceding elevation of the 'Hymn to Love'. This time the child is quoting the text, but he is also, like the little duchess, unlikely to comprehend the full meaning of the New Testament passage imposed upon him. The camera movement imitates the monotonous voice of Sergei, and in a leisurely manner tracks the characters inside the cathedral – again in contrast with the Chapter 13 episode, where movement (Rublev chasing the girl and flying doves) is crucial. The camera's main point of attention now is the holy fool who is hiding from the rain in the church where the icon painters work. Her inquisitive gaze and improper appearance (her face is covered in sores and her garments are unkempt) dominate the sequence. She is a stunning counter-example to Paul's rhetoric, since she is not only the 'disgraceful' woman who enters the holy place with head uncovered, but also a holy fool – a deeply respected irrational manifestation of Christianity in Russia. The woman, who may easily be classified as an unworthy sinner, is devastated by the sight of the desecrated wall in the holy place, and bursts into tears.

First Corinthians as a whole (apart from the 'Hymn to Love') is an attempt to impose order and to prescribe certain rigid patterns of behaviour. The subordination advocated is plainly revealed in the descending hierarchy of 'heads'. According to this hierarchy, the holy fool in *Andrei Rublev* exemplifies the ultimate disgrace, since she not only has her head uncovered but is also 'out of her mind'. In the longest version of the film she enters the cathedral and urinates inside the holy place. This act of disgrace and profanity puts her into a 'sinful' category even without reference to the Pauline doctrine, which prescribes proper and improper behavioural patterns. The consequence of profanity or even mildly improper behaviour always comes in the form of exclusion from the rest of the Christian community, and the Last Judgement is an act of exclusion per se: righteous people are separated from sinners, and both proceed to their respective domains.

At the same time, First Corinthians contains unequivocal praise for love as the principal Christian virtue. According to Paul, love cannot co-exist with the notion of judgement and punitive exclusion, since a Christian who has love does not lose patience or temper. However, this contention is not a characteristic feature of the text as a whole – the 'Hymn to Love' is a digression which falls beyond the boundaries of Paul's main argument. Rublev appears to utilize the very 'marginal' status of this quotation in order to challenge the idea of exclusion, which shapes some aspects of the Christian dogma and manifests itself clearly in the rest of First Corinthians, and most vividly in the passage read by Sergei.

In Chapter 13 of First Corinthians Love (*agapē*) stands for divine love, and differs from both *philia* (natural human affection, brotherly love) and *erōs* (desiring love). Rublev resolves his inability to give the Last Judgement pictorial representation by attaining the realm of *agapē* through *philia* and compassion for the holy fool – a marginal character in the film. The two quotations from First Corinthians thus discursively resolve Rublev's artistic block. The all-embracing *agapē* helps him to overcome the strictness and literality of the doctrine as such. Andrei's elevated tone returns, and he joyously announces: 'Daniil, it's a feast day, Daniil, a feast day! And you are talking about... How can they be sinners, even if they have taken off their kerchiefs!'

The icon painter realizes the impossibility of excluding the holy fool under the 'dubious' textual pretext, and he literally includes her in his own domain: she becomes his companion for years to come. Rublev now confronts Christian truth 'face to face' – he regains his spiritual vision. As a result of this sudden resolution, the icon painter manages to depict the 'feast day' scene from the Last Judgement: while no single image of it appears in the film itself, it is vividly described in the film script:

> One after the other, full of nobility and tenderness, their faces poignantly Russian, the righteous women glide forward.
>
> Their quiet eyes, full of hope, and their simple serene demeanour convince the beholder that they exist in reality, convince him of the sanctity of their womanly being. The radiant eyes of sisters, mothers, betrothed and wives – support in love and in the future.
>
> The innocent's [holy fool's] happy laugh re-echoes round the empty, clean cathedral.[26]

It is also important to note that the same resolution in the 205-minute version is preceded by a leap to another space and time: Rublev recollects a moment of leaving Andronikov together with Kirill and Daniil under heavy rain. A sole tree on the road gives them shelter – it literally covers their heads. The rain has a purifying function; water again connects the two disparate places and times. Rublev, visibly transfigured, goes out of the church to be soaked under the rain.

Visionary Iconostasis

When Dmitri Donskoi, the Grand Duke of Russia, died in 1389 his son Vasili inherited the throne. The latter was jealously opposed by his brother Iuri, who was based at Zvenigorod. The historical rivalry between the two shapes the storyline of *Andrei Rublev*. It serves as a background to 'The Last Judgement', but emerges into the foreground in the 'Raid' episode. More significantly, the sacking of Vladimir – the most action-driven novella – allows another character, apart from Rublev, to have visions and memories: the Duke of Zvenigorod suppresses the feeling of guilt, for he joins the Tartars and destroys the Russian city, by means of leaps to other spaces and times.

The first leap takes place at the beginning of the novella, when the duke meets the Tartar prince. The latter asks the former when he last made peace with his brother. The duke answers that he did not make peace with him: he was only summoned by the archbishop and made to swear that he would live with his brother in peace and harmony. These words call up a memory of a certain event – the viewer is transferred to a cathedral in a winter landscape, to which the brothers come to see the archbishop. The sacking of Vladimir brings the viewer back to the present time. The inhabitants of the medieval city are subjected to a terrifying ordeal, and at one point an Orthodox chant can be heard amid the scenes of murder and rape. What appears to be non-diegetic sound is gradually revealed to have a source within the cinematic frame: the chant is heard from the cathedral, which was the site of the forced reconciliation and is now being assaulted by the troops.[27] The monotonous noise of a battering-ram is mixed with the melodious song, and the combination of the two distresses the duke, who turns his back to the sacred place.

The principal flashback vision takes place inside the cathedral, when Tartars torture the key-keeper Patrikei. The vision is preceded by a spatial aberration: while the duke observes the scene of torture there is a heavy chandelier swinging behind him. The object appears and reappears in the camera's field of vision two or three times, and then, after it goes off the screen and the viewer expects it to come back, it disappears altogether in spite of the laws of nature. The pendulum of the present time stops and the narrative enters the domain of the past. After the swinging is interrupted without any reason, the duke enters the space and time of his traumatic memory. This small detail announces that the sacred space has entered an abnormal state.

The sense of devastation with a hint of abnormality is intensified in a further overtly stylized and improbable episode in the film. The destroyed cathedral, which is about to host another vision, is not a random place: it is the Dormition Cathedral in Vladimir, where Rublev painted his Last Judgement frescoes. Here he encounters the ghost of the deceased Greek master, his erstwhile teacher, inside the devastated building. The place of this meeting is of crucial importance: a dilapidated church or a damaged shelter is one of the recurrent themes in Tarkovsky's oeuvre, and it possesses great semantic potential for any interpretation of his cinematic language. The ruins, moreover, have a specific function, if one considers the phenomenon through the prism of Christian doctrine: the destruction of the Old Temple and the building of the new is a well-known biblical trope.

The cathedral in Vladimir, like the belfry from the 'Prologue', is a deformed building whose primary function has been challenged. The raid accomplished by the Tartars together with the Duke of Zvenigorod leaves the holy place in utter desolation. Its integrity is violated and it now contains unbefitting elements such as human corpses and animals (a stray cat and a horse are shown walking inside the church), and it is open to the natural elements – there is a fire, and it is snowing inside. The church's condition allows for borderline events to take place, such as Andrei's meeting with the ghost of the dead Theophanes. Heavy chandeliers, identical to the abnormal pendulum of time which launches the duke's leap in space and time, are visible at the background when the two men meet (Figure 2.4). It is also of crucial importance that the two encounter each other in front of the burnt iconostasis whose firebrands shape the whole scene. The iconostasis, according to Orthodox doctrine, is an obstacle separating the celestial and the terrestrial realms. As Pavel Florensky – a distinguished Russian Orthodox theologian and art specialist – describes it:

> The wall that separates two worlds is an iconostasis. One might mean by the iconostasis the boards or the bricks or the stones. In actuality, the iconostasis is a boundary between the visible and invisible worlds, and it functions as a boundary by being an obstacle to our seeing the altar, thereby making it accessible to our consciousness by means of its unified row of saints (i.e., by its cloud of witnesses) that surround the altar where God is, the sphere where heavenly glory dwells, thus proclaiming the Mystery.[28]

Florensky continues his train of thought by highlighting the capacity of iconostases to evoke holy apparitions: 'Iconostasis is vision. Iconostasis is a manifestation of saints and angels – *angelophania* – a manifest appearance of heavenly witnesses that includes, first

Figure 2.4

of all, the Mother of God and Christ Himself in the flesh, witnesses who proclaim that which is from the other side of mortal flesh. Iconostasis is the saints themselves.'[29] Theophanes comes to Andrei precisely by way of a holy apparition. The otherworldliness of the dead icon painter is referred to explicitly in the following exchange: '[Andrei:] Didn't you go to heaven? [Theophanes:] All I can say is that it's all quite different from what you all imagine.' The messenger represents the celestial realm and cannot disclose its nature to a still-living human being. The Greek icon painter is visibly transfigured: he wears a beautiful white robe, his facial features are to a certain extent pacified, and there is a hint of melancholy in his way of speaking. This last feature bears the greatest significance, since it is at odds with his fearsome misanthropic outbursts discussed above.

The spectral visitation finds Andrei already in an overwhelmed state; the scene opens with him kneeling in front of the burnt iconostasis and mumbling in a desultory manner. Once he notices Theophanes he expresses slight bewilderment, but then quickly yields to this far from ordinary situation. The first thing Rublev tells the ghost is of his recent dream, in which Theophanes himself features, together with the Tartars, thus further undermining the dichotomy between illusion and reality. He then complains to his teacher, in clear reference to their conversation which generated his own vision of the Russian Christ:

> [Andrei:] – Listen, what is happening? Killing and raping along with the Tartars, ransacking churches along with the Tartars. You were telling me…But now I'm worse off than you, you're dead already, whereas…
>
> [Theophanes:] – Dead…so what?
>
> [Andrei:] – That's not what I meant! What I mean is that I've spent half my life in blindness! Half my life, like that…It was for them, I was doing it all for other people, day in day out, night in night out…. Are they human beings at all? You were right then…
>
> [Theophanes:] – I said all sorts of things! You are wrong now, I was wrong then.

Rublev then confesses to Theophanes that he has killed a man – the Russian marauder who tried to rape the holy fool. The apparition of the Greek icon painter in the devastated cathedral in Vladimir dramatically differs from his previous encounters with Rublev. Theophanes radically reconsiders his vision of divine judgement. Though his speech still bears a discursive trace of his earlier, angry words, the idea of forgiveness emerges and overtakes the retributive discourse. Forgiveness is unambiguously affirmed. This episode – the sacking of Vladimir – draws the two icon painters closer together. The spiritually devastated Rublev tries to adopt Theophanes' former vision of people as an illiterate malicious herd, but it is now the turn of the Greek master to assert the opposite.

The result is Rublev's 'denial of the word and the image […] by disavowing speech and icon-painting',[30] and these are to be restored in the subsequent episodes. Meanwhile, Rublev meekly laments Russia's fate in his last speech:

> [Andrei:] – Rus', Rus'… She endures everything, this country of ours, and she will endure to the end…But how long is it all going to go on? Eh? Theophanes?
>
> [Theophanes:] – I don't know. Probably forever. [Looks at one of the remaining icons of the iconostasis] How beautiful it is!

[Andrei:] – It's snowing... There is nothing more terrifying than snow falling inside a cathedral. Is there? [Theophanes disappears]

Theophanes' response is of crucial importance to the discursive outcome of the scene: he appears to be indifferent to the cyclical evil shaping the human world that used to aggravate him so much. He also reaffirms the validity of and the need for iconography by one very simple but profound comment: that beauty cannot be resisted. In his very last sentence, Rublev refers to the cathedral as a deformed building. The horror he feels as a result of the murder he has committed and the massacre he has witnessed is intensified by the vision of the devastated church, which is no longer a holy place providing spiritual shelter for those who enter it. The snow falling inside the building is both an unsettling and a beautiful spectacle, and it mesmerizes the two characters. Theophanes disappears without responding to Rublev's last question; the affirmative statement about the art of iconography constitutes his last words. The viewer is nevertheless made aware that the two formerly conflicting visions have converged in the destroyed cathedral.

Casting the Future

In terms of storyline, the 'Bell' episode is the most coherent segment of *Andrei Rublev*. It is placed at the end of the film and allows a completely new character – an adolescent called Boriska – to emerge in the narrative foreground. The central character of the film is no longer an exceptional icon painter, but rather a sinful monk who has taken a vow of creative and physiological silence. The suppression of his artistic talent is an act of sacrifice and an attempt to terminate his own existence without ending his life. The aged and silent Rublev turns into a mere observer of events, though he still retains a capacity to have visions, and the episode resurrects him from oblivion. The meeting of the two evolves into the highest emotional point of the film: it delivers a life-affirming message which announces the return of the genius. Bachelard suggests that the 'imagination is not, as its etymology suggests, the faculty for forming images of reality; it is the faculty for forming images which go beyond reality, which *sing* reality. It is a superhuman faculty.'[31] The 'Bell' tells the story of a superhuman individual who transcends reality as such.

The 'Silence' episode concludes with an image of an incandescent stone, carried by Rublev to heat water, dropped on snow. The burning surface of the stone meets the iciness of snow and culminates in a violent interaction: the snow hisses and melts. The improbable outcome is 'dampened flames'[32] or 'burned water',[33] which is highly symbolic. Rublev, who is keeping a vow of silence after murdering the soldier, is also on the verge of a personal thaw: he is about to be drawn out of his physical and artistic silence by Boriska's natural genius. Indeed, the following 'Bell' episode opens with a spring motif – Boriska sitting by his hut and watching black strips of ground emerging from the snow bed. The adolescent has survived a plague and is about to resurrect the forgotten tradition of bell-casting.

The two characters 'meet' in the beginning of the episode, at a crucial point when Boriska finds the 'right' clay. The boy is on his own in heavy rain. He fiercely kicks the air, and one of his shoes flies off. After that he slides down a hill, and by chance finds a source of the 'right' clay. This desperately sought-for material stands for some kind of non-rational artistic need – a secret source of inspiration at which one arrives by intuition, for there are no guides. The camera finds Rublev far away; by this time no longer an icon painter, he is driving a horse-cart loaded with vegetables. Completely soaked by the rain, he sees Boriska in an ecstatic state from a distance. Rublev merely looks on.

The scene is followed by a cut to the laborious moulding process, during which Boriska stumbles upon Rublev and tells him to get out of his way. The bell-founder is confronted by his co-workers, who insist on adding an additional layer, while he is anxious to start burning out the form as soon as possible. The conflict is resolved by brute force: Boriska orders one of the workers to be flogged. Rublev pitifully observes the scene and is mocked by the young master. This is followed by a close-up of the former in the midst of intense labour. The idle monk is slightly disorientated. He turns his back to the viewer, and a sad tune enters the cinematic space announcing a leap to the past. Rublev recollects how he, Daniil and Kirill, then relatively young, aspiring icon painters, were leaving Andronikov and found shelter from heavy rain under a lone tree. The picturesque sequence shows the three figures on a winding road and then under an oak tree. The camera tracks the figure of Kirill with a jackdaw, Rublev silently looking off to the side, and a fluttering oak branch covered in leaves. What is peculiar in this memory leap is the fact that the sound of hammering made by the bell-founders is heard continuously up until the close-up of Rublev. The sound connects the two spaces in the same manner as the tree under which the monk-artists stand; the following cut returns the viewer to the present time, with Rublev standing under a leafless tree in late autumn snow as the sleeping Boriska is carried past him.

Flashbacks disrupt the linearity of the narrative, and they show 'how the temporal content of the narrative can seemingly contest or counter the irreversibility of the [cinematic] apparatus itself'.[34] The flashback is both in the present 'now' and the bygone past – it brings back to the present something significant from the past, it (re)collects. By this memory leap Rublev does not just bring back images of a certain space and time; he also consequently experiences a literal return of certain individuals from the past to his present life. The buffoon and Kirill, two central characters in the film's opening, have prominent appearances in the concluding 'Bell' episode. The former accuses Rublev of denouncing him to the authorities (the buffoon has been in prison for ten years and his health is ruined), while the latter persuades Rublev to start painting again. The holy fool, abducted by Tartars, also returns: she appears at the moment when the bell rings for the first time. The narrative circle closes.

Before the episode ends, Rublev appears as an observer two more times: during the process of filling the mould with molten metal, and during the chipping out of the bell. Each time, the icon painter is standing above the scene looking attentively at Boriska and his helpers. Once the bell is revealed, Boris lies on it completely exhausted. The 205-minute version of the film also includes a crucial addition – a brief vision-memory Boriska has while lying on the product of his hard labours. The adolescent dreams of three miniature landscapes: a tree with several buckets with fire 'decorating' it, snow with dark strips of earth, and sheets of material lying and apparently drying on earth. The last two images actually constitute memories of the moment when Boriska was taken by the Grand Duke's people from his hut to cast the bell; the snow and sheets are images connected with home. But all three are small visual poems glorifying combinations of natural elements: the fire-and-air image is followed by the two images of earth and water. All the four elements were crucial during the process of bell-casting.

The bell is raised: the ambitious adolescent bell-founder achieves the unachievable – he restores a forgotten tradition relying solely on his own ingenious instincts. Rublev forms a creative union with the young master in the concluding *pietà* scene: he consoles the weeping boy, breaks his silence, and proclaims his intention to go to the Trinity monastery and resume his craft. The brutality of the medieval era is miraculously transcended: Boriska's feat confirms that divinely beautiful icons, frescoes and bells could rise out of human filth, bestiality, cruelty, ignorance, with nothing remotely resembling an end in sight. These objects – miracles in themselves – violate norms, including those of space and time.

Iconic Poem

The resolution leads to a sequence of images of Rublev's icons accompanied by the poignant dodecaphony alternating with the tranquil melodies of Viacheslav Ovchinnikov's score. The cut to the icons is dramatically enhanced by the use of colour – the harsh medieval reality shot in black and white culminates in the images of unearthly beauty presented in their full colourful glory. The sequence, 'the poem, composed of icons',[35] is the ultimate avowal of artistic truth in the face of various doubts, silences and renunciations. Its positive message is even more notable given that the icon painter does not paint at all in the film. However, the purely formal qualities of the finale also play a prominent semantic role. The director's decision to present icons by framing them with the tracking camera in an overtly impressionistic manner resonates with the rejection of the notion of the 'immobile eye' in Renaissance perspective. The fragmented vision of the tracking camera corresponds to the real-life experience of a believer scanning the pictorial surface of icons with a moving eye.[36] Tarkovsky celebrates the concept of 'reverse perspective' and the multiplicity of vanishing points, instead of the singularity of the Renaissance perspective.

'Reverse perspective' is a term primarily associated with the work of Florensky,[37] and was further developed by Uspensky[38] and Zhegin.[39] The latter two define the aesthetic principles of iconography by contrasting it with Renaissance and post-Renaissance art – Zhegin by developing the idea of multiple vanishing points, and Uspensky by concentrating on the viewer's position. There is also an alternative view, and its proponents[40] claim that 'reverse perspective' is not a fully accurate term in relation to pre-Renaissance Italian, Byzantine or Russian iconographic pictorial space. The term presumes an intentional reversal or conscious distortion of linear perspective. However, the latter found its elaboration only in the fifteenth century in Leon Battista Alberti's treatise *On Painting*. Early masters did not negate any particular system of representation, but employed their own aesthetic preconceptions, which were different from the systematized pictorial space of the Renaissance.

The idea of *shifting point of view* reflecting the essence of reverse perspective is present in Tarkovsky's own reading of the film. In an interview in the late 1960s, he claimed that the perception of a painting requires a set of spatial and temporal characteristics different from what the cinema-goer can experience.[41] Thus, Tarkovsky saw an urgent need to present Rublev's icons in a fragmentary fashion:

> We enlarged some details because it is impossible to translate painting, with its own dynamic and static laws, into cinema. We thereby made the spectator see in short sentences that which he would have seen had he contemplated Andrei Roublev's icons for hours on end. [...] It was only in the presentation of *details* that we tried to create the impression of the *whole* of his painting.[42]

This stance echoes a textual description of the episode in the film script: 'Woven into the smoky, pure splashes, the very translucency of which is appealing, are the precise, measured decorations of the frescoes. Lines and contours repeat and multiply, converge and interweave, meet and eliminate one another, *with deliberate lack of sequence.*'[43] In the same manner in which the fragmented novellas present a vision of Rublev's biography, the fragmented parts of the icons present a vision of his entire artistic oeuvre.

The spectacular use of colour can also be explained by the fact that Tarkovsky wished to provide a fragmented vision of Rublev's art. Indeed, Tarkovsky's next film was *Solaris*, in which colour became an essential aesthetic element. Between the production of the two films he had an extensive discussion of 'colour dramaturgy' with the film critic Leonid Kozlov. Tarkovsky maintains that colour is a feature of an exceptional phenomenon: 'Whenever we encounter an unusual, previously unseen, exotic object, it is the colour that stands out.'[44] Moreover, he insists that the use of colour leads to the dissolution of figurative qualities: 'Colour, as a rule, dominates in painting. The texture of a depicted object – no matter how elaborate it is – dissolves in the texture of the colourful surface.'[45] As a consequence of this stance, the icons in *Andrei Rublev* are indeed treated as if their various textures constitute the most intrinsic artistic feature; the camera is not interested in the subjects depicted, in objects or visual narratives, and captures only fragments with different textures. As a result, most of the icons cannot easily be recognized even by a viewer with an interest in iconography; the fragments presented need to be closely examined and compared with the whole icons to be identified.

The last sequence of *Andrei Rublev* is an enactment of the principles of iconography by cinematic means. The sliding camera is never static, and explores the phenomenon of the icon not as a singular and exclusive system of perspectival vision but as a repository of multiple viewpoints. It imitates an authentic encounter with an icon as a devotional object during a liturgy – the worshipper is 'exploring' various individual sections of an iconostasis; moreover, each individual section does not presuppose a single viewpoint. Tarkovsky follows the optical rules of Russian iconography, whose core function lies in 'the nexus of image function and liturgical settings, within which temporal viewing processes of scanning are orchestrated by the painter's compositions in a way that precisely serves the spiritual and aesthetic needs of those to whom the images were directed'.[46]

In spite of the multiplicity of camera angles and of fragments of individual icons, there is one particular icon which dominates the sequence and functions as its visual culmination. Andrei Rublev's *The Old Testament Trinity* holds the camera's attention for a substantial two and a half minutes of the sequence's total duration of eight minutes. The serene beauty of the three angels is explored by the camera in great detail, and its effects are enhanced by the tranquil melodies of the soundtrack, which fade completely with the last images of the *Trinity*. It is worth noting that a reproduction of the icon appears in the director's next film – *Solaris*. Chris quietly contemplates *Trinity*, and its presence is marked by the same musical theme which accompanies the icon sequence in *Andrei Rublev*.

Abraham's divine guests are depicted as if engaged in quiet conversation. Rublev's circular composition conveys the unanimity of the three: the central angel does not overshadow the other two; the icon painter has managed to express the unity of opposites.[47] Rublev's *Trinity* can be read as a compassionate Christian vision born out of a violent and dark period of Russian history. The Old Testament angels challenge and cancel the horror of the Last Judgement. Rublev's reluctance to reflect the violent aspects of life constitutes an authentic quality of iconography since, according to Ouspensky and Lossky, 'At that time of martyrdoms, the sufferings are not shown, just as they are not described in liturgical texts. What is shown is not the suffering itself, but the bearing there must be towards it, as the reply.'[48]

Tarkovsky also emphasizes the importance of the *Trinity*'s unity, which he tried to convey in the final episode of the film:

> through a succession of details, we had the intention of leading the spectator towards a view of the entirety of *The Trinity*, the high point of Roublev's career. To bring the spectator towards this accomplished work by means of a sort of colored dramaturgy, making him wander through fragments towards a whole by creating a sort of flow of impressions.[49]

Figure 2.5

Nevertheless, the icon does not emerge in all its glory and the camera reveals only fragments, albeit substantial ones; it scans the wooden surface both vertically and horizontally, but never zooms out in order to include the whole image. The only one of Rublev's works to appear in its entirety is *Zvenigorod Saviour* – the last icon to feature in the film.

It is worth noting that the very first image of the colour sequence is a fragment of the *Saviour in Glory*, which depicts the right knee of Christ wearing a golden tunic against a red background. The close-up of this fragment does not give the viewer the slightest opportunity to identify the icon, and it remains an undisclosed artefact. The figure of Christ is also the subject-matter of the very last image of the sequence exploring Rublev's art, only this time the subject of the visual representation is fully revealed. The *Zvenigorod Saviour* is itself a fragment (the icon was heavily damaged, and Christ's face and neck are the only parts that have survived) but Tarkovsky allows this sacred 'texture of time' to emerge in its incoherent entirety. The principle of the simultaneous depiction of several perspectival planes is at work in this icon. The figure of Christ is presented in a three-quarter turn while his face is depicted *en face*. The two available vanishing points, and hence two points of view, highlight the unearthly reality presented before the viewer: the face of Christ is multi-sided in the literal sense.

The camera switches its attention to the empty wooden surface around the Saviour's head. The blank space is spattered with rain drops accompanied by the roar of thunder, and this vulnerability of the holy object to the natural elements underlines its materiality. The icon is a 'thing' or an 'object' which, unlike a canvas, exposes its physical parameters – it does not create an illusion of presence, but manifests a divine presence. An eternal, that is atemporal, deity imprints itself; celestial time finds its terrestrial form, it is spatialized. This emphasis on the materiality of the iconographic tradition allows the film-maker to return to nature itself. The same heavy fall of rain pours over horses standing tranquilly by a river (Figure 2.5). The image of horses is a fulfilment of the schema of a return to the beginning: it connects the concluding sequence with the opening prologue in which the stallion figures. The terrestrial and celestial planes converge, and this heralds the end of *Andrei Rublev*. The concluding metaphoric shifting of spatial planes through temporal leaps is explored further in the next film, *Solaris*. This time, an extraterrestrial phenomenon, the alien planet Solaris, is contrasted with a terrestrial entity: planet Earth.

3

PHANTASIES OF *SOLARIS*

The interaction between the real and the imaginary, addressed in *Ivan's Childhood* and *Andrei Rublev* by means of the tropes of dream and vision, finds its most acute realization in *Solaris* (*Soliaris*, 1972). The collision of the two domains is accomplished through a dichotomy between the real and rigid space of Earth and the hallucinatory and fluid surface of the giant ocean-planet Solaris, where there is no externally apparent temporal or spatial stability. The latter is a source of fluctuations and deviations from the norm: the planet is able to reproduce human beings based on the suppressed memories of the astronauts – it mirrors back events and phenomena from the past, and its 'reflections' have a traumatizing power. The Ocean Solaris, a fluid entity itself, moulds its inhabitants in the image and likeness of real earth-dwellers. However, the spatial concept of moulding gradually evolves into temporal displacement once Hari, one of the phantoms, regains memory – a human ability to remember past time. The film's plot gradually disintegrates and the viewer is no longer able to distinguish reality from mere hallucinations or a real entity from its 'reflection'. The circular shape of the station, which is revolving around the orbit of the alien planet, emerges as a site of apparitions and dreams: fantastic phantoms, in addition to conventional subjective visions, gain shape in its corridors and rooms.

Science fiction is the natural habitat for time travel (movement in space with temporal consequences) and the genre organically accommodates distortions of space and time. It also attempts to domesticate the future (to present it as present) which in itself is a form of temporal displacement. However, the spatio-temporal displacements that occur in *Solaris* are of a different nature from those in a typical sci-fi film. Time and space are extraordinary not because they are part of the miraculous world of science fiction but because they constitute the spiritual domain of human existence. That is, the conventions and limits of the established genre prove to be invalid for the director. The Second World War story (*Ivan's Childhood*), the medieval epic legend (*Andrei Rublev*) and the fantastic tale from the indefinite future (*Solaris*) all deal with the same issue: the main characters experience a metaphysical crisis and set out on a journey in the labyrinth of space and time.

Earthly Solaris

Tarkovsky's reading of Stanisław Lem's novel *Solaris* (1961) is very distinctive. The adaptation is marked by various distortions and digressions, similar to those found in the adaptation of Bogomolov's *Ivan*. These artistic breaches switch the semantic directions of the novel. The integral spatial and temporal framework of the text is subject to substantial violations. The very first sentences of the novel read:

> At 19.00 hours, ship's time, I made my way to the launching bay. The men around the shaft stood aside to let me pass, and I climbed down into the capsule.
>
> Inside the narrow cockpit, there was scarcely room to move. I attached the hose to the valve on my space suit and it inflated rapidly. From then on, I was incapable of making the smallest movement. There I stood, or rather hung suspended, enveloped in my pneumatic suit and yoked to the metal hull.[1]

The beginning of Lem's *Solaris* immediately informs the reader that he or she is entering the realm of science fiction – a highly mechanized world of inconceivable equipment and language. Chris comes into this space in a meticulously organized manner (precisely at 19.00 according to spaceship time, not to his own) and the capsule subsequently absorbs him (he is unable to move after 'entering' the space suit). The astronaut's actions lead him to a state where he constitutes a unified whole with the metal shell; before leaving Earth he has to abandon his human stance and be merged with a technical device. It is remarkable how these few sentences already provide the reader with the major thematic directions which will be pursued further over the course of the 200 or so remaining pages of the novel: the text will be dominated by wondrous technical gadgets shaping the human horizon, and it will be presented along a linear narrative axis.

If one were to compare the beginning of the novel with the opening scene of Tarkovsky's film *Solaris*, one would be surprised by the amount of liberty the film-maker allows himself during the process of 'adapting' the text by cinematic means. The scene depicts the same protagonist (Chris – a scientist and astronaut); however, he occupies a different space, a space which significantly contrasts the spaceship's fantastic and at the same time claustrophobic interior with what is all too familiar to the viewer: planet Earth. The opening four-minute sequence explores nature around Chris's parental home: a pond, waterweeds swaying in a stream, a willow tree, wildflowers, and a graceful stallion wandering around. Chris does not merely observe this natural habitat in a detached manner, he interacts with it by washing his hands in a pond, and later he lets rain pour upon his face (Figure 3.1). The soon-to-depart astronaut carefully explores the relatively vast landscape and collects some soil in a metal box, which he is going to take with him to the planet Solaris. This opening scene also provides the viewer with the major thematic directions which will be pursued further in the remaining

Figure 3.1

two hours: the film will be dominated by earthly imagery despite the fact that the main action takes place millions of miles away, on the planet Solaris.

The opening sequence accommodates various premonitions of levitation, which constitutes one of the key tropes in Tarkovsky's cinema. On his way back home Chris passes by a pond situated in front of the familial house. The camera 'looks down' on the protagonist and then tracks up to reveal a lone yellow balloon, which, in defiance of physical laws, hovers in the air above the pond. The balloon neither takes off nor falls to the ground – as a minor abnormal detail, it forebodes the protagonist's forthcoming flight to, and encounter with, an alien entity, the planet Solaris. Furthermore, the following interior scene reveals several lithographs, whose sole subject-matter is air-balloons from different periods of the history of aeronautics. There is also a cage with budgerigars placed between the lithographs. The house – an earthly artefact – and its contents forebode the forthcoming flight to Solaris. Indeed, this very house is emulated in an uncanny manner by the alien planet later in the film.

The Earth scene is followed by Chris's encounter with Berton and the latter's report about an accident that happened during an expedition to Solaris. It provides the viewer with the necessary basic information about the planet and the current state of its exploration. In contrast with the Earth we have already seen (which was introduced by means of somewhat meditative and beautifully photographed shots), we are here presented with opaque and cloud-obscured images of Solaris. The video sequence is delivered as a film-within-a-film (*mise-en-abîme*) and was not present in Lem's novel, where the report was communicated purely in words. This sequence can already be taken, even at this early stage, as a metaphor for the scientists' vain efforts to comprehend the alien planet. One may read these clouds and the fog as a veil obscuring the intellect of the explorers of Solaris.

The interfusion or clash between Earth and Solaris is already taking place in the video. The two topoi constitute a hybrid site – the alien planet imitates familiar Earth. The first hallucinatory image Berton encounters is a garden with a hedgerow, dwarf trees, acacias and footpaths. The earthly artefacts are not real; they are made of mucilage, Solaris's alien substance. The astronaut also claims that he has filmed an image of a gigantic child walking on the surface of the Ocean, but the viewer is presented with an ambiguous picture which contains nothing but waves and clouds. Although the mysterious child remains absent, this very absence further intensifies the viewer's anxiety, combined with the aesthetic pleasure of observing the wondrous textures of the unknown planet. As becomes obvious later (the child and the garden prove to be spatialized memories of a deceased astronaut), past terrestrial time gains a physical form on the alien planet.

The encounter with the child is a truly fantastic event, and at the same time it is a *phantasy* in its conventional meaning. 'Phantasy' is a Greek word that literally means 'a making visible' and it is defined by *OED* as 'imagination, visionary notion'. The dictionary also suggests that 'fantasy' and 'phantasy', in spite of their identity in sound and in ultimate etymology, should be apprehended as separate words: the predominant sense of fantasy being 'caprice, whim, fanciful invention', while that of phantasy is 'imagination, visionary notion'. The phantoms of Solaris are ultimate phantasies – visionary products of the astronauts' imagination. The guilt-driven men *make visible* phantoms of their past. It is worth noting that Chris, before his departure from Earth and before meeting the phantom of his dead wife, accused Berton of confusing his imagination with cognitive ability. As he says, 'the Solaris project ended up in a blind alley, precisely because of irresponsible f(ph)antasy'. The protagonist subsequently changes his stance, and tries to resolve his own spiritual crisis and the scientific task to cognize the alien planet by means of his imagination and intellect.

The quest for truth remains the main philosophical theme for both the film-maker and the writer. However, for Tarkovsky the anthropocentric stance, which is challenged by Lem, is by no means an obstacle to be overcome; rather, it is a natural intellectual and spiritual stance for a human being to occupy. It is not possible to think as if outside the human body, and humanity constantly explores the unknown through reference to the already familiar. The connection of a person with his or her natural habitat defines his or her philosophic horizon. This explains why the film-maker introduces an 'alien' spatio-temporal layer to the material offered in the novel, namely the planet Earth and memories connected with it: Earth is the natural environment in which thinking is grounded for a human being. Tarkovsky adds the topography of Earth (the real entity) to the purely imagined science-fiction world of Lem. He needs a real referent as backdrop against which the human drama can unfold, since it cannot do so in a (spiritual) cosmic void. The artistic device finds its justification in Bakhtin's discussion of divergences between the ethereal *future* and the material *present-past*: a reality 'when placed in the future is deprived of that materiality and density, that real-life weightiness that is essential to the "is" and "was".[2]

The first part of the film (a substantial 41 minutes 10 seconds) takes place on Earth, and Chris's home planet reappears in the form of video-sequences and dreams-hallucinations on Solaris: the familiar-familial spatio-temporal frameworks infiltrate the miraculous space-time of the alien planet. Moreover, the tin box with soil that Chris takes with him to Solaris appears several times throughout the film at decisive moments: the viewer sees Chris holding it in one of the very first shots, and it reappears in several sequences on the station and in dreams-hallucinations. The soil from Earth is transplanted to the alien domain. Towards the end of the film a crucial transformation takes place – a plant germinates from the soil, and the camera carefully explores the sprout. The plant close-up is followed by the return sequence, where the tin box re-emerges for the last time in the flooded familial home (Figure 3.2).

Answering a question about the film, Lem acknowledged that he was dissatisfied with the script written by Tarkovsky and Friedrich

Figure 3.2

Gorenshtein. The conflict between the two parties is crucial to the film in its final shape, for it still contains numerous traces of the original Lemian discourse. The Polish writer gives an extensive account of how dramatically different his views are from those of the director:

> This script proved a rather unpleasant surprise to me. In the long prologue that takes place on Earth, it introduces Chris's family and undue importance is given to his old mother. The mother's character symbolizes his family ties, but also the Motherland, Mother Earth, and this has very strong connotations in Russian folklore; as far as I was concerned, Chris's family connections were of little interest and should not have been bothered with in *Solaris*. After lengthy discussions, I managed to get rid of most of Chris's family in the script. But by then I knew for certain that Tarkovsky's film vision of *Solaris* and mine were quite different. I was expecting a visualization of the 'Drama of Cognizance', seen as a contrast between the images of 'home, sweet Earth' and the 'Cold Cosmos', a drama in which the characters affecting the men in the station originate from the ocean and symbolize the antagonism between the vast open spaces of the planet and the small enclosed Station. Unfortunately Tarkovsky took sides and favoured 'home, sweet Earth' against the 'Cold Cosmos'. For a drama of cognizance in which the people, the envoys from Earth, keep on struggling with the enigma that cannot be solved by the human mind, Tarkovsky substituted a moral drama *par excellence*, which in no way relates to the problem of cognizance and its extremes.[3]

The domain of Earth is crucial to Tarkovsky, while for Lem it scarcely exists; Earth as a space of human habitation is absent in the novel. From the moment Chris leaves it, not a single character is actually found there or expresses an aspiration to be there. The only time the earthly landscape is mentioned is in Berton's video – it is an uncanny replica of the garden with trees, acacias and a hedgerow all made of Solaris's mucilage. For Lem, Earth remains a visually abstract point of reference; it shapes the human capacity to comprehend, and this is perceived as an obstacle. As Snaut puts it: 'We don't want to conquer the cosmos, we simply want to extend the boundaries of Earth to the frontiers of the cosmos.'[4] Hence for Lem this all-too-powerful dependence should be overcome, and the writer interprets his work as a severe criticism of anthropocentrism. The same Snaut warns Chris upon his landing: 'We aren't on Earth.' The familiar ground should be abandoned.

By contrast with Lem, Tarkovsky is fascinated with Earth and entities related to it. The notions of landscape and nature in general dominate all of his films. The film-maker appears to follow the semi-pagan Russian cult of the Mother Damp Earth, as is evident from the following comment. Tarkovsky is referring to the person who is arguably his sole role-model from within the Russian filmic tradition: Alexander Dovzhenko (whose silent masterpiece is called *Earth*): 'I share [Dovzhenko's] love for my land, which is why I feel him very close to me. [...] His love of the land and of the people made his characters grow, as it were, from the earth itself. They were organic, complete.'[5] Žižek, in his discussion of Tarkovsky's 'cinematic materialism', also emphasizes the importance of the trope in question, and connects it with the concept of time – the embodiment of the film-maker's aesthetics: 'What pervades Tarkovsky's films is the heavy gravity of the earth, which seems to exert its pressure on time itself, generating an effect of temporal anamorphosis, extending the dragging of time well beyond what we perceive as justified by the requirements of narrative movement.'[6] Earth-space exerts its pressure and gravity on time, which undergoes distortion.

It is interesting to note that two prominent verbal references to Earth in *Solaris* are entirely products of Tarkovsky's imagination. First, Gibarian's last wish to be buried on Earth is cynically commented on by the 'astro'-biologist Sartorius, who says that his colleague 'wanted to be buried on Earth. But would space be such a bad grave for him? Gibarian wanted to go to the Earth, to the worms.' The second is also linked with Gibarian, this time his invention of attaching strips of paper to a ventilator so that their murmur will recall the rustle of leaves on Earth. Lem simply mentions in his text that Chris was aware of the murmuring of paper strips, but no connection whatsoever is made with Earth.[7] Tarkovsky's Gibarian, a man of Earth, would persistently reaffirm his human stance – his door is decorated with a child's drawing of a man with the awkward inscription *chelovek* ('a man').

For the Chris of Lem's novel, unlike for his namesake in Tarkovsky's film, Earth is not a beloved point of origin: there is a sense of something mundane and even undesirable in the idea of returning to it. As the text reads: 'Earth? I thought of the great bustling cities where I would wander and lose myself...I shall immerse myself among men.'[8] Tarkovsky's image of Earth is completely contradictory to that of Lem: it is realized first via nature imagery and then via the familial home. For the most part, there is nothing alien or mundane about Earth in Tarkovsky's *Solaris*; it is familiar and homely, and its presence in a science-fiction film is not a coincidence.

The topography of Earth and the non-linear time-patterns of the dreams and hallucinations related to it carry numerous emotional and moral concerns; they dramatically change the direction of the film's discourse. The coherent futuristic world is understated. Instead, the viewer is presented with the image of a confused state of mind inhabiting the borderlines between present and past. In general, it can be claimed that these temporal patterns (present and past), together with topographic references (Solaris and Earth), reveal the general dramatic dilemma of *Solaris*. The characters are tortured and torn by this spatio-temporal 'tensioner'.

The importance of the Earth–Solaris opposition for Tarkovsky is vigorously addressed in the film's travel sequences. Two characters – Berton and Chris – travel large distances, and the manner in which they perform these actions is extremely distinctive. Berton's journey from Chris's familial home to a city is ironically one of the most fantastic sequences within the film. It may be argued that, for Tarkovsky, alienation, as a source of spiritual confusion, also originates on Earth. The otherness of the highway (though the image possesses a real referent – Akasaka-mitsuke in Tokyo) is underlined by the long concrete tunnels, flyovers and clear-cut rectangular constructions surrounding it. Berton sits back in a detached manner and does not participate in the process of driving his car (which is apparently done by an onboard computer). His journey is accompanied by the disturbing sounds of the vehicle speedily progressing through the space of the city.

The extremely long (4 minutes 42 seconds) sequence, during which not a single word is uttered and no action takes place, explores the limits of cinematic contemplation: the viewer is given an opportunity to experience mechanical movement through space in its purity. The overextended sequence of images and sounds gathers intensity towards the end, and culminates in a strikingly tranquil image of Chris's house (shot with a blue filter) – the point of departure. Again, Tarkovsky counterpoises the sophisticated and technological world of equipment (accommodating the alienated and recumbent Berton) with nature (accommodating the active, interacting Chris, who washes his hands in the pond).

A few minutes later, another journey takes place in the film, namely Chris's actual flight to Solaris. This time the distance covered is substantially greater (the flight takes sixteen months, according to the book),[9] but to the viewer's surprise it takes only 2 minutes

22 seconds of cinematic time. The journey is rapid (Chris does not even notice that the spaceship has already taken off) and rendered with less visual ingenuity than the highway sequence. There is no image of movement, and the flight to Solaris appears to be extremely stylized. The journey ends with a shot of the neglected station, an artificial construction littered – that is, rendered habitable – by humans. The film-maker appears to display little interest in exploring the fantastic attributes of space travel: its alienating characteristics are visually downplayed and it is translated into the normality of the everyday.

It is clear that Tarkovsky attempts to subvert the miraculous quality of science fiction. The genre, as described by Sontag, either lifts the viewer out of the 'unbearably humdrum' or normalizes the 'psychologically unbearable'.[10] In Tarkovsky's case everything is reversed: the fantastic station is presented as a humdrum place, while its characters face psychologically unbearable situations. Chris comes to Solaris in order to help resolve the crisis facing the scientific expedition – the mystery of the alien planet – which constitutes an emblematic task within the genre. However, instead of surveying the fantastic nature of the Ocean, he explores his inner self. While he faces the uncanny phantom of his dead wife on Solaris, his mind constantly returns to Earth to resolve the moral problem: his personal guilt. The alien otherness of science fiction is internalized.

The topos of Earth functions as an all-permeating unsaid in science fiction and dominates the imaginary worlds. This is particularly distinctive in the case of *Solaris*, where Tarkovsky overcomes the alien nature of the genre of science fiction and attempts literally to bring it down to earth. Science fiction, like any other fiction, needs reality as such in order to evolve. The film-maker does not even endeavour to abandon his earthly point of view, and his visual vocabulary is dominated by familiar earthly imagery – autumn leaves fading, multicoloured waterweeds, and scuffed old surfaces all balance the Solaris station's otherworldliness. The recognizable landscape of Earth is preferred to fantastic spaceships in the style of Stanley Kubrick's *2001: A Space Odyssey* (1968). Tarkovsky's *Solaris* is one of the first epic space tales to make the satellite station look 'as anti-romantic as a kitchen or factory'.[11] The station in the film appears as an inhabited and littered place, and Chris is astonished by its unkempt state upon his arrival. The only sci-fi visual emphasis of the film is the planet Solaris itself. Its images repeatedly interrupt the narrative flow of the story without any apparent diegetic function; but even they, in their alien abstraction, resemble Earth as if seen from a distance.

Earthly Earth

Home video, as a recourse to another space and time, is a diegetic device which naturally disrupts the narrative flow. The images of Earth, once the protagonist reaches Solaris, manifest themselves primarily by means of this device. The family video in *Solaris* is made by Chris and his father, and consists of almost static shots of family members and nature. It emerges prominently in the middle of the film, following an image of the monotonous silver surface of the alien planet, and returns the characters and the viewer back to Earth. The projected images form a terrestrial enclave within the space-time of Solaris.

In addition to this general spatio-temporal 'otherworldliness', with Earth as the other of Solaris, the familial video registers temporal progression by spatial means. The alternating 'still lifes' reveal different seasons (winter, early autumn and late autumn) and show Chris at various stages of his life (as a young boy and as an adolescent). The passage of time is embodied. Every shot presents a single scene, and the video on the whole functions as a kaleidoscope of Chris's life that produces brightly coloured 'symmetrical' figures. The colour underlines the temporal progression by means of various rich textures; leaves changing colour and burning logs vividly register matter's ability to be transformed in the course of time. The video also concentrates on the figures of two women – Chris's wife and his mother. Both wear solid knitted dresses of pastel colours, and are captured standing still as part of landscapes. The women, as a true binary pair, belong to two discrete generations. They both played a crucial role in Chris's life on Earth, and they both enter his phantasmatic life on Solaris.

This recollection of past times is a human reminiscence recorded by technical means. This state of symbiosis is elegantly reflected in the soundtrack: Bach's prelude in F minor is performed on a MIDI synthesizer. The video contrasts with the guilt-driven memory revived by the Ocean and transferred into material form on the station. Yet, ironically, this very earthly recollection helps Hari, the phantom of Chris's departed wife, to regain memories of her own past, to rediscover her former reality when she was a real person. After watching the video the woman hesitates for a moment and then rushes to a mirror – an engine of memory – and declares: 'I don't know myself at all, I don't remember who I am. When I close my eyes, I can't remember my own face.' Hari's reflection in the mirror, as a memory of the present moment, helps her to delve into her own past: she performs an act of recollection, and remembers mundane details of squabbles with Chris. The verbal recourse to past time is followed by a minute spatial aberration: the woman looks aside, and the camera tracks in that direction to reveal a stream of water falling from above. Once again the integrity of an edifice – in this case the space station – is violated. The presence of the interior waterfall is not narratively justified (neither of the characters is taking or going to take a shower), and is elevated to a poetic level by means of accompanying tranquil choral music.

Two evident reference points, both personally cherished by the director – a poem by his father Arseni Tarkovsky and Pieter Bruegel the Elder's *The Hunters in the Snow* – define the aesthetic coordinates of the home video sequence. On 12 March 1971, during the shooting period, Tarkovsky made the following entry in his diary: 'It occurred to me that the film made by Kelvin the elder, which Chris takes with him, should be made like a poem. (Base it on one of father's poems).'[12] However, the poem he had in mind (supposedly 'As a child I once fell ill...', which later appears in *Nostalghia*) does not appear in its textual form. It appears as a spectral sequence of several images in the home video. These images were originally conceived as a separate short film, which is described in *Sculpting in Time*:

> Aerial view of a town; autumn or early winter. Slow zoom in to a tree standing by the stucco wall of a monastery. [...] A bonfire. [...The father] straightens up, turns, and walks away from the camera over the fields. [...] From out of the trees, and continuing along the father's path, appears the son. Gradual zoom in to the son's face.[13]

The video is a poem – a visual counterpart of the Japanese tradition of the haiku, which was highly valued by the film-maker and used as an inspiration for his philosophy of film.[14] The pure and subtle observation of life is a major stylistic trait of this ancient tradition. Its succinctness and an ability to extract poetic material from the most mundane scenes clearly inspired Tarkovsky's short film, which made its way to *Solaris*. The camera observes natural elements such as autumn leaves, frost and water, and allows time to manifest itself through space in the same manner as in the poem quoted in *Sculpting in Time*: 'As it passes by / The full moon barely touches / Fishhooks in the waves.'[15]

Another point of reference in the home video sequence is Bruegel's painting. Certain themes of *The Hunters in the Snow*, such as a landscape covered with snow which is panoramically observed from a hill, are animated and presented as ultimate visual impressions of Earth. The painting plays an even more crucial role at a later stage, when it is clearly linked with the home video. Hari looks attentively at its reproduction in the station's library and calls up images from the video. This moment in the film is narratively important, since Chris leaves Hari on her own and for the first time her phantom nature does not manifest itself in a feral manner: the woman calmly smokes and does not experience an uncontrolled urge to haunt her 'victim-husband'.

The Hunters in the Snow belongs to the cycle *The Months*, which probably consisted of six paintings of the months or seasons, of which five remain. Reproductions of the five remaining paintings are hung side by side in the library. The depicted temporal progression of seasons through space unites them with the home video. The painting is meticulously explored by the camera – several fragments of the canvas are scrutinized by unhurried tracking shots. The style of photography is similar to the concluding sequence of *Andrei Rublev*: *The Hunters in the Snow* does not appear in its entirety; the camera reveals only its fragments. The concluding point of this journey to another fictional space-time is a brief visual 'quotation' from the home video – Hari links Bruegel with the image of Chris as child on a snowy hill, and the two have an apparent visual affinity.

Bruegel's canvas helps Hari, a subjective perception of the real Hari conjured up from fragments of Chris's subconscious, to humanize herself. The Solaris-generated Hari does not recognize her own photographic image upon arrival; she declares: 'I've got a feeling that I've forgotten something.' However, later she proves that the essence of humanity lies beyond physical constitution, and regains her individual identity by developing an ability to appreciate art, to feel and consequently to sacrifice herself for her husband's sake. The climax of this is her 'interaction' with Bruegel's painting: while being taken into the realm of true existence by the painting, she starts to hear the authentic sounds of Earth: human voices, dripping water, birds, barking dogs, and so on. These sound-memories are crucial in the Heideggerian sense, since the truth possesses the qualities of memory – it is an act of remembering what is already there. Hari enters the space and time of Earth, and thus abandons her alien nature and stance.

The flight of imagination is followed by literal flight – one of the most memorable levitation scenes in Tarkovsky's oeuvre. Chris and his wife experience an extraordinary phenomenon: zero-gravity. The camera unhurriedly observes the transfigured interior of the station's library with its flying candelabra and books. The levitation sequence is punctuated by the images from *The Hunters in the Snow* and from Chris's home video depicting Earth. The unearthly experience of zero-gravity is seamlessly diluted by earthly images: Bruegel's Netherlandish landscape and Tarkovsky's Russian winter scene (Figure 3.3). This visual assortment with a complex spatio-temporal texture culminates in an extended vision of Solaris's surface; the mysterious alien matter wraps up the sequence.

Oneiric Space

The linearity and stability of space and time in *Solaris* are also subject to substantial deformation by means of extraneous literary material. The quotation from Cervantes' classic *Don Quixote* emerges prominently in the library scene, and constitutes one of the longest prose excerpts found in Tarkovsky's films. It is also one of very few quotations that is not delivered by a disembodied voice-over but presented diegetically – one of the characters reads aloud from the book. The

Figure 3.3

quoted text opposes dream with reality, and connects them with the notion of temporality, or rather with the ultimate end of it – that is, *death*. The discursive shift has profound semantic implications.

The presence of *Don Quixote* is not limited to the episode in which its passage is quoted. The book receives steadfast attention from the camera; it reappears several times apart from the reading scene itself, and is clearly connected with the trope of Earth. Unexpectedly, it emerges while Chris is still on Earth in his familial home. The book lies open on a table; its page is covered with soil and a key-chain is placed over it. Furthermore, the Cervantes volume is shown after Chris finishes reading the quoted passage aloud in the space station's library; on this occasion a herbarium is covering its page. Again, the book drifts past the camera during the period of weightlessness. An object flying in slow motion is bound to draw the viewer's attention. Finally, the volume of *Don Quixote* re-emerges towards the end of the film, again in the library: this time Snaut is holding the dry plant while leaning over it.

In all of these episodes the book emerges as an agent of Earth, for soil and the dry plant signify its earthly origin, and its presence is underlined. In order that it should immediately be recognized, every time it comes into view it is open at the same page, which bears a classic engraving by Gustave Doré. The illustration reveals the book's identity and shows that it is not chosen at random. The text by Cervantes is one of the earthly messengers, and is fully integrated into the ambivalent topographical dispute. Indeed, the book itself (as a material object) does not seem to have an ideological centre of gravity: it is shown literally both covered in earth and flying in the space ship after being released into zero-gravity conditions in the Solaris orbit. *Don Quixote* is an important, immediately recognizable earthly artefact, like other objects within the station's library – a depository of human cultural achievement. Cervantes' novel, a bust of Socrates and Bruegel's paintings all connect Solaris with Earth and, by extension, scientific discourse with art.

The great Spanish novel's insistent presence draws with it a set of connected discourses. They saturate the texture of the film and intermingle with its various semantic and general aesthetic concerns, thereby adding new layers to the interpretative readings of *Solaris*. The clash between the 'unhealthy' imagination of the character of Don Quixote and the reality of early seventeenth-century Spain is the first obvious Cervantic theme, which is interrelated with the dilemma astronauts face on Solaris, namely the nature of the phantoms. The presence of the latter is explained as a symptom of insanity in the first instance, but later the astronauts become convinced that what seems to be an illusion is part of their reality. In the novel, the reverse occurs: the protagonist is on his way to regaining his senses and to abandoning phantasies.

It should be highlighted that the phantoms on the planet Solaris do not follow the well-trodden path of the science-fiction genre and are not presented as monstrous figures. If there is monstrosity, it lies only in their complete resemblance to humans. Their presence is unbearable, and they are programmed by the Ocean to be constantly present around their 'victims'. Each individual conscience generates its individual phantom. The phantoms' individuality is crucial, since a moral issue cannot be resolved objectively in a detached manner and needs a particularized subject. There is no blood spilt or violence committed by the creatures – that is, created beings – of Solaris, since their cruelty lies in the mere fact of their existence, and it is this which undermines the dream–reality binary opposition.

A comparable effacement of the boundaries between imagination and reality takes place within both Cervantes' novel and Tarkovsky's film. The failure to differentiate real entities from imagined ones finds its highest development in the two female characters of *Solaris* and *Don Quixote*: Hari and Dulcinea. Both women have a peculiar ontological status: their existence is heavily dependent on the state of mind of their male partners. Dream-like subjectivism is a key to the existence of Dulcinea no less than of Hari. Don Quixote, according to his own contradictory accounts, has never seen his mistress and is 'enamored solely by hearsay'.[16] Nonetheless he has seen Dulcinea 'approximately' three times, and they scarcely exchanged glances. The contradiction is resolved by Don Quixote himself when he exclaims: 'To put the whole thing in a nutshell, I persuade myself that all I say is as I say, neither more nor less, and I picture her in my imagination as I would have her to be, as well in beauty as in condition.'[17] The knight-errant suggests that imagination makes it possible for reality to manifest itself in rather incongruous ways – this very situation is imposed on the scientists on Solaris, the only difference being that their conscience, and not imagination, serves as the key faculty.

Hari, in her turn, is a phantom, a product of Chris's guilt-ridden conscience and a mere interconnected assembly of unstable neutrinos. She is imposed onto Chris's reality by the Ocean. Following Freud's paradigm, Hari is an uncanny being: she is homely (*heimlich*) as an image of the beloved wife, and at the same time she is un-homely (*unheimlich*) as an embodied simulacrum of the dead person. The psychoanalyst's description of the modus operandi of the uncanny is perfectly applicable to her: 'an uncanny effect is often and easily produced when the distinction between imagination and reality is effaced, as when something that we have hitherto regarded as imaginary appears before us in reality'.[18] Furthermore, Hari is a palpable signifier which produces a hallucinatory or unreal signified – 'a super-copy, a reproduction which is superior to the original'.[19]

It is striking that the Lemian Hari never exchanges a single word with Snaut and Sartorius, and by and large adopts a very passive position, while the Tarkovskian Hari argues with the astronauts; the alien becomes human in the film while its otherness is maintained in the novel. By concentrating his discourse on Hari, who is a mere simulacrum, Tarkovsky gives preference to imagined, guilt-driven and purely internalized 'human' reality, whereas Lem is more concerned with outward manifestations of the alien phenomena and attempts to provide a solution to them. For the film-maker, the visions and 'guests', formed by the astronauts' consciences, constitute a tool to internalize the action, since their nature is always subjective, as opposed to the objective discourse of dehumanized science fiction. The dream or hallucination is never objective – it has to be lived through; and Chris lives through it together with Hari.

The content of the passage quoted from *Don Quixote* in the film touches upon the dream–reality issue only by implication. In one of the most vital scenes of the film, Snaut gives Chris a copy of Cervantes' novel and asks him to read aloud from it. The reading scene, completely invented by Tarkovsky and not found in Lem's novel, takes place in the library of the space station. The library possesses a peculiar quality – there are no windows – and hence the astronauts remain 'unseen' to the powerful glare of the Ocean. Chris reads a passage from Chapter 68 of Part II of *Don Quixote* in which Sancho shares the following thoughts with his master:

> All I know is that so long as I am asleep, I have neither fear nor hope, trouble nor joy. God bless the man that invented sleep, [...] the universal coin with which everything is bought, the weight and balance that makes the shepherd equal with the king and the fool with the wise man. Sleep, I have heard say, has only one fault, that it is like death.[20]

At this point Snaut breaks in and completes the quotation: '"Never have I heard thee speak so elegantly as now, Sancho," [said Don

Quixote].'[21] Sancho maintains that the firmness of our understanding of reality, which seems to accommodate numerous binary oppositions, is in fact unsteady, and it is loosened in sleep, which transfers us into a realm devoid of binaries. The mind of a sleeping person enters a *different* space – it is a fulfilment of Jacques Lacan's 'I think where I am not, therefore I am where I do not think.'[22] Then Sancho suddenly transfers his surprisingly eloquent discourse towards the notion of temporariness by comparing sleep with death, which culminates in the disappearance of the human capacity to experience time – that is, *to live*.

Dream, as has been discussed above, is a crucial instrument for Tarkovsky's reading of the novel, but what can one make out of 'mere' sleep, which 'is like death'? What is the rationale for Snaut to ask for this passage to be read aloud by Chris? The cybernetician enters the library in a devastated condition: he is drunk and one of the sleeves of his jacket is torn, but more importantly he seems to be mentally drained, resembling one who has been deprived of sleep. Before the passage is read aloud, Snaut exclaims: 'They arrive at night. But what about our sleep? That's a problem – a man deprived of sleep!' He reveals his reluctance to go to bed, since the phantoms materialize only when their victims are asleep. This may function as a diegetic justification to introduce the passage from *Don Quixote*. Snaut is afraid, and refuses to sleep since sleeping reincarnates phantoms of his guilty conscience.

Furthermore, the protagonist declares: 'We want to extend Earth to the utmost frontiers of the cosmos. We don't know what to do with other worlds. We...need a mirror.' The speech performs a crucial discursive shift from the dream–reality opposition to that of Solaris and Earth. Snaut regards exploration of alien spaces as utterly futile since anthropocentric attitudes cancel out the very possibility of meaningful contact with the ultimate Other. Moreover, he unexpectedly turns to the figure of Gibarian after suggesting that 'what man needs is man'. What is crucial is that Gibarian, whose door was decorated with the inscription *chelovek* ('a man'), is dead. Sleep and death, Solaris and Earth, are all brought together. The fact that dreaming is like death fascinates the disturbed mind of the astronaut. Both sleeping and dying are unavoidable aspects of human life.

While Snaut tries to remain as vigilant as possible, Chris indulges himself in sleep, and the film is governed by his dreams and hallucinations. The idea of not sleeping, and hence not reincarnating Hari, does not occur to him, and he seems to be reconciled to his guilty conscience. In addition, sleep, or rather the inability to sleep, is an important aspect of Hari's existence, as she confesses, 'I don't know how to sleep. No, actually, it isn't sleep. It's something that's around me, rather than within me; something much further away.' To which Chris replies: 'I expect it's dreams.' Dreaming and sleeping are inherent constituents of human life. Hari gradually learns how to sleep, and this becomes one of the major aspects of her gradual humanization.

In the same fashion in which Sancho reconciles the general binary nature of life (via sleep), Chris resolves the conflict between rational science and his own unscientific morality through contact with Hari – a mere simulacrum of the real. He declares his unconditional love to her: 'But what does it matter, if you are dearer to me than all the scientific truths which have ever existed in this world?' The phantom-woman is the ultimate embodiment of the conflict between epistemology and ethics. Chris sleeps and dreams without limits, and thus arrives at some kind of resolution: the 'rediscovered woman' leads him to the 'rediscovered dwelling'.[23] He restores intimacy with his wife literally by sleeping together with her, but the pinnacle of his immersion in the domain of Morpheus is the delirium scene towards the end of the film.

The entry to the hallucinatory site is again accomplished through an abnormal spatial manifestation. After Hari's suicide attempt, the couple lie on the bed and reconcile. This is followed by a cut to Chris who is sleeping restlessly, covered in sweat, on his own but next to Hari's shawl. The camera tracks to one side – it 'scrutinizes' the man in his sleep and then zooms out to reveal, to the attentive viewer's amazement, that instead of the shawl, Hari is in the bed: the woman is sleeping peacefully beside Chris. This aberrant apparition, accomplished by means of the camera's continuous movement, signals that the protagonist is gradually entering the space and time of hallucination. Chris gets up and wanders in the station's circular corridors. After meeting Snaut, and delivering a rather dense monologue while staring at Solaris's seething surface, he is escorted back to the room by his colleague and wife. The walk is visually 'interrupted' by the blinding glare of the corridor's illumination devices.

One of the dazzling shafts of light transports Chris for a brief moment back to Earth. For a few seconds the camera sweeps around the interior of the protagonist's earthly home. The peculiar detail of the sweeping shot is that the director uses an orange camera filter, so the home appears in an unfamiliar light. This is followed by a cut back to the station, though Chris's room's interior is transformed – the walls, the ceiling and the floor are all made of mirrors. The effect is that the protagonist's bed is placed into infinity. The viewer sees the infinite reproduction of Chris's image; the protagonist's singularity is undermined.[24] The interior is transformed once again in the next shot – the walls are now wrapped in plastic, and Hari approaches a delirious Chris. The woman stares into the camera and another glare of light functions as a cut.

The following vision is the pinnacle of the hallucination. It presents Hari as an even more uncanny being: the woman is multiplied. The singularity of the phantom is undermined: there are six Haris walking, standing and sitting in the room. Tzvetan Todorov suggests that among the fantastic genre's fundamental themes are 'multiplication of the personality [and] collapse of the limit between subject and object'.[25] The six Haris of Chris's vision indeed fulfil this aspect of the genre, and their inhuman nature obliterates the borderline between subject and object.

More importantly, the six Haris are juxtaposed with the appearance of Chris's mother, who wears the same nightgown as one of the phantoms. The multiple apparition scene is followed by the episode which brings the viewer back to the house. Chris gets up from his bed but finds himself back on Earth: he is in the house – the familiar familial space. The tropes of house and mother-wife figure are harbingers of *Mirror*, and both will dominate Tarkovsky's next film. However, the hyper-realism of the latter contrasts with the fantastic setting of the former. The protagonist of *Solaris* 'returns' home and establishes contact with his apparently deceased mother, an action which, though imaginary, is still curative. He 'meets' her in the house with rooms full of objects wrapped in plastic, and one of his massive suitcases from Solaris is put on a table. The blue monochrome colour scheme underlines the uninhabited nature of the place and its otherworldliness. While there is an apparent discrepancy in age (the mother looks too young), the tenderness between them is still that of mother and child: she washes his dirty arm and lovingly kisses his head, and the latter gesture brings Chris to tears.

The emotional outburst erases the borderline between Earth and Solaris; the two planets negotiate their real and at the same time hallucinatory status. The artist-creators of the 'discontinuous Baroque fold', who, according to Deleuze, accomplished a leap from the domain of space to that of time, were aware 'that hallucination does not feign presence, but that presence is hallucinatory'.[26] For Chris the dichotomy is not valid, for the opposition between the two is reconciled on – or rather by – the alien planet: the Earth-inspired hallucinations do feign presence, while the Solaris presence is indeed hallucinatory. The subjective and objective realms are indistinguishable either in reality or in dream.

Bruegel's *The Hunters in the Snow* emerges once again in the film; this time it is found not on the Solaris station but in the earthly familial home, hanging half-wrapped in plastic on a television screen. Chris's mother calmly contemplates it. The 'dysfunctional' and abandoned condition of the painting reveals its own artificial state – it is a mere representation of a certain space, a Netherlandish village. However, this artificiality prompts the director to use it in order to reconcile two seemingly disjoined spaces and realities: those of Solaris and Earth. The conclusion seems to be that only art, and by extension imagination and even hallucination, are able to resolve the conflict between the present reality of Solaris and the distant memory of Earth. For Tarkovsky, truth lies beyond the rigid boundaries of scientific discourse and is situated in the artistic (artificial) realm.

Following a few routine exchanges, the mother notices that Chris's arm is dirty. She brings a bowl, a towel and a jug, and washes his hand. After completing this gesture of motherhood the woman disappears in the darkness of a door aperture, and when the camera emerges from this obscurity we are already in Chris's room on the station; the two incongruous spaces are merged into an indissoluble whole. The sound of water, which enters the diegesis when Chris's mother washes his hand, lingers during the woman's departure and stays on in the protagonist's room on the station. The water also has a diegetic reason to be present in Chris's room: the viewer sees two glass vessels with boiling water by the bed. Moreover, when Chris awakes he sees on an armchair the jug with the towel which his mother used in the hallucination-dream sequence. Material objects and natural elements are means by which the characters step over the threshold of dream.

Upon his recovery from these vivid hallucinations, the protagonist emerges a renewed person. He learns that Hari has ceased to exist: she has committed her second suicide by the process of voluntary annihilation – 'the heroic act of the self-erasure of her very spectral undead existence'.[27] The abortive and the successful suicides on Solaris mime the real event, which took place on Earth. Hari and Chris are given another chance to redeem their earthly abortive marriage, and the woman emerges from the situation by setting a new standard of compassion and love: she 'kills' herself for the second time, and relieves her former husband of her unbearable presence. The phantom created by the hallucinatory powers of the Ocean ceases to exist immediately after Chris's own vision-hallucination. The transformation is evident, since the director withdraws the filters and disturbing sounds which accompany the dream-hallucination sequences. Even the beams of one of the two Solaris suns resemble earthly light. However, when he awakens, Chris notices the jug and the towel which his mother used during the dream sequence, and the vision is rather disturbing to him. The reverse mechanism is at work here: the spectral material objects materialize in reality while the phantom of Hari leaves it. The astronaut also learns that, after his electroencephalogram was sent to the Ocean-Solaris, it stopped generating phantoms and instead started creating islands on its surface. Solaris imitates Earth itself, and the solidity of the islands augurs an end to spectral visitations.

The Return

The concluding, mesmerizing episode of the film depicts Chris's 'second' homecoming. This time the protagonist meets his father. The reunion is also accomplished through physical contact in a familiar space: the father and son embrace by the steps of the familial house. The finale, however, is preceded by two encounters with Snaut on the station orbiting Solaris. Sitting in the library, Chris stares at Hari's shawl and talks about the value of the imaginary contact with the Ocean via the phantom of Hari. He also delivers a long 'edifying' monologue, a prominent feature of Tarkovsky's late films, while the screen is filled with images of Solaris. The protagonist realizes that there is no place like home. The last verbal exchange of the film is a short conversation between Snaut and Chris. The former suggests: 'It is time for you, Chris, to go back to Earth.' To which the latter replies: 'Do you think so?'

The 'last' unearthly image before the departure is the tin box with soil, from which a plant germinates. The uncomplicated symbolic image transfers the viewer back to Earth. The film ends where it began – waterweeds swaying in a stream announce Chris's return home. However, the space around the house is transfigured: it looks deserted. More importantly, the pond is covered in frost, trees are stripped of their leaves, and vegetation is scarce. The spatial transformation reveals a temporal progression: Chris left his house in late summer and 'returns' to it in late autumn.

The final episode of the film once again reveals how Tarkovsky minimizes the fantastic world of Lem. The director introduces striking spatio-temporal displacements. Just as the beginning of the novel contrasts glaringly with the first sequence of the film, so too the final passage of Lem's *Solaris* is at odds with Tarkovsky's vision of it. The last action depicted in the original text consists of Chris trying to touch the Ocean:

> I went closer, and when the next wave came I held out my hand. [...] the wave hesitated, recoiled, then enveloped my hand without touching it, so that a thin covering of 'air' separated my glove inside a cavity which had been fluid a moment previously, and now had a fleshy consistency. I raised my hand slowly, and the wave, or rather an outcrop of the wave, rose at the same time, enfolding my hand in a translucent cyst with greenish reflections. [...] The main body of the wave remained motionless on the shore, surrounding my feet without touching them, like some strange beast patiently waiting for the experiment to finish.[28]

This pseudo-contact between the man and the Ocean, which lacks an inherent haptic quality, can be interpreted as a final metaphor for the Solarists' vain efforts to comprehend the planet and to establish meaningful contact with it. The contact is a mere appearance; it refutes the possibility of any convergence. The human mind cannot reach the stage where it is palpably aware of Solaris. The planet resists physical interaction by stepping back and then mirroring human movements. The discursive emphasis in this scene is on the purely external attributes of contact: the human mind is unable to get in touch with the Ocean.

Tarkovsky's cinematic interpretation switches this discursive emphasis to the internal register. The film-maker distorts Lem's final passage, in which the unity of space and time is adhered to closely, in an explicitly allegorical way. Contact – or, to be more precise, a simulacrum of contact – is established: Chris comes back to his beloved corner of Earth which, however, is accommodated in the Ocean's 'waters'. This recalls the opening sequence of the film, and in particular the very first shot – water plants swaying in the stream. Tarkovsky once again contrasts the Ocean with Earth; the watery fluidity of both planets is underlined as a unifying feature. This island constitutes Chris's vision of the earthly home, to which he strives to return in order to regain his roots. He contemplates his parental house, with his father inside it arranging a pile of books. The seemingly mundane scene contains an uncanny feature: inside the house it is pouring with warm water, and it does not seem to bother the man. The integrity of the house is violated, and it belongs to the same lineage of dilapidated edifices which precede and follow *Solaris*. In a manner visually reminiscent of Rembrandt's *Return of the Prodigal Son*, Chris kneels before his father, and hence is reunited with him and the home planet in general, although in a hallucinatory-imagined way (Figure 3.4).[29]

Thus the initial metaphor's intention is switched from the external impossibility of contact to the internal actuality of contact: two completely detached minds, that of the astronaut and that of the Ocean in Lem's novel, are contrasted in Tarkovsky's film with Chris's mental images being imitated by the Ocean. The last scene of *Solaris* puzzles the viewer, since it is impossible to identify the 'producer' of this vision: it may equally well be created by Chris or by the Ocean. The question of whether Chris dreams his reunion with the father or whether a simulacrum of this homecoming is created by the Ocean is bound to remain open. The planet Solaris does not just allow atemporal events to take place, but also celebrates aterritoriality. The concluding episode is both an atemporal and an aterritorial event. This shifts the finale into the realm of the parable:

Figure 3.4

Chris's return to Earth concludes the film, which began with earthly imagery. The return of the protagonist to his own domain via the alien entity – the planet Solaris – is a purely symbolic act: the man approaches his inner human self through palpable contact with spectral phenomena.

In his diaries, Tarkovsky provides an elaborate image of a bonfire which explores further the impossible possibility of contact between the earthly human mind and the alien intellect.[30] The passage describes the phenomenon in three guises: real (where Chris burns his papers on Earth, and which enters the film in the beginning); hallucinatory (which Chris dreams in his delirium, and which is inspired by his own feverish condition); and Solaris-generated. The bonfire produced by the alien planet is cold, and an object thrown into it does not burn since the planet imitates the appearance of phenomena, not their nature. The bonfire generated by Solaris is a spatial abnormality per se; it belongs neither to the domain of the real nor to the hallucinatory plane. Like Chris's contact with Hari and his parents, it allows the protagonist to reconsider the nature of earthly matters.

* * *

In his classic hymn to postmodernity, Jean Baudrillard suggests that 'the conquest of space constitutes an irreversible crossing toward the loss of the terrestrial referential'.[31] Tarkovsky reverses Baudrillard's vision, since in his film he aims to obliterate the all-too-powerful presence of science fiction – a genre which includes a conquest of space in its pure form – by restoring the terrestrial referent. However, this referent is of a different order, since it has already experienced the alienation of space; it is not a mere homecoming, but a dreaming about homecoming which is powerfully depicted at the end of *Solaris*. The film-maker tries to reconcile the irreconcilable: he is desperate to humanize the fantastic genre and to undermine the rigid opposition between the real and the hallucinatory.

The infiltration of the fantastic space of Solaris by the familiar images of Earth is a symbolic distortion. It helps Tarkovsky to reorientate semantic directions by transferring the scientific quest into a spiritual journey. As he declares, 'What is important for me is a view of Earth from space.'[32] The astronauts on Solaris are translated from stable and mundane consciousness to a mode of awareness dominated by guilt-driven images. The phantoms they face are not extraterrestrial monsters, though they are produced by the alien planet, but emerge as all-too-familiar earthly beings. Moreover, the constant subject of Chris's dreams and hallucinations during his term of service at the Solaris station is his parental home on Earth, though the cherished space is constantly presented literally in an unfamiliar light, and appears as an uncanny topos.

The coherent linear narrative form of Lem's *Solaris* is distorted in Tarkovsky's film of the same title by means of seemingly disjointed narrative blocks, which all strive to turn the action (observed in the text as if from outside) into a purely internal discourse. The epistemological questions which shape the text of the novel are transmuted into a quest to regain self-knowledge through the prism of ethical judgement. The internalization of the narrative flow allows time – a more subjective concept than space – to govern the film. Memories (the home video from Earth), dreams and hallucinations all manifest a non-objective and hence ambivalent aspect of temporal reality: they literally materialize on the alien surface. This dislocation of time, however, leads to spatial confusion. The Solaris base ceases to be the sole ground on which the narrative is rooted. Real Earth and imaginary spaces – those where Chris 'meets' his parents – emerge as alternative topoi. Moreover, islands start appearing on the surface of the Ocean after Chris's encephalogram is sent to it. The planet Solaris now includes earthly manifestations; 'dry land' makes its landscape more familiar. The aesthetic strategy of overcoming the rigidity of space (the topos of the Solaris station is constantly mixed with earthly imagery) and time (the present time of the narrative is constantly mixed with memories from the past and timeless dreams and hallucinations) is developed further in *Mirror* – a film that is almost solely dedicated to the spatio-temporal aspects of human existence.

4

MEMORIES OF *MIRROR*

*M*irror (*Zerkalo*, 1975) is one of the most daring and influential cinematic projects to have come out of the Soviet Union. Unlike the director's three preceding and three subsequent films, *Mirror* consists solely of disparate spatio-temporal frameworks which are not unified by a single narrative line. One may define the film as a complex exercise in counterpoint consisting of a series of recollections of a dying man, though this would be an oversimplification. Memories of childhood and scenes from the man's present life are intermixed with dreams and 'unmotivated' leaps into the historical past by means of a documentary chronicle. This makes any linear reading of the film's narrative impossible, and leads the diegesis beyond the conventions of traditional storytelling. All of these place *Mirror* in the domain of highly experimental cinematic endeavours shared by Alain Resnais' *Last Year in Marienbad* (*L'année dernière à Marienbad*, 1961), Federico Fellini's *8½* (1963) and Ingmar Bergman's *Persona* (1966). The four films perform a radical deconstruction of normative space and time.

Spatial dislocations and temporal abnormalities are the defining features of *Mirror's* unique style – they dominate its reflecting surface. The general complexity of the film and its aesthetic significance arise primarily from the way the director approaches its narrative structure. Various episodes from the lives of three generations of one family are blended with seemingly unrelated historical events. As a result, the divergent spatio-temporal frameworks form a relatively homogeneous yet complex narrative texture. The fact that several of the characters are played by the same actors adds further confusion: Margarita Terekhova plays the roles of Maria/the Mother and Natalia/the Wife, and Ignat Daniltsev is Aleksei/the narrator as a child, as well as Aleksei's own son Ignat. These multiple identities are scattered throughout the narrative of the film as splinters of a broken mirror. The characters' actions do not obey the rules of chronological sequentiality. Due to their constantly shifting and elusive identities, the notions of space and time as such become the main characters of the film.

In addition to its formal experiments, the film is richly infused with cultural references – distorted reflections of other artefacts – which render it even more intricate. Bach, Pergolesi and Purcell dominate the soundtrack of the film, while images by Leonardo and landscapes inspired by Bruegel appear throughout. *Mirror* also contains a broad selection of literary quotations and allusions. Four poems by Arseni Tarkovsky, together with the first lines of Dante's *Inferno*, provide a pronounced reflection on the notions of space and time. Spatial and temporal categories function as dominant tropes in the poems and actively interact with the general filmic discourse.

The film opens with Ignat, the narrator's son, switching on a television set and watching a staged documentary episode during which a psychologist cures a stammering adolescent. The two – a rather stereotypical Soviet doctor and a polytechnic student – perform an almost miraculous act of healing in front of the camera. To begin with, the young man is not able to articulate a single word clearly. His stammering is distressing to watch, and the woman uses hypnotism to cure him. After her therapeutic intervention, the young man is able to speak loudly and clearly. He proclaims his ability to communicate – 'I can speak' – and this gives the filmic discourse permission to start evolving.

The style in which the encounter between the two is filmed is remarkable: the glaring spotlights and the shadow from a microphone in the background present the event as belonging to the factual, not imaginary, realm. The process of mechanical reproduction is revealed. The psychologist, her patient and the cure are real but, at the same time, the whole episode is staged – it is re-enacted in front of the camera, and the film crew does not even attempt to hide the evidence of this re-enactment. This intermediate position, somewhere between reality and its artistic impression, heralds the general aesthetic approach employed by the director in *Mirror*: real-autobiographical elements, the newsreel footage, and the presence of family members are infused with poetic abstractness. The borderline between fiction and documentary undergoes a process of erasure, and this transformation becomes a key characteristic of the film.

Mirrors in *Mirror*

The 'autobiographical' nature of *Mirror* can also be compared to an act of contemplating one's own image in the looking glass. The author's *reflection* in the mirror initiates a mental *reflection* on the past and the world around him. Reflection is, of course, also 'the action of turning (back) or fixing the thoughts on some subject; meditation, deep or serious consideration' (*OED*). The act of looking into a mirror stimulates the author's distant memories, which are revealed by different temporal segments closely connected with various spaces seen or inhabited in the past.

As Marcel Proust writes, describing the famous episode of the madeleine – the ultimate moment of remembrance: 'the whole of Combray and its surroundings, taking shape and solidity, sprang into being, town and gardens alike, from my cup of tea'.[1] The grace of the memory of a particular time manifests itself by spatial means. Space in this search for lost time is an even more important category, for memories, according to Bachelard, 'are motionless, and the more securely they are fixed in space, the sounder they are'.[2] The word 'memory', defined as '[s]enses relating to the action or process of commemorating, recollecting, or remembering' (*OED*), presumes a certain gathering of objects, people and experiences, which are already devoured by time, in a mental space. Memory is therefore situated somewhere between the realms of reality and dream. To remember is to recall phantoms of the real past, and this liminal quality is echoed throughout the film.

Explicit spatio-temporal discontinuity is what makes *Mirror* such a renowned cinematic project. While Tarkovsky's other films do contain 'confusing' non-narrative sequences, *Mirror* relies upon them entirely. There is no major narrative line from which leaps are accomplished. The film does not differentiate between past, present and future events, and, moreover, confuses sequences representing reality, dreams and memory. In 1982, several years after the completion of *Mirror*, Tarkovsky discovered an epigraph for the film – it is drawn from the first page of Hesse's novel *Demian: The Story of Emil Sinclair's Youth*: 'Mine is not a pleasant story, it does not possess the gentle harmony of invented tales; like the lives of all men who have given up trying to deceive themselves, it is a mixture of nonsense and chaos, madness and dreams.'[3] The lack of narrative harmony and the presence of chaotic elements are exactly what characterize

Mirror. However, according to the director, the cinematic reflecting surface, though it may appear to be shattered and disjointed, still offers a whole image, for

> [c]inema in general is a way of gathering some sort of shattered fragments into a unified whole. A film consists of shots in the same manner as a mosaic consists of distinct parts of different colours and textures. It is possible that each part does not make any sense at all individually, if you remove it from its context. It exists only as a whole.[4]

Tarkovsky's insistence on the wholeness of cinematic experience is understandable, for he prefers the smoothly edited continuous long take, which reveals the way time flows in the shot – the 'pressure of the time that runs through [it]'[5] – to the aggressive rational cuts of montage. Disjointed unit-shots evolve into a complete aesthetic experience only once they join the mainstream of cinematic time. Thus, the integrity of the reflecting 'surface' is essential. The mirror, as a symbol and artefact, emerges in its full glory as a unified whole in the film. It becomes a tool to facilitate *Mirror*'s journey in time and space: various displacements are accomplished by reflecting surfaces of different kinds.

The prominence of the mirror metaphor in the film cannot be overestimated. The looking glass, as an object, is one of the most resonant aesthetic devices, able to overcome the imposed homogeneity of space as perceived by the human eye. It is a natural means of displacing spatial categories. Even a straightforward reflection reverses, at the very least, the right–left axis – a mirror always reflects distortion back to the subject. In addition, the point of view in relation to the mirror (for instance, that of a camera or of an eye) inevitably tilts the reflected object; the resulting image is bound to misrepresent its physical source. The impact is even more considerable in fiction, where a mirror is often used as a means of shifting spatial categories and revealing alternative worlds (for example, in Alexander Pushkin's *Tale of the Dead Princess and the Seven Knights*, 1833, and Lewis Carroll's *Through the Looking-Glass, and What Alice Found There*, 1871), and as a means of presenting alternative temporal frameworks (for example, in Andrei Bely's *The Return: The Third Symphony*, 1904).

Moreover, affinities between the mirror and cinematic apparatus are too apparent to be ignored. Christian Metz compares the mirror to a shot, which frames a particular spatial fragment.[6] The looking glass reproduces an image while projecting it in the same manner as the camera does – with inevitable distortions. The ontological essence of the process of mechanical reproduction, where the filmed object or person is always already real and fictional, unites the two. Foucault suggests that the mirror is unreal since it is a 'placeless place [where] I see myself there where I am not, in an unreal, virtual space that opens up behind the surface',[7] and at the same time it is real because 'the mirror does exist in reality, where it exerts a sort of counteraction on the position that I occupy'.[8] Indeed, the reflecting surface of the mirror, like the cinematic apparatus or photography, exists on the borderline between reality and fiction (reality's distortion or impression).

In addition, mirrors and reflections do not perform the function of spatio-temporal 'stabilizers' in *Mirror*. On the contrary, they seem to displace, disorientate and confuse the notions of space and time. Mirrors do appear as conventional devices for self-admiration, and the female characters are seen casting an eye into the looking glass. However, cinematic reflection on the presence of mirroring surfaces, and their unconventional use, is what makes *Mirror* a daring project – a film that addresses the ontology of film-making.

There are multiple mirrors that produce different types of reflection with different textures. The very first shot presents Ignat curiously looking into the blank screen of a television set in whose grey surface a reflection of a room is visible. Increasing sensitivity to the mirror as a physical object finds its utmost manifestation in the wall of mirrors in the scene where the author dies (his death symbolically signified by the gesture of freeing a bird). At least eleven mirrors of different sizes and designs are placed on the wall as purely aesthetic objects – as elements of the room's decoration. The mirrors on the wall do not seem to perform their designated function of providing reflections. The author-narrator ceases to exist, and the possibility of his recognizing his own reflection expires concurrently with him. The eleven mirrors remain 'empty' and cannot accommodate his reflection. What makes the sequence more problematic is the fact that it is Tarkovsky himself who is lying on the bed in the sequence. Though shots which unambiguously revealed the director's presence in the film were deleted at the editing stage, this presence–absence of the real author inevitably situates the film in the realm of autobiography.[9]

However, there are other, more innovative uses of mirrors and reflections in the film. In some scenes, mirroring surfaces are not crystal-clear, and the reflected images they produce are blurred or distorted as in Shakespeare's 62nd sonnet – 'beated and chapped with tanned antiquity'.[10] Water, dust or refractions of light undermine the linearity of reflections, and the characters must confront slightly disfigured versions of their own appearance. In other scenes, the camera reveals the presence of a mirror in a shot (either by focusing on its surface instead of on a mirrored image or by showing a mirror with the boundaries of its frame); but then the reflected images start to dominate the screen and appear to be not reflections but fragments of filmed reality (the camera changes its focus from the mirror's surface to the image, or it zooms in and 'hides' the mirror's frame). Thus the image is shown as commingling reflection and reality – its spatial coordinates become difficult to discern (Figure 4.1).

Finally, in one of the scenes towards the end of the film, the camera itself functions as a mirror. The episode reveals the Mother's inner tension, and occurs immediately before she abruptly hurries away from a wealthy doctor's house. It is filmed as a sequence-shot, and the viewer's/camera's point of view is treated as a mirroring surface. The first image to appear is that of the doctor's wife trying on earrings and looking straight into the camera as if it were a mirror. The camera then tracks to the right and shows the Mother, who is apparently troubled by something and looks quite indifferently at her own 'reflection'. The doctor's wife emerges again from behind the Mother, draws nearer to the camera while still out of focus, and then disappears altogether from the camera's field of vision. The viewer is presented for a few seconds with a blurred, dark screen, which then develops into the image of Ignat looking sadly to one side – the transformation of the shot is accomplished by means of the change in focus. The camera is designated the role of omnipresent mirror in this highly complex and brilliantly orchestrated *mise-en-scène*.

Reflected images in Mirror are never faithful to the given reality they reproduce. They are almost always distorted visions of something or someone. This process of displacement is part of a general aesthetic strategy to present an alternative multiplicity of spaces and times – that of childhood, and of a time contemporaneous with the making of the film. The multiplicity of reflections – that is, of identification – and their resistance to being captured are inherent characteristics of the genre of autobiography, in which the self's plurality reigns supreme: 'what is fetishized is not a stable mirror-image of the self, which can be exported from text to life, but the profusion of signs, tokens, and traces of selfhood which are generated as the autobiographer "processes" memories, conjectures, and documents'.[11]

Deleuze's argument that Tarkovsky's *Mirror* explores crystallized, not simply mirrored, spaces furnishes a very productive interpretative stance. It echoes to an extraordinary degree the director's own statement that '[a]ll artistic work relies on memory, and is a means of

Figure 4.1

crystallizing it'.[12] Crystal, unlike flat, reflecting surfaces, presents a multiplicity of reflections due to its complex internal pattern extending in all three spatial dimensions. Deleuze writes:

> *Mirror* is a turning crystal, with two sides if we relate it to the invisible adult character (his mother, his wife), with four sides if we relate it to two visible couples [...]. And the crystal turns on itself, like a homing device that searches an opaque environment: what is Russia, what is Russia...?[13]

The metaphor used by Deleuze is functional, since it brings into the discourse of the film the physical and mythical qualities of crystal. Apart from the above-mentioned ability to provide a multiplicity of reflections (space), the crystal of fairytales is able to reveal different temporal frameworks (time). Crystal, with its multiple planes, is a spatio-temporal labyrinth.

It could be suggested that Tarkovsky's project is ultimately a leap from the territory of space to the realm of time. However, this leap into time is possible only by means of deconstructing space. The extensive use of documentary chronicle, the character-doubling, the reliance on sequences such as dreams or memories in *Mirror* – all contribute to the constantly shifting topography. The ensuing instability of space liberates time and generates a non-linear vision of temporal relations – time becomes visual and almost palpable. As Tarkovsky describes the narrator's apartment in *Mirror*, 'this was a flat where time itself lived'.[14] The metamorphosis or even complete disappearance of spatial coordinates means that time becomes a material entity, and the viewer encounters the spatialized flow of time – its passage.

In the light of the role of time in the film, a comment by Grigori Chukhrai, a prominent Soviet film-maker, regarding *Mirror* is highly intriguing. During an official Goskino meeting, at which the first cut of the film was discussed, Chukhrai put forward the following argument: 'this film by Tarkovsky is a failure. He wanted to tell a story about time and about himself. He succeeded, perhaps, in telling us something about himself, but not about time.'[15] Chukhrai accuses Tarkovsky of narcissism; according to him, *Mirror* reflects his colleague's obsession with his own image and has nothing to offer in terms of exploring human experience in historical time. Ironically, *Mirror* is a film which directly tackles the issue of time. For Tarkovsky, time is a conceptual, abstract entity, and he presents it primarily by merging and confusing the spaces of private and social-historical, temporal frameworks, thus loosening the classical narrative cause–effect relationship. Events are no longer perceived as a progressive chain of occurrences, but presented as abstract chunks of drifting time.

The role of literature in the process of spatial and temporal destabilization in *Mirror* is crucial. The film in a way began as a work of literature: in 1970 Tarkovsky published a short story that was divided into several novellas.[16] These novellas, based on childhood memories, would eventually become a literary preamble to *Mirror* and form its core. Moreover, the presence of numerous literary quotations in the aesthetic texture of the film is also significant. The literary intertext is by definition an entity which has been borrowed from another space and time: first, the artwork occupies a specific physical space, and also refers to other spatial locations within itself; secondly, it possesses its own authentic temporal qualities – the historical era to which the text belongs or the conceptual time it represents. The substantial presence of literary quotations in *Mirror* enhances its spatio-temporal 'ambitions' within Tarkovsky's cinematic project. Meditations on and conceptual models of space and time contained in the poems help the film-maker to break away from cinema's classical narrative representational strategies. The poems used in the film are explicitly non-diegetic. However, they interact with various elements of the narrative line in a contrapuntal fashion.

Disembodied Voice

The heard voice of Arseni Tarkovsky reciting the four poems shapes the film and plays a complex role in its aesthetic texture. The voice-over does not overlap with the images presented, and does not coincide with a particular body. The lack of unity between voice and image intensifies even further the incoherence of the storyline, since sound synchronization is one of the predominant features of narrative cinema. A voice emanating from a source outside the frame is a phantasmatic phenomenon. It does not satisfy the viewer's urge for lifelike representation, according to the schema of 'heard voice corresponds to seen body'. Arseni Tarkovsky's voice is not anchored by a visible body in the filmic space, and consequently cannot be located. The voice-over transcends the spatio-temporal limitations imposed on the seen body. However, the resulting asynchronism – the disembodied body – does not destroy the perceived unity of *Mirror*: as Mary Ann Doane puts it, 'the body in the film becomes the body of the film.'[17]

Furthermore, the voice reading the poems in *Mirror* is not just a randomly chosen one; it is the voice of the author of the poems, who is also the director's father. The present voice of the father with his absent body inevitably invites psychoanalytic interpretations. The Lacanian interplay between the imaginary and the symbolic (with the unattainable real in the background) can be easily located in *Mirror*.[18] The voice-over of the absent father (the imaginary) is the ultimate source of the language (the symbolic) in the film. Separation, redeemed by language, functions as a means to attain oneself.

More generally, Arseni Tarkovsky's poems delivered by his own voice-over are part of the overall aesthetic strategy of *Mirror*; that is, to create an abstract autobiography which would strive to present general reflections on the human condition: the artists transform 'empirical facts into *arti*facts'.[19] The autobiographical-confessional character of *Mirror* (which at earlier stages was even called *Confession* and was also referred to as a 'film-questionnaire') is suggested by Tarkovsky's original intention to interview his mother, Maria Nikolaevna, and to film her with a hidden camera. Although the idea was eventually abandoned, she nevertheless appears in the film playing herself. Furthermore, photographs of the family taken by Lev Gornung, among which were several images of Arseni and Andrei Tarkovsky shot beside mirrors, influenced many of the film's *mises-en-scène* and provided visual inspiration for the film.[20] The real plane framed the process of making *Mirror* at every stage.

Although somewhat commonplace as far as literary references are concerned, the importance of Proust's monumental *In Search of Lost Time* to the discourse of *Mirror* is nevertheless worth mentioning. Tarkovsky appears to follow the French writer in so far as he perceives autobiography to constitute an act of textual production that dissolves the steadfastness of such concepts as subject, self and author. Moreover, the director considers autobiography to be a creative act, through which the author attempts to overcome the rigidity of established genres. The fact that Tarkovsky rewrote the script for *Mirror* almost a decade after the film was shot tends to confirm the nature of the autobiographical enterprise, which should remain 'an endless prelude'.[21]

The autobiographical tone of the film is inevitably intensified by Arseni Tarkovsky's aural presence. The narrating father, the acting mother,[22] together with the almost motionless body of Tarkovsky himself, all constitute a strong aesthetic statement: the real, together with its familial relations and private anxieties, enters the fictional space of cinema. Similarly, the poems address the real lovers of the poet Arseni Tarkovsky, but they do not conform to the standard sender–recipient pattern. The communicated romantic message becomes an aesthetic statement. The first poem in *Mirror* – 'First

Meetings' – appears early, in the eleventh minute of the film, towards the end of the first episode. Its early introduction establishes a register which will dominate the film all the way through: overtly non-diegetic poetry generates abstract artistic meditation on the fate of an individual as dominated by historical events.

'First Meetings'

We celebrated every moment of our
First meetings, like an epiphany,
Alone in the entire world. You were
More daring, and lighter than a bird's wing,
On the stairs, like dizziness,
Running down over the step and leading
Through the moist lilac to your domain,
From that side of the mirror's glass.

When night set in, grace was given
To me, the altar gates
Were opened, and in the darkness
Nakedness shone and slowly bowed,
And, waking up: 'May you be blessed!'
I said and knew, that my blessing
Was audacious: you slept,
And the lilac reached out from the table to touch
Your lashes with the universe's blue
And the lashes, touched by the blue,
Were calm, and your hand was warm.

While in the crystal, the rivers pulsed,
The mountains smoked, the seas glimmered,
And you held a crystal sphere
On your palm, and you slept on the throne,
And – righteous God! – you were mine.

You woke up and transfigured
The daily human vocabulary,
And your speech was filled to the throat
With a full-bodied force, and the word *thou*
Revealed its new sense and it meant: *ruler*.

In the world everything was transfigured, even
Simple things – the basin, the jug – when
Between us stood, as if on watch,
The stratified and solid water.

We were led, not knowing where.
Before us stepped out, as if mirages,
Miraculously built cities,
The mint itself lay down beneath our feet

And birds were following the same path as us,
And fish were jumping out along the river,
And the sky opened out before our eyes...

When fate followed behind us on the trail,
Like a madman with a razor in his hand.²³

The poem functions as a kind of initiation; it allows the viewer to enter the imaginary world of *Mirror*. The film's aspiration to present the author-director's personal autobiography, which would mirror the viewer's own human condition, is clearly revealed in the poetic text. The private lyrical message reaches a metaphysical domain. The amorous encounter of the first lines is transformed into the agonizing anticipation of fate. Furthermore, 'First Meetings' unambiguously refers to mirroring devices: the mirror figures prominently in the case of 'You were [...] leading [...] to your domain, / From that side of the mirror's glass', and crystal is mentioned in the following passage: 'While in the crystal, the rivers pulsed, / The mountains smoked, the seas glimmered, / And you held a crystal sphere / On your palm...' Mirror and crystal, as has already been pointed out, are two artefacts of the utmost importance for the filmic discourse. Their ability to dislocate and present alternative temporal frameworks is deployed heavily in the quoted passages. A mirror reveals an alternative place of human dwelling, while crystal presents a discrete miniature universe consisting of its own rivers, mountains and seas.

Before the male narrator of the poem delivers the lyrical message, the theme of absence is highlighted by means of images of the woman waiting for her husband. The waiting proves to be in vain; he does not come. However, a bizarre and somewhat unsettling encounter takes place with a stranger, played by Anatoli Solonitsyn. The meeting is marked by the abnormal incident occurring in the field near the house. A wind of unnatural origin prepares the ground for the relocation into the poetic world. The husband does not come and the poet (in real life he is the husband who never returned) starts reading the poem, while the woman withdraws to the house and is reunited with her children.

The accompanying visual sequence in its everyday domestic simplicity balances the metaphysical leap accomplished by the poetic text. The lover of the poem leads the poet to her 'domain, / From that side of the mirror's glass', while the female protagonist of the film (the abandoned lover, the Mother) leads the camera and the viewer to her everyday domain: the house. A sexual encounter between the lovers in the poem is counterpoised by images of the children at their most common activities – playing and eating. The camera then carefully observes the Mother while the two-level transfiguration occurs within the poem: a linguistic transformation of everyday vocabulary (particularly of 'thou' into the 'ruler') and a metamorphosis of common objects (the basin and the jug). The transfiguration opens up miraculous horizons ('We were led, not knowing where') and allows a new magic universe to emerge. The latter is explored by the lovers, who are nevertheless followed by fate 'Like a madman with a razor in his hand'.

'First Meetings' was initially conceived as a diegetic quotation – Terekhova, playing the Mother, was supposed to open a notebook and read the poem to herself.[24] The trace of this idea can still be found in the final product. The actress sits near the window with an open notebook, which is then closed and put aside once the poem ends. However, the diegetic treatment of the poem's presence in the film was abandoned; a more extreme and abstract form of quotation was preferred. The voice-over is used as a separate aural image, since it is literally disconnected from the visual sequence presented. The ultimate loneliness of the woman in the given situation is redeemed by the disembodied voice. Though the latter is not spatialized, and hence does not guarantee 'the singularity and stability of a point of audition',[25] it still provides some kind of consoling presence.

The visual sequence accompanying the poem concludes with shots of the Mother looking out of one of the windows in the house. The view from the house comprises a glade with a bench on which random objects lie in the summer rain. The reverse-shot exposes the woman silently crying as if echoing the rain outside. The camera lingers for a few seconds on her beautifully lit face. The shot is the pinnacle of the sequence; it creates a dramatic aura, since it effectively delivers a sense of emptiness and loss and communicates to the viewer the pain of futile waiting. The house is the sole refuge for the Mother with her young children, and is a topos to which it is impossible for the director to return.

The role of the house is crucial both in this episode and in the film in general, for 'the house shelters daydreaming, the house protects the dreamer, the house allows one to dream in peace'.[26] Built especially for the set on the foundation of the real house where the Tarkovsky family used to live, the house inhabits the borderline between the real and the fictional; it is an impression of a real entity. The place which appears in the film accommodates a memory – that is, space houses time. As with Thoreau's fields, which the writer claimed were engraved in his soul, Tarkovsky's memories settle in his own soul, for he writes: 'Time cannot vanish without trace for it is a subjective, spiritual category; and the time we have lived settles in our soul as an experience *placed* within time.'[27] The director's memory of his place of dwelling materializes in his most intimate film project; again, time is given a spatial form.

The episode following the reading of the poems includes Tarkovsky's favourite combination of natural elements: fire and water. The Mother hears cries and dogs barking, and goes outside to find out what is happening. She tells her children that there is a fire nearby, and they rush outside. The camera lingers inside the house: it attentively observes the table from which the glass part of an oil-lamp suddenly falls. This is a mundane and at the same time rather strange event, for the lamp was lying still, accompanied by the loud sound of a cuckoo clock. The camera tracks aside to reveal a reflection of the two children looking at the fire. The looking glass 'with tanned antiquity' appears to be out of focus for a few seconds, before disclosing a meticulously composed *mise-en-scène*. The camera then discovers the neighbours' son, Klanka, and follows the boy outside. The burning construction, a wooden barn or a house, is engulfed by flames, and its former inhabitants and neighbours stand in the rain engrossed by the scene of destruction. The image, with its intense sound of burning wood and the surrounding dampness, heralds the finale of Tarkovsky's last film, *Sacrifice*.

The fire is immediately followed by the image of the narrator as a child lying in bed. The boy wakes up in the middle of the night, sits up and attentively listens out for something. The scene, photographed in colour, is followed by a slow-motion shot of a wood with swaying bushes photographed in sepia. The combination of the house, the wood and the wind, which recurs throughout the film several times, recalls Tarkovsky's own dream, which he discussed with his students during a series of lectures on film-making and which also made its way into the script of *Mirror*:

> I have a recurring dream which is amazingly regular. It is as though my memory does not let me forget the most important things. Sometimes this even makes me want to revisit heart-rendingly dear places, which I have not been near these last twenty years.
>
> I dream that I am walking through Zavrazhe, past the birch grove, the ramshackle, abandoned bath house, past the small, old church with the flaking plaster and torn bags of lime and broken weighing scales from the collective farm visible in the porch. And among the tall birch trees is a wooden, two-storey building. The building where I was born, and where my

> grandfather [...] delivered me, on a starched tablecloth thrown over the dining-room table forty years ago. And this dream is so accurate and convincing, that it is more real than actuality.[28]

This dream that is 'more real than actuality' also participates in the film's intricate deconstruction of the reality–dream pair. The cinematic screen, which does not differentiate between the two, functions as a site of re-enactment of past events. It also makes the director return to the cherished topos of childhood. The house and the wood are defining artefacts that accomplish the return. Bachelard singles out the concept of the house in his book *The Poetics of Space*. For the philosopher, the familial space is a source of comfort:

> When we dream of the house we were born in, in the utmost depths of revery, we participate in this original warmth, in this well-tempered matter of the material paradise. This is the environment in which the protective beings live. We shall come back to the maternal features of the house.[29]

However, the house recreated in *Mirror* is not just a cherished domestic place for Tarkovsky. The edifice in the first dream is gradually transformed into something uncanny. The cut back to the boy in bed, after the wood interlude in sepia, is also accomplished in monochrome, and the disappearance of the colour signifies a shift of realities. The boy murmurs for his father and gets up from his bed. He sees a shirt thrown across the adjacent room, and then observes his father helping his mother wash her hair. The woman with long wet hair bends over a washbasin and the sound of dripping water, as if in an empty space, dominates the soundtrack. She gets up without exposing her face, and after a mysterious noise effect the camera zooms out to reveal that neither the washbasin nor the father are in the room, and that the room itself is not part of the wooden house, but of a flat. The bending Mother stands in isolation with the wet hair covering her face. The room undergoes a transfiguration – it is no longer an ordinary room where domestic experience is possible. Water streams down the walls, wet plaster falls down from the ceiling and hits the flooded floor by a lit gas stove; the two antagonistic elements, fire and water, meet again.

The Mother, now with backswept hair, passes by the camera. The movement is accomplished against the walls, still covered in streams of water, of different texture – made of dark plaster and bricks. The camera unhurriedly observes the scene: it tracks the woman, her reflection in the wet mirror, the dark wall, and then the woman again. The tracking shot undermines the singularity of the character – one of Tarkovsky's stylistic devices which occurs repeatedly in his films. However, the uniqueness of the sequence lies in the following doubling of the double. The Mother looks into the camera as if it is a mirror, and the camera bypasses her to reveal the looking glass. The following cut shows her reflection as an old woman (played by the director's real mother), surrounded by a maze of diverse reflections and refractions. The streams of water and flames are visible in the reflection, and suggest that it is the same space as in the preceding seconds. The spatial abnormality reveals a temporal progression: the woman meets her own old self. The aged Mother touches the mirror's surface; her hand meets her reflection on the surface of the faint glass (Figure 4.2). The dream episode concludes with a colour shot of a hand placed against the fire.

After the highly abstract and rather disturbing beginning, the film continues with its narratively most conventional episode. Various themes dominating the appearance of 'First Meetings' and the following dream sequence come into sight in normal, everyday circumstances – in the printing house. Unlike most of the other parts of the film, this episode has a comprehensible linear storyline. It presents an incident that took place during the period of the Stalinist purges. The Mother believes she may have made an unforgivable proofreading error in a very important state publication. This doubt becomes almost unbearable in conditions dominated by the constant fear of arrest, which would be tantamount to an agonizing death. She rushes to her workplace in heavy rainfall to find out about the typing error and, therefore, to learn her own fate. The wetness of the woman's hair meets the disembodied voice of Arseni Tarkovsky in 'From the morning I was waiting for you yesterday...', the shortest and the most abstract poem to appear in *Mirror*.

The poem is delivered by Arseni Tarkovsky's voice-over and visually accompanied by the tracking shot of the heroine walking in the long corridor of the printing house. She has just learned whether her fears about a fatal printing error were justified or unfounded, but the viewer remains uninformed of the outcome at this stage. The poem reads:

> From the morning I was waiting for you yesterday,
> They guessed that you wouldn't come,
> Do you remember the weather?
> Like a feast day! And I went out without a coat.
>
> Today you came, and they have fixed for us
> An especially gloomy day,
> And the rain, and the especially late hour,
> And the drops are running along the cold branches.
>
> They can't be calmed with a word, nor dried with a cloth...

Figure 4.2

The accompanying visual sequence is perfectly homogenous. It simply shows the Mother walking along the corridor. As a result, the represented cinematic space and time are uniform and the images are endowed with a clear intelligibility. The camera recedes while the actress advances towards the viewer. However, the barely perceptible slow motion of the sequence, together with the voice-over delivering the poetic text, rescues the scene from its everydayness and transfers it into the realm of myth or parable. Both slow motion and voice-over are purely artistic and artificial devices which cannot be experienced in real life. They are in keeping with the general capacity of art to displace a world-view imposed by common sense.

It should also be noted that the laconic style of the poem, written in Russian in regular amphibrachic trimeter followed by an iamb,[30] organically corresponds to the straightforwardness of the visual sequence accompanying it. The plain images of the sequence absorb every line of the poem, thus making significant every word it contains. The apparent simplicity of 'From the morning I was waiting for you yesterday...' is surmounted by the signifying potential of the lapidary language of the text.

The poem appears at a point when it is not clear whether the error has taken place or not. This uncertainty is eliminated and at the same intensified by the lyric message of Arseni Tarkovsky's text. The dramatic tension of the episode, achieved by the presence/absence of the printing error (everyday reality), is suddenly switched by means of the poem onto another level (the presence/absence of a lover). In both worlds (those of the poem and of the film) the weather weeps: the verse 'They can't be calmed with a word, nor dried with a cloth...' is echoed in the heavy rain that followed the heroine on her way to the printing factory, and her wet hair bears witness to this. The poem's laconic but complex poetic world is contrasted with the minimal cinematic set of the printing-house episode. The weeping, present both in image and word, is about something which neither the poem nor the filmic episode reveals to its full extent, and this uncertainty organically ties them together, though they remain separated.

The interaction of the poetic text with the printing-house episode is an illustrative example of Deleuze's vision of modern cinema as implying the collapse of the sensory-motor schema. Speech ceases to be a connecting point between image and narrative. 'From the morning I was waiting for you yesterday...' belongs neither to the domain of action nor reaction; it is situated beyond a web of diegetic interactions. As a result, *Mirror* reconfigures the poetic word into the cinematic medium in a fashion unparalleled in contemporaneous narrative cinema. The film constitutes a leap away from the clichéd use of poetry whereby text is fully appropriated by the diegesis. Arseni Tarkovsky's poems appear as if from nowhere, and the voice-over is explicitly disembodied. Fused with visual imagery, the narrated text acquires a new weight and force.

The reading of the poem is followed by the Mother's encounter with one of her colleagues and her close friend Elizaveta Pavlovna, the memory of whom offered diegetic justification for the whole printing-house section to enter the narrative of the film. The unexpected hysterical clash between the two functions as an emotional resolution; it releases the tension accumulated by the presence/absence of the fatal error. The impenetrability of the episode reveals and at the same time obscures a complex relationship between the women. The Mother ends the quarrel by locking herself in a shower room. The intermittent water supply does not allow her to take a shower, and she starts giggling and then bursts into tears. The theme of washing again enters the film – a mundane event, which is accompanied by some kind of abnormal manifestation. This time washing is suddenly interrupted by a brief, and dramatically unmotivated cut to a countryside view: a buckwheat field with a fire in the distance. The short leap to another space connects the episode with the opening sequence in which the Mother and her children observe the fire engulfing their neighbour's place. It also serves as an intermission before the leap to a radically other space and time – a Moscow flat in the 1970s.

Chronic Chronology of Chronicle

The first image of the narrator's present incorporates the same actress, Margarita Terekhova, in the guise of his former wife Natalia. The woman carefully observes her reflection in a mirror while her divorced husband points out that she resembles his mother. This comment again allows the narrative to execute a leap into an alternative space and time, to a short and rather mundane scene by the familial house surrounded by the wood. The man remains invisible in the course of the whole conversation between the two. He is another disembodied voice in the film but his function, contrary to that of the reader of the poems, Arseni Tarkovsky, is prosaic – he argues with his former spouse. The visual absence of the interlocutor makes Natalia talk while looking off-screen, or facing her own reflection in the mirror and window. Her and the narrator's gazes do not meet on the cinematic screen, and most of the time the woman's *reflection* talks to the *disembodied* voice. The two therefore do not interact; the conversation is maintained only by traces of their presence.

The encounter evolves into the densest fragment, in terms of alternation between various temporal and spatial frameworks: the episode with the Spaniards. A voice talking in Spanish is heard towards the end of the conversation, and the narrator asks Natalia to go to another room and distract 'him'. A middle-aged Spanish man passionately recalls and mimics Palomo Linares, and his engrossing story is preceded by a documentary chronicle, which shows the famed matador during a bullfight. The Spaniard and his extensive family – who, as children from Communist families, were evacuated from their motherland to the Soviet Union during the Spanish Civil War – are either guests or neighbours in the communal apartment. Irrespective of their real status, the war victims inhabit and share the space with the narrator. The flat makes them also recall certain memories of their childhood. Memories of that distant time and space are delivered by means of sounds of flamenco music and the documentary chronicle showing heartbreaking partings of parents with their children in a Spain, devastated by the war.

The train departure of the 'Spanish childhood' chronicle is followed by footage of a Soviet stratosphere balloon – the giant, slow-moving structure served by soldiers on smaller balloons. The mesmerizing flying sequence is emotionally elevated by the soundtrack, a fragment from Pergolesi's 'Stabat Mater'. Tarkovsky fuses the modernist discourse of technical progress with the classical tradition of sacred music. The image of the balloon, disappearing in the height of the sky, is followed by the documentary chronicle depicting the Soviet aviator Valeri Chkalov's triumphant return to Moscow after his 63-hour flight across the North Pole in 1937. Thousands of leaflets scattered in the air celebrate the pilot's feat of endurance and create a lyrical atmosphere. By introducing this patchwork of various chronicles and private memories, the director explores clashes and incongruities between systematic public and experiential private space and time. Ignat leafing through a monograph commemorating the artistic exploits of Leonardo ends the documentary journey and returns the viewer to the flat and the present time. The book holds the attention of the camera for a long time. This is echoed later in the film when the same boy, this time in the role of the narrator as an adolescent, carefully looks at another drawing by Leonardo, which is followed by a close-up of a reproduction of the 'Portrait of Ginevra de' Benci'.[31]

The episode continues with Natalia's attempt to leave in haste, which is delayed by her dropping her bag on the floor. The boy helps his mother to gather the various items scattered on the apartment's floor. The mundane scene includes two mild abnormalities: Ignat gets an electric shock from something lying on the floor, and then he experiences a *déjà vu* moment – a remnant of the Proustian madeleine makes him realize that he has already lived through this very moment of gathering coins in this very space, though he notes to himself that he is in the flat for the first time. The woman, after asking her son to stop fantasizing, finally leaves. The camera tracks an empty room adjacent to the corridor and then reaches Ignat, who is on his way to close the door behind his mother. The two exchange a few remarks (the mother tells him to ask Maria Nikolaevna – Ignat's grandmother and Tarkovsky's real mother – not to leave if she comes by), and the boy is left on his own.

The encounter between the two is accomplished in a single sweeping movement, the continuity of which, in a truly Tarkovskian manner, reveals a spatial abnormality with temporal consequences. The astonished boy hears some noise from the previously empty room, and discovers that there is now a middle-aged woman sitting at a table with an elderly maidservant serving her tea. The mysterious woman-visitor behaves like a confident host and invites Ignat in. Her manners and appearance testify that she belongs to a different age, perhaps to the nineteenth century. She may be a former pre-revolutionary owner of the flat who enters it as a ghost, which can be defined as a temporal condensation manifesting itself through spatial means. Her appearance reconfirms the status of the flat as a space 'where time itself lived'.[32]

The visitor asks Ignat to read aloud a passage from a notebook, and warns him that they do not have much time. The boy reads a short quotation from Jean-Jacques Rousseau's 'Discourse on the Arts and Sciences', which turns out to be the wrong passage, and then reads aloud an extensive extract from Alexander Pushkin's letter to Peter Chaadaev, written on 19 October 1836. The overtly slavophilic discourse, ironically originally written in French, is read for the woman's pleasure. The extract does not seem to have any aesthetic value: it functions rather on the level of discourse, in that its rhetorical force exceeds its aesthetic merit. However, in spite of its semantic straightforwardness, the letter can be correlated with the complex discourse present in the direct literary quotations, which all deal with spatio-temporal categories. Pushkin talks about history – 'the formal record of the past [i.e. *time*]' (*OED*) – and unambiguously refers to Russia as a *space* which saved the Christian world: the Mongols, according to the great Russian poet, did not dare to leave Russians behind them.

However, the content of the exchange between Ignat and the woman-visitor is of secondary significance. What is important is her status as an apparition. The director describes her sudden appearance in the following way:

> These are some kind of cultural roots of this house, of this man who lives in it – the author's. And his son also in some way falls under the influence of this atmosphere, of these roots. [...] This is simply a woman who knits together the broken thread of time like in Shakespeare's *Hamlet*, as you might remember.[33]

As it is clear from the director's words, time, which is 'out of joint', is fixed by a spatial apparition.

The episode concludes the way it began – in an unexpected and abrupt manner. Ignat finishes reading the extract from the letter and hears a doorbell. The woman-visitor gives him permission to go and see who is there. The boy opens the door and, to the viewer's surprise, fails to recognize his own grandmother standing outside, while she also fails to recognize her grandson; the woman leaves thinking that she has called at the wrong apartment. There is a small detail in the preceding sequence which complicates and even muddles the narrative coordinates of the scene: Ignat, while reading Pushkin's letter, stood below a photograph of his grandmother and the director's real mother – Maria Nikolaevna. The photograph, like the body of Tarkovsky's mother, represents ultimate reality, and the two enter the aesthetic domain of *Mirror* (at a later stage in the film Natalia leafs through a set of photographs of herself with Maria Nikolaevna, taken on the shooting location, and the two look alike). The dyads of actuality–fiction and reality–hallucination intersect in the episode. Ignat, slightly puzzled, returns to the room and is genuinely astonished to find it empty. The thread of time, which functioned as a juncture between the present and the past, manifests itself again by means of space: through a gradually disappearing patch of condensation from a cup of tea.

A telephone call from his father 'awakens' the boy. The father tells his son a story about how, at his age, he was in love with a red-haired girl with lip sores. The disembodied voice, this time delivered through a telephone receiver, transfers the filmic narrative to the post-war Soviet Union. An image of the girl from the story is followed by an episode with Asafiev – an orphan and survivor of the Leningrad siege – during shooting practice. The child is the ultimate victim of warfare, illustrated by his disorientation, in a literal sense. He challenges the logic of military commands and refuses to understand military terms: he interprets the 'turnabout' command (the Russian *krugom* literally means 'turn around') as a 360-degree turn. Moreover, it seems that the war chronicles that precede and follow the episode are narratively associated with him, as Tollof Nelson observes: 'Through the rebellious eyes of [Asafiev] – a figure of disorientation and dislocation – viewers are taken through a series of three separate apocalyptic sequences of war: the hand-grenade prank, the Lake Sivash crossing, and the end of World War II.'[34]

The hand-grenade prank is an episode in which Asafiev, after being scolded by a military instructor, takes a dummy hand-grenade out of his bag. Children seize it and inadvertently pull out the pin. The boy falls down, squeezing the 'hand-grenade' in his hands, and then throws it away. The military instructor quickly orders the children to get away, and covers the dummy with his body. His cap and a plastic protective cover fall off his head, revealing a pulsating, boneless patch of his head – apparently a shrapnel wound sustained during the war. The camera pauses on the close-up of the instructor's head so the viewer can see the pulsating flesh in its full vulnerability, intensified by the amplified sound of the beating heart. The man gets up after realizing that it is a prank and gently reproaches Asafiev. He sits down in exhaustion, and this is followed by a brief return to the redhead with sore lips. The close-up of the girl, Tarkovsky's stepdaughter in real life, is followed by the most memorable sequence of the film: a poem accompanied by documentary footage of the Sivash crossing.

The enactment of 'Life, Life' in *Mirror* is probably the most remarkable combination of Arseni Tarkovsky's poetry and Andrei Tarkovsky's cinematic techniques. The fictional space of the filmic diegesis accommodates two 'real' and distinct artefacts: the poem by the director's father and the documentary footage, shot by an anonymous cameraman, depicting Soviet troops during the Second World War attempting to ford the shallow bays of Sivash. This Ukrainian lake is known as the Rotten Sea because of its putrid smell, and the chronicle registers the superhuman efforts of the soldiers crossing it in harsh weather conditions.

The words and images in the sequence create a very dense artistic texture which presents an array of semantic possibilities. The text vigorously interacts with the visual material. The actual appearance of the poem is preceded by almost two minutes of footage of the fording of Sivash. The images of soldiers struggling with nature are first accompanied by occasional splashes of water, before some disturbing drum music enters the scene. Then Arseni Tarkovsky's voice starts reciting the following lines:

'Life, Life'

1
I don't believe in presentiments, and signs
Don't frighten me. I run from neither slander
Nor poison. In the world, there is no death:
All are immortal. Everything is immortal.
One should not be afraid of death at seventeen,
Nor seventy. There is neither gloom nor death
In this world, only clarity and light.
We are all already on the shore of the sea,
And I am one of those who pulls in nets,
When immortality swims by like a shoal.

2
Live in a house – and the house won't collapse.
I will summon any of the centuries,
I will enter it and build a house in it.
Here is why your children and your wives
Are seated with me at a single table –
At a single table, your ancestor and grandson:
The coming time is being enacted now,
And if I raise my arm up just a little,
All five of the rays will remain with you.
I propped up every day of the past,
Supporting with my collarbones.
I measured time with a surveying chain,
And passed through it, as if through the Urals.

3
I picked the age according to my stature.
Going south, we held dust over the steppe;
The tall weeds smoked; the grasshopper made mischief,
Touched horseshoes with its whisker, and prophesied,
And threatened me with destruction, like a monk.
I fastened my fate to the saddle;
And now, in the coming times, like a boy,
I raise myself up halfway in the stirrups.

For me my immortality is enough,
That my blood should flow from age to age.

> For a faithful corner of unchanging warmth
> I would pay wilfully with my own life,
> Whenever its flying needle
> Would lead me, like a thread, around the world.

The accompanying chronicle presents the soldiers advancing through the boundless space of Lake Sivash while the idea of movement, in both the literal and metaphorical senses, dominates the poetic text. Several lines of 'Life, Life' describe transitions from place to place and from one situation or state to another.[35] This diversity of allusions within the poem saves the visual constituent from the non-artistic disambiguity and straightforwardness of the documentary material. As a result, the men depicted are not just overcoming a concrete obstacle by crossing the lake – they are entering and moving within metaphysical grounds.

The broad waters of Sivash become a reservoir of time: the Heraclitean river. Time, in a conventional metaphor, is indeed represented as a dynamic or stationary object through which one moves. Water in this case is an ideal symbol, since it can naturally appear both still and flowing. Two of the most memorable time-metaphors used in the poem deal directly with liquid entities: 'We are all already on the shore of the sea, / And I am one of those who pulls in nets, / When immortality swims by like a shoal', and 'For me my immortality is enough, / That my blood should flow from age to age.' The power of these two passages lies in an attempt to 'own' immortality – hence, eternity. Immortality swimming by like a shoal of fish is caught in the poet's nets, and his own blood enters the realm of the eternal by flowing from age to age.

The fact that the ultimate goal of the soldiers – the other bank of Sivash – is not made visible in the sequence adds further ambiguity, and allows the episode to remain open-ended. The crossing of the waters by the army becomes a doomed act that is destined to continue into eternity. The black-and-white footage emerges as an illustration of the impossibility of reaching the desired shore. What it depicts is a mere 'aimless' movement. The episode does not aspire to offer narrative input, since most viewers are not aware of the historical background of the chronicle and do not know *why, where, when* or even *whether* the soldiers accomplished the crossing. Human suffering is portrayed as an abstract category: it is not a consequence of a certain event, but a general human condition.

The ambiguous role of space is further illustrated by the concluding lines of the second stanza of 'Life, Life'. Time here materializes as a principal category, but still retains spatial correlates: it is measured by a surveying chain, and is passed over as over the mountain ridge of the Urals. Further destabilization of the notion of uniform and stable space takes place by means of Arseni Tarkovsky's voice-over. The poet's declamation appears again as a disembodied voice; it emerges from outside the homogenous diegetic space. It is precisely because the voice is not localizable and cannot be related to a specific body that it is capable of shifting accents in the viewer's perception of the film; time, as a more abstract category, attempts to free itself from the apparent visibility of space.

The role of the documentary chronicle in this spatio-temporal tension is crucial. One of the manifest qualities of the documentary footage is its concern with the notion of memory. The filmed material presents not staged but 'real' life, and can be viewed as an objective memory. *Mirror* attempts to explore the relationship between past (history) and present by 'confusing' the realms of social and individual memory. As a result, the rigid boundaries between the social and individual domains are eliminated by the contraposition of the visual documents with the narrative episodes. The result is that the viewer is uncertain whether historical shifts serve as a background to private human dramas or vice versa.

The footage used in the film is manifestly authentic – its quality is flawed, and no attempts were made to restore and refine it. The texture of the film bears witness to the past and to the harsh conditions endured during the shooting process. Hence its historical significance plays a vital role in the filmic narrative; the documentary images introduce a degree of veracity to the purely fictional parts of the film, which are supposed to correspond to the present time. Furthermore, the chronicle in *Mirror* is a quotation of space and time in the literal sense. The documentary footage, as such, does not belong to the realm of the fictional diegesis, but represents the discrete spatial and temporal frameworks which have a straightforward relation with reality: the events presented took place in real life.

These 'real' units are brought into the texture of the film, and their alien nature is consciously exposed. This can be extended to a claim that Tarkovsky treats fictional footage as documentary material in his major features. The documentary approach unexpectedly creates a possibility for 'contingent encounters, coincidences and unexpected mysterious links'.[36] Thus, the film-maker proposes a certain pre-mimetic condition where the artistic realm is approached not by means of imitating nature, but by pointing to something which is already there and naturally creative: the viewer is invited, in Žižek's words, 'to experience reality itself as a fiction'.[37] The distinction between documentary and fictional material collapses. In addition, linear threads of biographical and historical time are interwoven, and subsequently used to hold together patches consisting of dreams and visions of certain 'real' spaces.

The final images of the 'Life, Life' sequence bring the viewer back to the imaginary world of the filmic diegesis from the documentary material of 'real' history. These images depict a landscape ostensibly inspired by Bruegel – a hilly winter scene with carefully dispersed moving figures in the distance which, with some modifications, has already appeared in *Solaris*. Asafiev approaches the camera; he is calmly crying and at the same time whistling a tune. His eyes, filled with tears, are the eyes of a seer. The lone child, wearing clothes that are too small for him, is the ultimate bearer of wartime memories and visions. The documentary material depicting the fall of Berlin and an atomic bomb detonation disrupts the narrative flow once again. These historical documents reveal at once the end of the Second World War and its violent echo-finale – the bombing of Hiroshima and Nagasaki. The narrative goes back to the Bruegel landscape, and the slow-motion shot shows an anomalous event: a sparrow flies towards the boy and lands on his hat (Figure 4.3). Asafiev grabs the bird and the narrative is interrupted by a documentary chronicle once again: footage depicting the events of the Cultural Revolution and the territorial dispute between the Soviet Union and China over Zhenbao-Damansky Island in 1969 concludes the episode. The history of military conflicts does not end with the fall of Berlin, and Asafiev's memories evolve into premonitions of future hostilities.

The Wood

The remaining third of the film does not include a single documentary shot, but the narrative flow nevertheless remains highly unstable. Various spatio-temporal dislocations and lapses dominate the ending of *Mirror*. The split identity of the actors and the yet more prominent real plane, which manifests itself through the presence of the figures of the director and his mother, wife and stepdaughter, disorientate the viewer even further. The encounter between the narrator and Natalia, his divorced wife, mirrors the scene in the first half: the man's presence manifests itself through the disembodied voice, while the woman moves around the room and various reflections of her face prevail on the screen. The conversation is also followed by a memory of the house and a dream sequence with the wood. In addition, there is a symmetrical equivalent to the

Figure 4.3

narratively linear printing-house episode at the end of the film. The sequence depicting the Mother's attempt to sell her earrings to the wealthy doctor's wife is the last 'coherent' fragment of *Mirror*.

The doctor's well-to-do household provides a location for the interplay between various reflections and refractions, including the transformation of the camera itself into a mirror, as discussed above. The vulnerable image of the Mother struggling to feed her children is contrasted with the stout, house-proud figure of the doctor's wife. The irreconcilability of the two worlds finds its culmination in the scene with a cockerel. The doctor's wife asks the Mother to kill the bird for dinner before she leaves. The woman, who apparently has never done this before, reluctantly agrees. The off-screen act of killing leaves its traces – flying feathers – on the host's face. The camera tracks aside and lingers on the Mother's face, unrealistically illuminated from a lighting source below. A spatial abnormality – water flowing on the wall's surface behind her – manifests itself and announces a forthcoming spatio-temporal leap. The woman stares straight into the camera in this slow-motion close-up, and the director once again uses a modification of the shot/reverse-shot technique to establish a connection between two incongruous spaces and times. The Mother's gaze finds an answer in the gaze of her former husband, who stands by her 'bed' half naked. The doctor's house, as the domain of the real, shot in colour, merges with a room of the dream shot in black and white.

The half-naked man appears to be standing by a bed with the woman lying down on it. The camera zooms out to reveal that the Mother is in fact raised in the air above the bed, with her hair scattered as if on an invisible surface. Her husband suddenly disappears and she is left on her own, floating in the dark room – the same space that appeared in the first dream at the beginning of the film. The improbable levitation, a desperate attempt to evade the cruelties of mundane life, is accompanied by a dove flying across the screen. This expressionist scene is clearly a vision – the woman's voice-over announces that she 'sees' her husband only when she is not well. The return to reality is accomplished in a very abrupt fashion: the narrator as an adolescent and his mother open the door to leave the house. Unable to stand such an inappropriate display of prosperity in wartime, the woman decides to walk home without selling her earrings.

The departure is accompanied by 'Eurydice', the final poem by Arseni Tarkovsky to appear in *Mirror*. The poem is another textual agent of spatio-temporal dislocation in the film. Together with her son Alexei, the Mother walks along the damp and cold bank of a small river. Arseni Tarkovsky's voice, which is also disembodied as in the previous instances, starts reading the poem:

'Eurydice'

A human has a body
Just one, like one alone,
The soul has had enough
Of its continuous frame
With all its ears and eyes
The size of a silver coin
And skin like scarves on scarves,
As if hung on a rack.

It flies out through the cornea
Into the heavenly clearness,
Upon the icy spoke,
Upon the bird-drawn chariot
And listens through the bars
Of its own living prison
To the crack of woods and fields,
To the horn of seven seas.

A bodiless soul is shameful,
Like a body without its garment –
No reasoning or deed,
No impetus or line.
A riddle without solution:
Who will return again,
From dancing on that stage,
Where nobody is dancing?

And I dream of another
Soul dressed in different clothes:
It burns and runs across
From timidity to hope,
With fire that leaves the earth,
Like spirit without a shadow,
Leaving a bunch of lilac
On the table for remembrance.

Run, child, don't lament
For poor Eurydice,
And chase your copper hoop
With a stick around the world,
While, still hardly audible,
Joyfully and dryly,
In answer to each step
The earth resounds in your ears.

The theme of the poem, in spite of its inspirational tone, is death. The level of abstraction allows the poet to talk about mortality in a non-figurative manner. Death in 'Eurydice' is not a tragic event in a particular person's life, but is instead represented as an abstract category. Moreover, it seems that the soul struggles to free itself from the limitations of the earthly frame. It strives to reach the celestial realm. The poet goes on to describe the state of the disembodied soul and its subsequent transfiguration. The poem ends with an address to the 'child' to stop lamenting Eurydice and to live on.

The role of Eurydice, the mythical character, is not very prominent in the poem. She is taken as a mere object of lamentation – as an abandoned bodily frame. In addition, discourses surrounding the tale of Orpheus' lost love do not reverberate prominently within the text: art's ability to overcome death (Orpheus' music softened steel-hearted Hades, the overseer of the underworld) or the notion of distrust and impatience (Orpheus failed to obey Hades's precondition not to look back at Eurydice as he ascended to the land of the living) are not touched upon. Instead, 'Eurydice' offers a mixed impression: it is a celebration and lamentation of life and death at the same time. This intermediary and somewhat contradictory condition is intensified even further by the accompanying images of the sequence. The continuous single shot of the Mother walking with Alexei along the bank – a residue of the previous sequence with a clear and linear narrative line – is followed by abstract, mystifying images of the house surrounded by the wood (Figure 4.4).

The wood and part of the house are shot in sepia. The shift from the colour photography of the preceding images to monochrome has radical aesthetic consequences. The absence of the everyday colour palette introduces dream connotations. Moreover, the images are shot in a clearly perceptible slow-motion regime. Movement, once slowed down, encourages the viewer to sink into the presented image and see the reality from a different, unfamiliar angle. The wood and the house immediately take him or her to the visionary domain, where temporal features remain uncertain: is it the director's remembered past or his re-enacted present dream?

The three visual segments complementing the poem (the bank of the river, the wood, and the house) are not linked to one another by means of conventional narrative techniques. The episodes do not form a coherent visual manifestation of a single narrative line; they lack a logical connection and are not motivated by plot developments. This constitutes Tarkovsky's attempt to represent the sublime region

Figure 4.4

of childhood on the cinematic screen. The sublime is something which lies beyond ordinary experience, and is defined by Hegel as 'the attempt to express the infinite without finding in the sphere of phenomena an object which proves adequate for this representation'.[38] The visual sequence accompanying 'Eurydice' attempts to reach the level of the 'unattainable' or infinite, and thus it has to use unconventional techniques in order to overcome the vicious circle of representation of things that cannot be adequately represented. As Hegel continues, 'Precisely because the infinite is set apart from the entire complex of objectivity as explicitly an invisible meaning devoid of shape and is made inner, it remains, in accordance with its infinity, unutterable and sublime above any expression through the finite.'[39]

Tarkovsky thus tries to utter the unutterable, and the impossible return to childhood is accomplished by means of the destruction of 'finite' categories that include stable characterization and linear narrative with strict delineation of represented space and time. The result is what Frank Kermode calls a 'feeling of bright confusion'[40] – the viewer ceases to perceive the represented spaces as stable bearers of narrative information, instead facing an impression of a particular non-figurative imagery that aspires to give an impression of the director's lost childhood.

One should emphasize that the resulting patchwork assembled from disparate narrative units does not obey the logic of flashback or recollection. Tarkovsky's cinematic language avoids the 'trap' of the latter devices, which observe strict chronology and in which recollection or flashback is only a former present. Instead, the director deals with far more complex spatio-temporal structures, and goes beyond the spatially bound sequence of past–present–future historical time. The aesthetic strategy employed in *Mirror* finds its fulfilment in what Deleuze calls 'a coexistence of distinct durations, or of levels of duration; a single event can belong to several levels: the sheets of past coexist in a non-chronological order'.[41] Time is dislocated and found on the multiple shuffled sheets.

Tarkovsky's preoccupation with the notion of time, serving an attempt to overcome the limits of space, is highlighted by two themes that shape *Mirror*: childhood and death. They are both present in the 'Eurydice' episode: the text of the poem addresses the notion of death, while the accompanying visual sequence presents memories of childhood – a childhood that is already in the past and to which it is impossible to return, and a death in the future which cannot yet be experienced. The director finds himself in the impossible void of his present situation, and one may argue that this is precisely what motivates him to exceed narrative conventions. The film is encompassed by movements back and forth (past–present) which are not motivated by the consistency and linearity of the units of plot construction.

Both childhood and death are also deeply autobiographical themes. Childhood recollections are not mere neutral memories of a distant past – they are always approached from the critical stance of the present moment, and death seems to be Tarkovsky's ultimate preoccupation in *Mirror*. The metaphors in 'Eurydice', as mentioned above, centre upon the idea of mortality. Moreover, one of the succeeding episodes presents the author-narrator on his death-bed. The scene is highly ambiguous in terms of its temporal location, since it is not made clear whether it is taking place in the present time of the film itself (the Soviet Union of the 1970s) or in some distant past. The protagonist is surrounded by a doctor and two women, the mysterious visitor and her maid, who are clearly characterized in a previous episode as coming from the nineteenth century, and the interior of the room does not bear any clear temporal markers. Thus the death depicted becomes a purely symbolic and stylized event: the act of freeing the bird (echoing the lines from the poem '[The soul] flies out through the cornea / Into the heavenly clearness, / Upon the icy spoke, / Upon the bird-drawn chariot') is an allegorical way of announcing the protagonist's death, while the setting does not unambiguously situate the event within the chronology of the narrative line.

The link between death and autobiography seems to be natural. Philippe Lejeune, for instance, takes a radical position by claiming that mortuary aspects of the self-portrait should generate a new term – a 'self-mortrait'.[42] This stance is shared by Joseph Brodsky who, in an essay dedicated to Eugenio Montale's last book of poems, asserts in lapidary fashion: 'death as a theme always produces a self-portrait'.[43] The Russian poet goes even further by suggesting that Aristotelian mimesis ('art imitates life') should be reversed to 'art "imitates" death'; that is, 'realizing its own brevity, art tries to domesticate the longest possible version of time'.[44] An autobiographical reflection is a battlefield between reality and art, as well as life and death.

Thoughts about death in the first place are thoughts about one's own mortality: the fate of being constrained by time. The leap to the temporal is thus an inevitable precondition of any autobiographical endeavour. One can supplement the suggestion that an autobiography is 'a polyphony of the different kinds of discourse – historical, essayistic, psychological, ideological, factual, lyrical, investigative, conjectural'[45] – by saying that all these discourses are perceived through the prism of death. The significance of transforming one's own life into a text derives from the preoccupation with mortality; it is a doomed attempt to challenge invincible time, which consumes and at the same time gives birth to everything.

Mirror is an autobiography in images which explores spatio-temporal links between generations as well as the general human submission to history's temporal flow. The poems of Arseni Tarkovsky are active agents in this exploration. The themes of the poems, together with the way they emerge within the film (never as mere illustrations), allow time to move to the foreground and to accomplish a desperate, and vain, attempt to evade the concept of space. As a line from 'Eurydice' expresses it: 'The soul has had enough / Of its continuous frame'. One could argue that this preoccupation with time is not merely dictated by the film-maker's taste and aesthetic strategy, but derives from the nature of the content itself. Meditations on memory, autobiography, history and mortality all necessitate the emergence of time as a primary category at the expense of space – they all try to accomplish a leap to the impossible domain of the past and the realm of the imaginary. Tarkovsky uses the recurring image of the wood as a dense trope realizing the leap. The wood is a topos that signifies both past time and the unreal in *Mirror*.

The overbearing presence of the wood is not confined to the visual plane. The first lines of Dante's *Divine Comedy*, which also approach the idea of autobiography through the themes of death, space and time, prominently enter the film in the publishing house sequence. The opening lines of *Inferno* are read a few seconds after the confrontation between the Mother and her friend Elizaveta Pavlovna. The quotation is very brief, is not related to the storyline (like the diegetic passage from Cervantes in *Solaris*) and does not receive abstract visual treatment (unlike the extract from Revelation in *Stalker*). Elizaveta Pavlovna walks back to her workplace after the Mother has locked herself in the shower room. As the former moves away from the camera, apparently cheered by something since she gives a happy little jump, she enthusiastically recites the canonical lines:

> Midway in the journey of our life
> I found myself in a dark wood,
> [for the straight way was lost.]

> Земную жизнь пройдя до половины,
> Я заблудилась в сумрачном лесу,
> [Утратив правый путь во тьме долины.]

Nel mezzo del cammin di nostra vita
mi ritrovai per una selva oscura
[ché la diritta via era smarrita.]⁴⁶

The first lines of Dante's *Divine Comedy* indicate two beginnings: the beginning of a journey through hell, purgatory and paradise, and the beginning of the poem itself. But the lucid simplicity and straightforwardness of the opening is deceptive. The poet provides an immediate indication of his aesthetic strategy – the value of the authorial 'I' and the individual human being are underlined; the poetic voice gains flesh – the moving body.

The quotation contains a peculiar Russian mistranslation, which has significant semantic consequences. Mikhail Lozinsky, the author of many canonical translations who received the Stalin Prize for his version of the *Divine Comedy*, has omitted the possessive pronoun *nostra* ('our'), which qualifies the noun 'life'. The importance of *nostra* in the Italian original should not be underestimated. Dante refers to *our* life – though the poet finds himself alone in the wood, he dwells in a common time which he shares with others. The first adjective of the poem, in the guise of the possessive pronoun, is allegorical and succeeds in merging the realms of private and public. Such a collapsing of boundaries might have been desired by Tarkovsky: the film-maker attempts to appeal to common spiritual dilemmas by means of his private recollections. Moreover, the line in *Mirror* contains a modified version of the Russian rendering of *ritrovai*; while Lozinsky has translated the word slightly inaccurately as *ochutilsia* (in the same way, the English version of the *Divine Comedy* translates the word as 'I found myself'), Tarkovsky changes it to *zabludilas'* ('I lost myself'). The feminine gender can be explained by the fact that it is Elizaveta Pavlovna who recites the line, but the use of *zabludilsia* instead of *ochutilsia* is less easily justified. The rendering of the Italian text by Tarkovsky thus contains negative connotations: 'I lost myself' in place of the neutral 'I came to myself'.

The visual sequence that accompanies the lines from *Inferno* is relatively simple. Walking through a corridor and reciting the poem, Elizaveta Pavlovna provides a complete and unambiguous image. The only salient feature of the episode is its barely perceptible slow motion. This aspect of the scene shifts the viewer's perception – the scene is stripped of its everyday crudeness and simplicity. Elizaveta Pavlovna's slow-motion walk, combined with Dante's poetry, creates an undeniably enigmatic impression.

The vision of the woman reciting the poem while walking is remarkable for its discursive implications. The monotonous rhythm of the human strides seems to be an organic visual accompaniment to the poetry, with its strict observation of metrical patterns and tendency towards rhyme. All of the poems in *Mirror* appear in episodes containing human movement: the Mother withdraws from the viewer and leads the camera back home in 'First Meetings'; in 'From the morning I was waiting for you yesterday...', on the other hand, she advances towards the viewer; 'Life, Life' reveals Soviet soldiers attempting to ford Lake Sivash; 'Eurydice' begins with images of the Mother and Aleksei walking along a small river, and ends with the child entering the house. The Dante episode is no exception. What is more, Elizaveta Pavlovna's walk may have additional relevance in view of Mandelstam's reflections on the relation between Dante's poetry and human walking: for the Russian poet, *Inferno* and *Purgatorio* 'glorify the human gait, the measure and rhythm of walking, the footstep and its form. The step, linked with breathing and saturated with thought, Dante understood as the beginning of prosody.'[47]

In spite of its fleeting and 'erroneous' nature, the presence of Dante's verse is significant, as the quotation interacts with *Mirror*'s general semantic preoccupations. The film and the poem employ a similar narrative technique: the central character and the narrator of the story are one and the same. The grand narratives of history and the spiritual realm are approached in an explicitly subjective manner. The *Divine Comedy* is a reservoir of visions dominated by Dante's public and private memories. The idea of recollection is crucial to the poem, since Dante re-remembers departed friends, teachers and acquaintances. Erich Auerbach claims that Dante substantially changed the way in which the human being is perceived: the poet turned away from the legendary and morally abstract stance (an ethical type), and introduced a living individual who is bound by his historical reality and living memory (a concrete individual).[48]

However, perhaps more important is the fact that the opening lines of the *Divine Comedy* indicate the crisis Dante was facing at this time – a personal state that can also be seen to influence the aesthetic strategy of *Mirror*. Dante was 42 years old when he started writing the *Divine Comedy* (circa 1307), while Tarkovsky was 42 years old when he finished *Mirror* in 1974. Both men, approaching the middle of their lives, appeared to feel an urge to recall the past and to interweave it with imagery that strove towards spiritual ideals. The artists accomplish their respective autobiographical projects by historicizing their own selves. In both works, the temporal flow of an individual's life shaped by history becomes a principal aesthetic category. Tarkovsky's preoccupation with time is revealed through autobiographical gestures and recurring references to immortality in poetry. Time in the *Divine Comedy* is also objectively precise (for instance, his journey takes exactly seven days) while, at the same time, striving for abstract infinity ('I, who to the divine from the human, / To the eternal from time had come'[49]).

The preoccupation with time manifested in the first lines of *Inferno*, and in the poem in general, is frequently combined with unequivocal references to spatial categories. 'Midway in the journey of our life' (time) is immediately followed by 'I found myself in a dark wood' (space). The wood, which has often been seen to stand for 'the social influences which darken a man's perception of the truth, and prevent him from seeing the right path',[50] is one of the most memorable allegories of the *Divine Comedy*. The poet finds himself surrounded by the corrupted world of human existence, which conveys a sense of spiritual confusion.

Dante's lines appear to have relevance, given the recurring image of the wood that surrounds Tarkovsky's childhood house in *Mirror*. The wood sequence appears several times in sepia with a slow speed of projection. This feature allows the film-maker to emphasize the movement of bushes gently swaying in the wind, and to create the impression that the viewer is sleep-walking through the scene. This walk repeatedly ends near the house, and only towards the end of the film (in the 'Eurydice' sequence) does the child feature in it. It is clear from the director's diaries and comments that the images of the wood and the house have intensely private associations. The house was built on the same spot as Tarkovsky's own childhood home near the village of Ignatievo, thus providing the temporal aspect of memory with its spatial realization. This move is natural, since the process of remembering involves a recreation of familiar topography – a map of past existence. The wood-topos was assigned an even more prominent role in the original, where it had an explicit textual presence: 'First Meetings' in fact replaced another of Arseni Tarkovsky's poems, 'Ignatievo Forest', as the first poem to appear in the film. Instead of this verbal representation, the wood instead emerges in *Mirror* as a recurring, mysterious image.

The forest, as a boundary-space of dislocation, is also present in the crucial sequences preceding 'First Meetings' and following 'Eurydice' – the first and the last poems to appear in the film, respectively. The cluster of trees in which the camera 'hides' is contrasted with the openness of the field, where characters gradually disappear by walking away from the viewer. These wood–field images, placed

Figure 4.5

at the beginning and the end, frame *Mirror*, holding its reflective surface together. The two episodes, however, differ in their semantic orientation; they represent different sets of interrelationships between space and time.

The first sequence after the prologue contains an abnormal spatial phenomenon. The doctor, played by Anatoli Solonitsyn, leaves the Mother after an abortive flirtation and walks across the field surrounded by the wood. Suddenly a sharp gust of wind catches him in the middle of the grassland, and he stops and glances back to meet the woman's eyes. The first gust is followed by another, even stronger one. The strong wind, which was most likely produced by a helicopter during the shooting process, does not look like a natural phenomenon: it dramatizes the action and transforms the scene from its everydayness into the realm of mystery. Space manifests itself in its full, mystifying glory.

Towards the end of the film, after Arseni Tarkovsky reads 'Eurydice', the same field reappears (filmed with a similar shooting regime). This time, the spatial abnormality has clear temporal connotations. The Mother is surrounded by her young children, who already featured in the opening episode; but she emerges as an old woman, played by Tarkovsky's own mother. Moreover, the young Mother played by Terekhova is found in the field too. Initially she is shown lying with her husband and discussing whether she wants a boy or a girl, and then she is shown standing far away looking at her children – the boy and the girl – and her own old self (Figure 4.5). By explicitly obscuring the characters' identities and aligning the two incompatible temporal segments in a single space, the episode immediately puts the sequence into the domain of an abstract parable: the pressure to provide a coherent narrative pattern adhering to a linear concept of time is overcome.

The importance of the wood is further highlighted in the very last images of the film. The camera follows the old Mother with her small children into the field, and then gradually withdraws back to the wood. The Dantesque wood – the image of confusion – reappears for the last time, though in a different light (in both literal and metaphorical senses). The scenery is shot in twilight and presented at the normal speed of projection. The allegory of the wood, in some sense, becomes a reality: it literally materializes.

5

REVELATIONS OF *STALKER*

The production history of *Stalker* (1979), the film which explores the ruined landscape of human civilization, was marked by a technical disaster. Errors made during processing after three months of filming meant that more than half of the film stock used up to that point had to be scrapped. The production turmoil profoundly influenced the dramaturgy of the film and, as a consequence, *Stalker* has at least nine dramatically different scripts.[1] All of the versions were written by Arkadi and Boris Strugatsky, cult Soviet science-fiction writers at the time, under the close supervision of Tarkovsky himself.[2] The earlier versions retain more affinities with the source novel by the Strugatsky brothers – *The Roadside Picnic* (*Piknik na obochine*, 1972) – while the final product has almost nothing to do with the initial idea. The figure of Stalker underwent a drastic reformulation: the cynical vagabond of the novel became a meek seeker of spiritual truths, almost a holy fool; a rather conventional figure in Tarkovsky's cinema.

Retrospectively, it may seem odd to the viewer of *Stalker* that the director envisaged the film as having a coherent narrative flow – that is, as being devoid of any digressions or leaps in space and time. Tarkovsky discusses his approach extensively in his book:

> I felt it was very important that the film observe the three unities of time, space and action. If in *Mirror* I was interested in having shots of newsreel, dream, reality, hope, hypothesis and reminiscence all succeeding one another in that welter of situations which confronts the hero with the ineluctable problems of existence, in *Stalker* I wanted there to be no time

lapse between the shots. I wanted time and its passing to be revealed, to have their existence, within each frame; for the articulations between the shots to be the continuation of the action and nothing more, to involve no dislocation of time, not to function as a mechanism for selecting and dramatically organizing the material – I wanted it to be as if the whole film had been made in a single shot.[3]

The viewer should be highly sceptical of any correspondence between the film-maker's intentions and the final result. Though *Stalker* can indeed be conceived as a single shot – Tarkovsky with all his artistic might tries to avoid montage cuts (there are only 142 shots in 161 minutes) – the film is filled with a variety of narrative digressions which function on temporal and spatial levels that are different from the main storyline. Dislocation of time does take place. According to Boris Strugatsky, Tarkovsky deleted the 'time-loop' scene – 'a monotonous repetition of a tank column that had perished in the Zone; it repeatedly crossed a little, half-destroyed bridge.'[4] But even in the final cut, spatio-temporal instability is still prominent: the nature of the Zone, with its traps, the essence of which is beyond human reason, and Stalker's recurring semi-delirious visions do not allow the narrative to evolve in a linear manner while observing 'the three unities of time, space and action'. At the same time, the film-maker, who 'wanted time and its passing to be *revealed*', indeed succeeds in revealing the passage of time: a *temporal revelation* housed by the *abnormal space* of the Zone is a predominant theme of the film.

Revelation, defined as a 'disclosure or communication of knowledge, instructions, etc., by divine or supernatural means' (OED), is a spatio-temporal category in the Christian sense. It provides accounts of visionary experiences or journeys to celestial spaces, and describes future events, including the end of time. The Book of Revelation of St John, also known as the Apocalypse of John, is the last book in the New Testament canon, and an extract from it is quoted prominently in *Stalker*. The quotation is accompanied by one of the most memorable visual sequences in the film, and probably in Tarkovsky's oeuvre. The biblical text was also a constant source of inspiration for the director, and he even gave a lecture on his own reading of it at St James's Church in London. One of the first sentences of his address reads: 'Perhaps Apocalypse is the greatest poetic text created on Earth. This is a phenomenon which essentially expresses all laws imposed on man from above.'[5]

The apocalyptic end of temporality and the spatial transformation of the terrestrial realm develop into a major theme in late

Tarkovsky, and one can even claim that his last three films – *Stalker*, *Nostalghia* and *Sacrifice* – form a single apocalyptic trilogy. The end of the world as we know it figures in each of them, and the late director becomes manifestly preoccupied with the sense of ending. It is also noteworthy that the chapter of Tarkovsky's book which directly addresses the key concept of time (Chapter III, 'Imprinted Time') is preceded by an apocalyptic allusion through a quotation from Dostoevsky's *The Possessed*:

Stavrogin:	…in the Apocalypse the angel swears that there'll be no more time.
Kirillov:	I know. It's quite true, it's said very clearly and exactly. When the whole of man has achieved happiness, there won't be any time, because it won't be needed. It's perfectly true.
Stavrogin:	Where will they put it then?
Kirillov:	They won't put it anywhere. Time isn't a thing, it's an idea. It'll die out in the mind.[6]

The Book of Revelation and Fyodor Dostoevsky – the two major literary sources for Tarkovsky's oeuvre – merge into an intertextual amalgam which strives to predict the degree of transformation of the notion of time in liminal circumstances. Apocalypse delivers the ultimate end of time and the irreversible transfiguration of space, and the two suicidal characters of Dostoevsky's most apocalyptic text confirm this stance. This eager acceptance of the fact that 'there should be time no longer' (Revelation 10: 6) from *The Possessed* precedes Tarkovsky's elevated and assertive discussion of time as the core element of film aesthetics. The paradoxical combination not only underlines the director's artistic stance, developed in the contradictory concept of 'sculpting in time' (as impossible possibility), but also highlights the general human condition as depicted by the biblical text – the waiting in time for time to cease to exist.

The Zone's Gravity

The film opens with credits appearing on a static monochrome shot of a messy, dark bar. The haunting soundtrack, an electronic score punctuated with Eastern motifs, accompanies the first images. The camera captures three rugged walls and the stained floor of the interior, thus creating a claustrophobic feeling; the room is transformed into some kind of cave. An idle bartender, emerging from the entrance in the corner, is joined by a tall customer, who will later be revealed as Professor. The latter orders a cup of coffee and waits for his companions, Stalker and Writer. The three will gather here to embark on their quest to the Zone – a mysterious site defying human reason and logic, or, as Fredric Jameson puts it, 'a kind of magical Gulag in real physical space'.[7] The proximity to the Zone makes the bar of the opening sequence a liminal topos. The characters use it as their base before entering the inexplicable space, and they return to it after their journey is accomplished.

The immobile shot of the bar is followed by a passage of text on the screen – a quotation from a fictional Nobel laureate – which puzzles the viewer rather than providing basic, orientating information about the Zone: 'Was it a meteorite? A visit of inhabitants of the cosmic abyss? One way or another, our small country has seen the birth of a miracle – the Zone...' The textual intermission transfers the viewer to Stalker's flat, where the protagonist and his family are all asleep in one bed. The camera regains the ability to move, and enters the bedroom. This unhurried forward motion creates a sense of embodiment; the filming device draws the viewer into the fabric of *Stalker*. The camera explores various objects on a bed-side table, including a glass moved by the vibration created by a moving train – a premonition of the telekinetic act at the end of the film – and then tracks the sleeping people from right to left and back again. The interior of Stalker's bedroom is haunted by the sound of dripping water, as in *Ivan's Childhood*, while the texture of the wooden floor and the plastered walls in the flat and the bar are clear echoes of *Mirror*. Another self-quotation appears a few minutes later: the hysterical outburst of Stalker's wife is apparently inspired by Hari's suicide attempt and her subsequent 'resurrection' in *Solaris*. During the very first minutes the film provides a sense of artistic continuity; nevertheless, Tarkovsky's cinematic language acquires new inflections in *Stalker*.

The protagonist – a shaved and poorly dressed man in his forties – is about to sneak out of the flat without his wife and daughter noticing. The camera stares right at his nape, with its half-lit uneven texture, while he tries to close the bedroom doors without making any noise (Figure 5.1). The close-up of the back of Stalker's head, which goes against the conventions of classical scenography, evolves into a major stylistic device in the course of the film. Writer's and Professor's faces and the napes of their necks are also meticulously explored by the camera. These non-uniformly lit, wrinkled and usually soiled surfaces function as miniature landscapes that are scrutinized by the interfering gaze of the camera. *Stalker* is dominated by the use of these obtrusive close-ups, and the camera is turned into an invisible but omnipresent observer. Its haunting presence, intensified by the fact that it consistently approaches the main characters from behind and breathes down their necks, dominates the film. Tarkovsky's 'observant' long take evolves into the tracking shot, which creates a sense of embodiment and *stalks* the characters.

Stalker finally leaves the apartment after an emotional exchange with his wife. His sole aspiration is to escape his mundane reality and to enter the Zone – the cherished other space which is guarded by armed forces. The entry to the sacred topos is accomplished with his co-travellers on a rail car, and the journey amplifies the stalking qualities of the filming. The steady movement is marked by a succession of close-ups; the camera follows the backs of the characters' necks and their half-turned-away faces; it slides along with the men and watches them. The three travellers are silent and endure the transition from ordinary space to the extraordinary Zone with bated breath. The monotonous sound of the moving rail car gradually evolves into the mesmerizing electronic soundscape composed by Eduard Artemiev.

Stalker, Writer and Professor illegally enter the space that is supposed to be devoid of human presence. The transition from normal reality to the mysterious realm of the Zone is, in a rather unexpected way, marked by colour photography. The sudden change from the bleak monochrome of the bar and Stalker's flat to the lush colour of the Zone, after the characters' journey on the rail car, gives the viewer a sense of relief. The Zone – the other space – is not so alien, according to the colour dramaturgy of the film. It is an intermediary topos located somewhere between the industrial and rural domains. Meadow meets concrete in *Stalker*. Nature is blended with artefacts right at the entrance to the Zone, where the viewer finds a miniature landscape inside a dilapidated factory. The vast puddle in the centre appears as a pond, while tall grass and weeds give an impression of trees surrounding a reservoir. The artificiality of the landscape is only revealed by window openings reflected in water. Nature is 'housed' by the building.[8]

The materiality and gravity of the Zone is extremely important. Concrete tunnels, abandoned railways, dilapidated factories and office buildings (in which some telephones and lights still work) constitute the topography of *Stalker*. The Zone and its surroundings are manifestly heavy: muddy and probably contaminated water and various kinds of litter defile the territory. This spatial decrepitude has temporal implications: the passage of time in *Stalker* reveals itself through the space of the Zone, which is immersed in the process of decay. The post-industrial wasteland, which is at the same time an enclave of wild vegetation, accommodates numerous decomposing

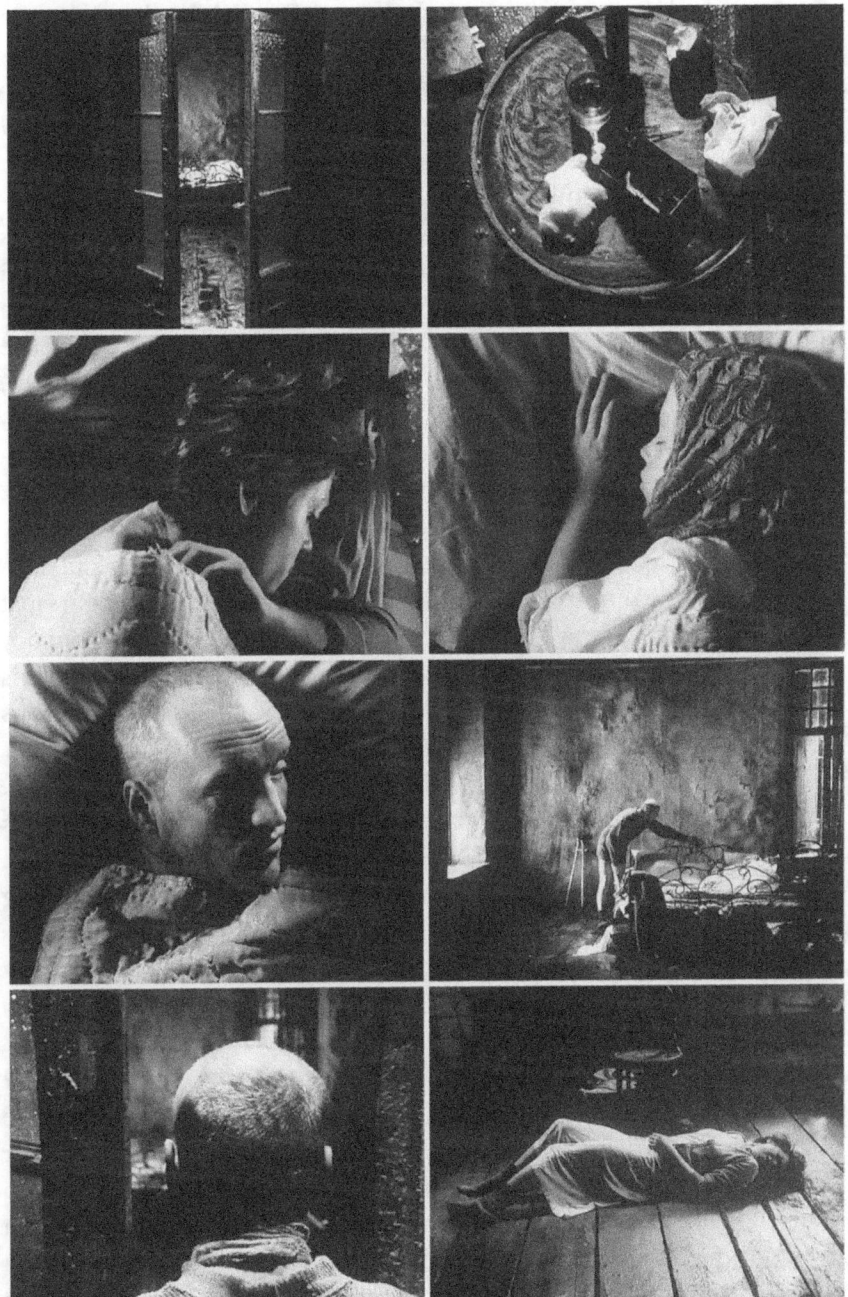

Figure 5.1

artefacts and polluted lakes and forests. For Žižek, the film is a masterpiece precisely because of 'the direct physical impact of its texture',[9] and the given texture reveals decomposition.

However, the outwardly 'heavy' appearance is deeply connected with the inward consciousness of the observer: the Zone, like the planet Solaris, is the miraculous and ultimate *other* topos which modifies itself according to the inner state of the characters. The origins of the Zone are dubious, but apparently it possesses supernatural qualities which attract adventurous explorers. The space shelters the otherworldly – the wish-room. The latter concept derives from the magic object trope (for example, magic wand or magic tablecloth), which is often employed in fairytales. Magic objects create an abundance of desired things in one's life and symbolize the human inability to submit to a divine will – thus one dreams of a simple and quick device that fulfils all desires instantly. Professor and Writer, led by Stalker, are engaged in a quest to reach the desire-fulfilling site.

Though the semi-ruined building with the wish-room appears just a hundred meters away at the very beginning of the film, the journey to reach it takes several hours, for there are no direct routes in this abnormal space. The vast surrounding territory consists of numerous death traps, which are beyond any logical comprehension. Stalker carefully guides his followers through the debris, failing only once. But before the characters enter the trap, the narrative undergoes its first leap in space and time. The coherent, rather linear narration of *Stalker* is interrupted by a black-and-white insertion: a stone falling into a dark well enters the screen completely unannounced. Stalker's voice-over, which accompanies the sequence and quotes Laozi's *Tao-te Ching*, also adds to the general dislocation: the man is moving silently in the field of vision of the camera, but the viewer hears his voice. Tarkovsky explores the photogenic qualities of water: its stillness and movement. The darkness dominates this short sequence, and the dropped stone disturbs the motionlessness of the water; but after some time it calms down and returns to its initial tranquil state, with a silver gleam. The weak and fluid water absorbs the harsh and violent stone. Indeed, verse 78 of *Tao-te Ching* reads: '[N]othing is more soft and pliable than water, yet for attacking the hard and stiff, nothing can beat it, so it is impossible to take its place'.[10]

Soon after the 'Taoist' well sequence the characters fall into the 'dry tunnel' trap, which consists of a ruined factory building with arches and lamps hanging down. This deformed topos is a spatial abnormality per se – it shelters a waterfall. Water is once again shown in its struggle with hard matter. Heavy and wild waters flow through the edifice and form small 'islands', one of which bewilders Writer since its surface is covered with burning coals (the recurrent combination of fire and water). The 'dry tunnel' does not lead anywhere and turns out to be a looped passage: Stalker and Writer return to the point of their departure and are reunited with Professor, who has secretly returned there to retrieve his bag. The mistake devastates Stalker, and functions as a breaking point in the film.

Revelation to Stalker

Stalker is not just a tour guide in the Zone, he is also a spiritual guide. The holy fool-like man cannot stop preaching, and most of his monologues carry a clear religious message. His world-view is shaped by the Taoist tradition but his meek philosophy of non-violence is infused with visionary apocalyptic-transfigurative themes. The protagonist cites Luke 24: 13–18, and 'experiences' the quotation from Revelation 6: 12–17, and the two intertextual insertions explicitly deal with an idea of disclosure of Christian truths. At the same time, the two New Testament texts do not have a merely discursive significance. Their theological content is, in fact, overshadowed by the visual plane. The cinematic techniques employed by the director complicate, enrich and transcend the quotations' message. The way in which the text is presented, or even enacted, remains a bewildering cinematic experience.[11]

The Revelation sequence takes place right in the middle of the film, when a shallow pool with scattered objects enters the narrative. The appearance of the pool itself represents a spatio-temporal dislocation, for the viewer is given neither its physical location nor its temporal placement. The uniform narrative flow breaks down as soon as the characters decide to rest after emerging from the 'dry tunnel'. Alternating monochrome and colour photography launches the dislocation in space and time. While Professor and Writer are squabbling Stalker lies on the ground, and his location and position are shifted from one sequence to another. At one point he is found lying on rocks by a 'mountain' torrent, and at another on a small 'island' in the flooded area next to a black German shepherd.

The dog's presence is significant, and it materializes here for the first time in the film – though its howling is heard by the characters immediately after entering the Zone and its whimpering enters the soundtrack from time to time in the course of the approach to the wish-room. The black dog, the Zone's untamed spirit, which cautiously approaches the men in the preceding sequence, obediently lies down by Stalker's side. There is another mysterious manifestation of the Zone before the Revelation images enter the screen: a light whirlwind on a marshland with flying dust. The undulating ground creates a surreal impression; the stability of the site is literally undermined.

The physical presence of various artefacts and natural phenomena as objects on the cinematic screen is central to Tarkovsky's aesthetics; he does not subject natural phenomena to vulgar metaphorization. The director is known for his attack on symbolism, though his understanding of this practice of representing ideas and things in art is largely based on misconception and confusion of terms, which is found in the contraposition of symbol and image in his discussion of Revelation. While the symbol, according to Tarkovsky, always stands for something – that is, it symbolizes – the image is never fully defined because instead of signifier–signified linearity it is governed by infinite possibilities:

> [I]t is impossible to interpret Revelation, because there are no symbols in it. It is an image. That is, a symbol can be interpreted while an image cannot. A symbol can be deciphered, or more precisely, one can extract from it a certain meaning, a certain formula while we are not able to understand an image, but we can experience and accept it. It has an infinite number of interpretative alternatives. It expresses, as it were, an infinite number of connections with the world, with the absolute and eternal. Revelation is the last nexus of this chain and in this book [the Bible] it is the last nexus, in a spiritual sense, completing the human epic journey.[12]

The last line of the argument appears to be self-contradicting: the never-finalized image of the Revelation originates from the text, yet it ultimately concludes the history of humanity. Revelation is the ultimate definitive statement, yet it has indefinite interpretative possibilities. Something paradoxical, akin to Tarkovsky's discourse, takes place in the Revelation sequence in *Stalker*. The temporality presented is not purely 'atemporal', but it decisively overcomes the linearity of the conventional and familiar world; the sequence 'sticks out' of the relatively stable space-time progression of the film. The camera sliding over the pool creates an illusion of movement which is inaccessible to human experience – it explores the debris of human civilization. The biblical text fuses with artefacts, objects and natural elements, such as water or mud, in an intricate interplay lying beyond the traditional hermeneutic framework. The items placed under the water appear to the viewer as if they are tired of signification. They restore the sign to its wholeness – no longer signifier and signified, but a single, integrated entity – and simply bear witness to the passage of time.

As a result of this semantic 'exhaustion', it is the texture of objects and natural elements, not their semantics, that is of utmost importance for the Revelation sequence. The fragment of the altarpiece, Rembrandt's etching 'The Three Trees', coins, syringes, the submachine gun, the coiled spring, the broken clockwork mechanism, the page of the calendar, all emerge in an unfamiliar setting – in water covered with mud (Figure 5.2). The calendar page and the clockwork mechanism are literally chunks of time captured in their spatial glory: the chronographic instruments no longer function, and are simply scattered in space. By being placed in the water, all of the artefacts lose their utilitarian quality. The only genuinely aquatic entity that appears in the sequence is a fish tank, although it also emerges in an unfamiliar light: the aquarium is freely floating above the stable ground. Water in this case can be read as an attempt to overcome the celestial–terrestrial binary. Its fluidity envelops the objects and gives an illusion of surmounting gravity, while mud serves as a reminder that they belong to the realm of the earth.

However, the sequence also contains a purely intellectual artefact – the highly ambiguous text of Revelation, which was referred to by D. H. Lawrence as an 'orgy of mystification' containing 'imagery which cannot be imagined'.[13] The last book of the New Testament is a text whose authorship and origin are unknown, or at least debatable. The seer of the imposing complexity of visions remains unidentified. However, the problem of authorship is not the main dilemma for theologians. Scholars tend to be more concerned with ways of dealing with the text's menacing images: should one try to decipher them and apply them to historical discourse, or should they be left on the metaphorical plane and read as certain figures of speech that have the potential to illuminate some Christian doctrines?

Various attempts to apply the text of Revelation to particular episodes within the history of humankind are akin to some critics' attempts to view *Stalker* as a prophetic vision of the forthcoming Chernobyl tragedy – 'ecological Apocalypse'[14] – or even Tarkovsky's prediction of the day of his own death[15] (the calendar leaf in the sequence reads '28 December' – the last day, it proved, of Tarkovsky's life: he died on 29 December 1986). However, these attempts are exceedingly self-limiting, since they dispense with the purely aesthetic or imaginative qualities of the film. Tarkovsky's treatment of Revelation is a multifaceted interaction with a holy text on the plane of abstract ideas and artistic images. His aesthetics struggle with the dictatorship of single meanings (rigid symbolism, according to his understanding of the term), and attempt to reach the realm of supra-symbolism. For Revelation,

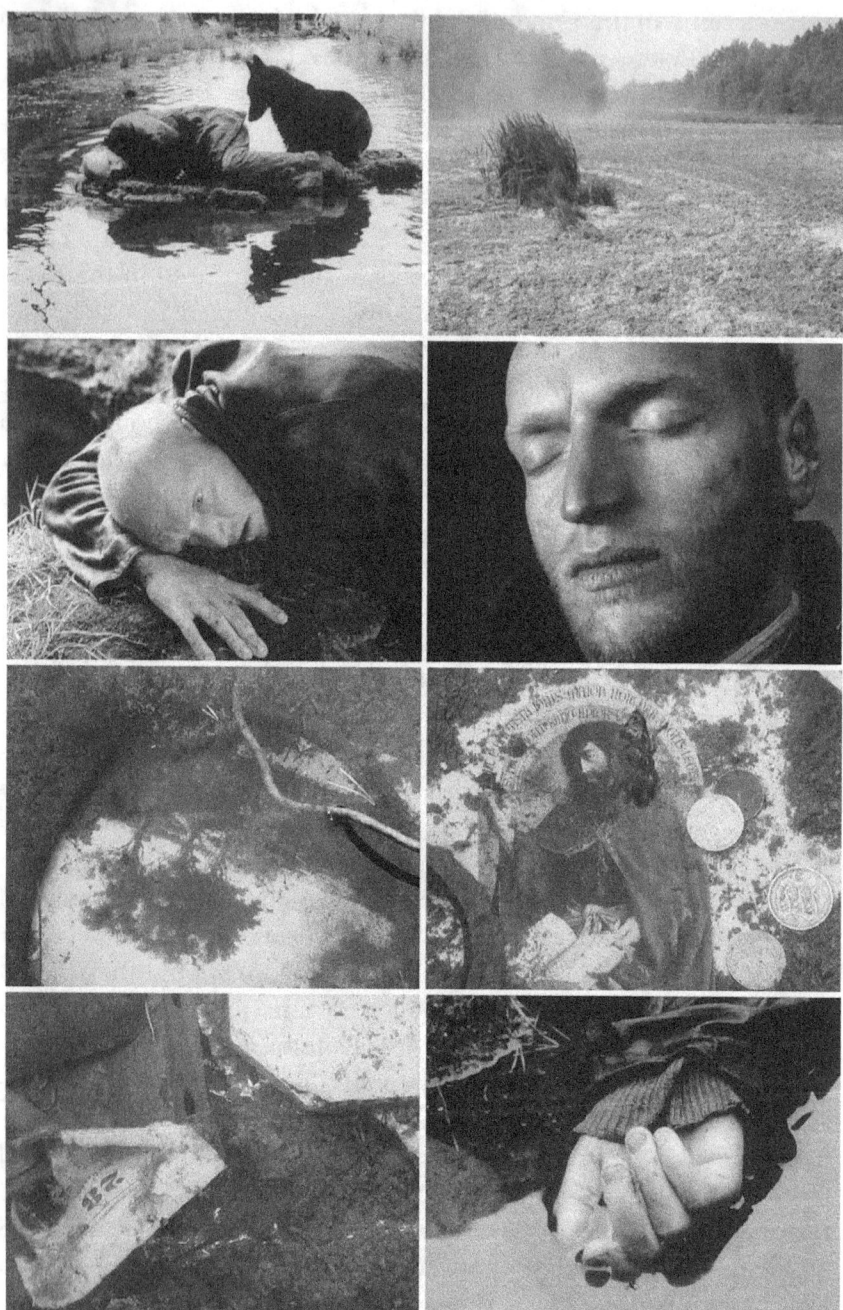

Figure 5.2

having influenced many artistic productions, may itself be regarded as a stimulus for the imagination rather than as a repository of truths about the course and end of history.

The word 'revelation' (*apokalypsis* in Greek) is used in literature contemporaneous with Revelation to describe the 'unveiling of God or divine secrets'.[16] However, the highly ambiguous nature of the text suspends its ability to unveil secrets in an ultimate and finalized way. The genre of Revelation aspires to reveal some kind of knowledge, while its text seeks to conceal it. The fantastic images and metaphors of the last book of the Bible are more likely to puzzle the reader than to disclose a secret message. This may be why Luther advised readers in his later *Preface to the New Testament* 'to read this book and to learn to look upon Christendom with other eyes than those of reason'.[17]

The Revelation sequence in the film starts with a shot of Stalker staring anxiously at some abstract spot far away. After this establishing shot in colour, the camera slides over his face with its closed eyes and over what seems to be a shallow pool which contains numerous artefacts. It ends its uninterrupted movement with Stalker's hand lying in the water, and thus undermines the protagonist's singularity. His body in the sequence is absolutely still; it ceases to be a subject of movement or an instrument of action – it becomes what Deleuze calls 'the developer [*révélateur*] of time'.[18]

The long take is accomplished in sepia, which allows the viewer to concentrate on the shapes and textures of the scattered artefacts. The text of Revelation is read by Stalker's wife: she whispers the first few sentences, thus creating a sense of secrecy, and then her narration becomes highly unstable; she takes long pauses, and finally bursts into a neurotic giggle. The otherworldliness of the sequence is emphasized by the soundtrack: dripping water, together with bird cries, creates a sense of agitated tranquillity. Stalker imagines John's highly unstable imagery when the following passage is cited from the New Testament:

> [A]nd, lo, there was a great earthquake; and the sun became black as sackcloth of hair, and the moon became as blood; and the stars of heaven fell unto the earth, even as a fig tree casteth her untimely figs, when she is shaken of a mighty wind. And the heaven departed as a scroll when it is rolled together; and every mountain and island were moved out of their places. And the kings of the earth, and the great men, and the rich men, and the chief captains, and the mighty men, [and every bondman,] and every free man, hid themselves in the dens and in the rocks of the mountains; and said to the mountains and rocks, fall on us, and hide us from the

face of him that sitteth on the throne, and from the wrath of the Lamb: for the great day of his wrath is come; and who shall be able to stand? (Revelation 6: 12–17)

The sixth seal, which is the quotation's core point, is interpreted in many different ways: from Anselm of Havelberg's time of the Antichrist and end of the world to Francis Lambert's revival of the Gospel.[19] However, it is difficult to disagree with the fact that the genre of Revelation contains *tragic* elements that are rendered through ultimate catastrophe. The word *apocalypse* has ceased to signify a mere revelation or disclosing of something. The last book of the New Testament has given the word a strong sense of *ending*: Apocalypse within popular discourse stands for the end of history. The sense of ending prevails in the text; it is also intensified in the film by the images of the remains of Western civilization decaying in the pool.

During the long take, the camera slides across a fragment of the upper central part of Van Eyck's Ghent Altarpiece (or *Adoration of the Mystic Lamb*), which depicts the enthroned figure of St John the Baptist sitting on the left-hand side of the deity with the Virgin on the right. Unlike other objects in the pool, the fragment is a complex semiotic micro-world of its own. Its relevance to the whole sequence is quite straightforward: St John the Baptist is a symbol of Christian initiation – he was the first to instigate the baptism of repentance; at the same time he is also perceived as the prophet of judgement (punishment), which makes him a symbol of the Last Judgement and Apocalypse. The Ghent Altarpiece portrays him in this latter role (this is also supported by the inscription on the edge of the dais, on which the deity's seat is placed – 'Untroubled joy at His right hand [the Virgin]. Fearless security at his left hand [St John the Baptist]').[20]

Nevertheless, in spite of its numerous embedded meanings, the altarpiece transcends the symbolic level by the mere fact that it is presented in an extremely abnormal setting: it lies in the water, covered with mud and coins. It constitutes an abandoned icon which no longer plays a part in Christian rituals. The fragment is distanced from the altarpiece, where it is used to perform certain semantic functions carefully prescribed by the Christian system of signification. Its texts are visually present, but they cannot perform their primary role: to deliver meaning. The illegibility of the texts transfers them from the realm of semantics into the realm of texture. Their physical presence becomes more important than their signifying potential. With its present and at the same time absent texts, the image of St John lies under the water, with the sediment both framing and obscuring it. Thus the icon becomes a multifaceted image of Apocalypse in Tarkovsky's sequence – its prophecy is revealed, but its meaning is concealed.

The height of this ambiguity (disclosing–concealing) can be found in Chapter 10 of the text of Revelation, where its author unambiguously says that something has been withheld from humans: 'And when the seven thunders had uttered their voices, I was about to write: and I heard a voice from heaven saying unto me, Seal up those things which the seven thunders uttered, and write them not' (Revelation 10: 4). This enigmatic passage fascinates Tarkovsky in his discussion of Revelation:

> It is interesting, what did John conceal from us? And why did he reveal that he had concealed something? What is the purpose of this strange interlude, of this remark? All these vicissitudes of interrelations between the angel and St John the Evangelist? What was it that man wasn't supposed to know? After all, the purpose of Revelation is precisely that man should know. Maybe the notion of knowledge makes us unhappy? Do you remember: 'knowledge increaseth sorrow'? [...] This detail has some kind of incredible, absolutely inhuman generousness, in front of which man feels himself a defenseless and at the same time protected infant. This has been done in order to make our knowledge incomplete, not to desecrate eternity and to leave hope. In human ignorance lies hope. Ignorance is noble. Knowledge is vulgar. That is why the kind of concern that is expressed in Revelation gives me hope more than it frightens me.[21]

This passage illuminates the Revelation sequence in *Stalker* in several ways. The ambiguity of the images and the director's representational strategy, a long steady take, do not strive towards consummation. They leave gaps in the viewer's perception and, at the same time, they pass on 'hope', to use Tarkovsky's vocabulary. The suspension of direct knowledge is the key to Revelation, and it also becomes the ultimate aesthetic strategy of the sequence. The director's lengthy citation of the text in the middle of the film and his visual enumeration of various artefacts, combined with the anticlimactic but mesmerizing soundtrack, all contribute towards speaking without saying anything concrete: as Jacques Derrida writes, 'Speaking in order not to say anything is always the best technique for keeping a secret.'[22]

The Road to Emmaus

The Revelation episode is immediately followed by another quotation from the New Testament – the Emmaus story from Luke's

Gospel. While the Revelation segment constitutes one of the most sophisticated visual treatments of a text in Tarkovsky's oeuvre, the reference to Luke is illuminating on a more subtle level – as a delivered text, accompanied by a highly complex interplay of gazes. On the surface level, the quotation in the film deviates from the biblical original by several expressive omissions. When Stalker awakes from a short sleep, during which he experienced the Revelation of St John, he mutters the following passage from Luke:

> And, behold, two of them went that same day to a village called [Emmaus], which was from [Jerusalem] about threescore furlongs. And they talked together of all these things which had happened. And it came to pass, that, while they communed together and reasoned, [Jesus] himself drew near, and went with them. But their eyes were holden that they should not know [him]. And he said unto them, What manner of communications are these that ye have one to another, as ye walk, and are sad? And the one of them, whose name was [Cleopas]... (Luke 24: 13–18)

The references to Christ by name (Jesus) and to one of his followers (Cleopas) are left out.[23] Moreover, the place names (Emmaus and Jerusalem) are not pronounced clearly; Stalker appears to 'swallow' them. The protagonist whispers the passage in a delirious manner, and the canonical allusion to Luke is transformed into a secret: the viewer does not know *who* is going *where* and *why*.[24] Proper nouns undergo a kind of erasure – they are banished from the text and make it, to a certain degree, unfamiliar. It should also be stressed that proper names as such are completely absent in the film.[25] Stalker, Writer, Professor, Stalker's wife and Monkey are all invented nicknames. This fact in a way signifies some kind of antagonism towards social conventions: naming, defining, registering are all banished from *Stalker*'s secretive discourse. The viewer may, in fact, repeat the fate of the two disciples and fail to recognize the famous biblical tale, since proper names clearly signal the origins of the passage, and once they are removed they liberate the text from the rigid boundaries of signification. However, the viewer who is aware of the origins of the passage shares a secret knowledge. He or she performs the act of recognizing a text about a failure to recognize.

Stalker stares at some undefined point in the distance while reciting the text – he is clearly out of place. The passage functions as a monologue, or even as a prayer. The protagonist is surrounded by water and damp earth, and his gaze is unfocused. However, in spite of the vagueness and the secret mode of delivery of the uttered words, they are nevertheless heard by his fellow travellers. The words spoken into the emptiness eventually find their recipients, though unintentionally. The whole scene bewilders Writer and Professor, who stare at Stalker in bemusement. Writer and Professor thus turn, as it were, into the two biblical characters who fail to see or comprehend reality, though they are presented directly with its manifestation – they are not fully spiritually awake. As if suspecting that this is the case, Stalker looks at his companions after finishing the quotation, and asks, 'Are you awake?'

The ability to *see*, as described in the Luke passage, is a spiritual quality. It belongs to the same realm as the gift of witnessing a revelatory experience: it is a form of anomalous perception of everyday reality. It becomes clear in this light why Tarkovsky was preoccupied with Carlos Castaneda, who describes practices that enable awareness to be increased. For the director, the Zone in *Stalker* 'is simply a place where we live. I just want to say that we don't know the world in which we live, though we naively think that we have studied it completely. Carlos Castaneda's *The Lessons of Don Juan* is immensely interesting to me in this context.'[26] In 1979 – the year that *Stalker* was released – Tarkovsky also made the following entry in his diary: 'Reread Castaneda's *The Lessons of Don Juan*. A marvellous book! And very true, because – 1. the world is not at all as it appears to us. 2. under certain conditions it could well become different.'[27] The Peruvian-born American anthropologist and writer claims that there is an unknown realm, which he calls *nonordinary reality*,[28] indicating that this realm is indeed a reality, but is essentially different from the ordinary reality experienced by human beings engaged in everyday activities. Or, if one is to take a more extreme position: 'the reality of the world we know [...] is merely one of many descriptions'.[29] A human is able to enter the domain of 'nonordinary reality' by developing the capacity to attain a level of heightened awareness.[30]

The Luke sequence is indeed about seeing and perceiving phenomena in a new light. The three characters seem to occupy different realities. The rational and sceptical minds of the Zone's tourists are not convinced by the visions of their guide. The sequence starts with Stalker's sideward stare, which is then invaded by Writer's and Professor's gazes of non-comprehension. The way the latter are filmed, however, creates an intricate interplay of gazes. The cut to Professor shows him lying down in his soiled coat with his eyes closed. The camera then tracks along his body to reveal Writer, also with his eyes closed, resting his head on Professor's abdomen. Writer suddenly opens his eyes and the camera, after lingering on his face for a few seconds, tracks alongside again and reveals Professor also looking at Stalker with bewilderment. Are the characters eventually awakened by the biblical words?

The stalking-haunting mode of camerawork in the film reaches its pinnacle in the Emmaus sequence. The characters stare into the camera's lens for prolonged periods of time with little or no diegetic motivation at all. This 'interaction' turns the filming device into the Zone's embodied envoy, which oversees the invaders' progress in the mysterious space. The very first gaze after the Revelation sequence displays a rather abnormal awareness of the camera: Stalker stares directly into its lens before he begins citing the text from Luke. The gaze is completely unmotivated by the *mise-en-scène*, since Stalker looks attentively upwards into the sky while lying on the ground, and the viewer is not aware who the intended recipient of this gaze is.

Tarkovsky yet again breaks the conventions of the shot/reverse-shot technique at a later point in the Emmaus sequence. The camera explores Writer's bewildered gaze, which is supposed to be directed at Stalker, and the director delays establishing the logical connection between the men. Instead of immediately returning to Stalker's reverse gaze, a move which would create a connection between the two disparate spaces, the camera lingers on Writer's face and then tracks aside to Professor's head. The camera's tracking movement is manifestly preoccupied with the men who are observing Stalker quoting the passage from the New Testament. The two stare right into the camera lens and again make the viewer aware of the presence of the filming device: he or she witnesses a complex interplay of gazes, which accompanies the text about gazes that fail to see.

Even more arresting is the fact that the camera also *reveals itself* in the sequence, though this revelation was very likely unintended. When it slides along Professor's body there is a reflection in one of Professor's coat buttons of a spotlight and of the camera with its operator (Figure 5.3). The small circular reflective surface captures the movement of the filming crew and of devices on the set, and evolves into a metafilmic construction.[31] This otherworldly plane, in relation to the given fictional reality, reveals itself voluntarily or involuntarily. The mirroring button compensates for the limits of the camera's field of vision, and the viewer can see what lies beyond the camera lens. The reflective surface holds 'the mirror up to nature',[32] which, according to Hamlet, was the purpose of mimetic arts.

For Deleuze, 'the sole cinematographic consciousness is not us, the spectator, nor the hero; it is the camera – sometimes human, sometimes inhuman or superhuman'.[33] The manifestly superhuman camera in *Stalker* exploits the reflective properties of the shiny button and reveals itself to the attentive viewer when the Emmaus story, in which Jesus reveals himself to Cleopas and to his companion, enters the film's diegesis. The revealing or exposing reflection of the camera also disappears once the button ceases to be a centre of the composition in the course of the tracking movement. The presence of the filming crew – the 'transcendental' other – is revealed only for a moment.

The fact that the camera's reflection appears just a few seconds before Writer opens his eyes, after hearing Stalker utter the words 'But their eyes were holden', is very significant. The quotation from Luke, which already transforms the text in complex ways through omission, is elevated to another realm by means of intentional or unintentional gazes and reflections. The central subject of the story – Christ, or the transcendental other – reveals itself only for a moment, and then disappears altogether. A theological interpretation suggests that the story of the encounter near Emmaus is not concerned with the two men inexplicably failing to recognize their teacher; it is about the way they remove their veil of unawareness by sharing the Eucharistic meal: 'And it came to pass, as he sat at meat with them, he took bread, and blessed it, and brake, and gave to them. And their eyes were opened, and they knew him …' (Luke 24: 30–1). Breaking bread is the action which realizes and discloses Christ's presence after the Resurrection. However, what is striking is that immediately after disclosing himself, Jesus 'vanished out of their sight' (Luke 24: 31). The secret divine presence is only momentarily revealed, and it resists complete solidity and permanence.

The small, circular, reflective surface in *Stalker* is in many ways, in terms of form and semantic potential, similar to the convex mirror of Jan van Eyck's celebrated *Arnolfini Portrait*. There is a mirror behind the couple in the painting, and in its circular reflecting surface one can see the backs of the two sitters and a silhouette of the painter with a strong source of light behind him. The reflective surface within the portrait is consciously used by the artist as a reflection on the process of artistic creation. Van Eyck imitates the interior of the room, and at the same time captures his own reflection as the agent who performs this very process of imitation.[34]

The reflection in *Stalker* also brings into focus the agent and the process of production itself, and it does so in a literal manner. The button makes the invisible visible and breaks the real–fictional borderline. It continues the discourse initiated by *Mirror*, the film that precedes *Stalker*. *Mirror* consistently explores the same violation by

Figure 5.3

slightly different means: mirror reflections, documentary chronicle, the presence of Tarkovsky's own body and the acting family members all diffuse the viewer's perception of the cinematographic fictional reality. The resulting disorientation is an excuse for self-reflection. As Borges asks in his discussion of the phenomenon of *mise-en-abîme* in 'Partial Magic in the Quixote',

> Why does it disturb us that the map be included in the map and the thousand and one nights included in the book of *The Thousand and One Nights*? Why does it disturb us that Don Quixote be a reader of *Don Quixote* and Hamlet a spectator of *Hamlet*? I believe I have found the reason: these inversions suggest that if the characters of a fictional work can be readers or spectators, we, its readers or spectators, can be fictitious.[35]

The End of the Journey

The Revelation and Emmaus sequences disturb the narrative flow and halt the characters' progression in the Zone. The entrance to the 'meat grinder' trap-tunnel appears straight after the revelations and reflections of Emmaus. Writer is chosen to lead the way, and the camera follows him – it again breathes down his neck. After a few metres the camera faces Writer from the front and reveals his exhausted and soiled face. The man traverses a room adjacent to the tunnel filled with water, and enters a building with sand hillocks inside; this time, the industrial space shelters sand, not water. Writer crosses the boundary that he is not supposed to cross, and the Zone manifests itself in a mysterious way: after Stalker throws a screw, its fall is filmed in slow motion; there is a blinding flash of light and two flights of a bird, one of which is interrupted halfway. Writer is found lying on the ground in a puddle. He rises up, throws a stone into something akin to a well and delivers a rather recondite monologue.

To 'reward' the tormented man, who leads their way out of the 'meat grinder' trap, Stalker recites the poem 'So summer has passed....' The film continues the tradition initiated in *Mirror* of merging Arseni Tarkovsky's poems with the filmic material. However, the highly complex interconnection of image and word in *Mirror* is virtually absent in the film that follows it. The presence of the poetic text is diegetically motivated in *Stalker*. This literary allusion does not pose any danger of over-interpretation in terms either of its content or of its representation. The protagonist presents it as if it were written by his mentor's young brother, whom he describes as a delicate young man.

Tarkovsky does not introduce unrelated abstract images to accompany the poem. While it is read, the unity of time and space is not violated; Stalker expressively recites the lines while leaning on a wall with the camera attentively observing him. The episode is shot without a single cut. It does, however, contain minor zoom movements, which, together with the changing lighting, overcome the static character of the sequence. Stalker recites the poem and experiences a moment of emotional excitement – he and his fellow travellers have managed to escape from the most arduous trap in the Zone.

> So summer has passed
> Like it never had been
> It is warm in the sun
> But it's no consolation.
>
> All that might have come off
> Landed right in my hand
> Like a five-fingered leaf
> But it's no consolation.
>
> Neither evil nor good
> Were expended in vain
> All was burning and glowed
> But it's no consolation.
>
> Life arched over its wing
> It took care and preserved
> And, in truth, I was blessed
> But it's no consolation.
>
> The leaves were not burned
> The boughs were not broken
> The day's rinsed like glass
> But it's no consolation.

The poem is written in a 'simple' and lapidary anapaestic dimeter with high tolerance of verbal rhymes, suggesting avoidance of prosodic sophistication. It explores how the layers of existential anxiety and the themes of fading autumnal nature intersect with spiritual unrest; together they serve as dominant images for Arseni Tarkovsky. The line 'But it's no consolation', repeated in every quatrain, refers to something hidden, not present in any material form but nevertheless eagerly anticipated and actively sought after. The discourse of the poem bears a resemblance to the tactics of negative theology, by which a phenomenon is described not in affirmative words but by means of negative statements (*via negativa*) – that is, in terms of what may not be said about a given phenomenon. The poet draws a circle around something which is needed but which he is unable, or refuses, to name.

The absence of this actively desired *something* develops into a presence, into a core idea, in a paradoxical manner. The need and yearning for something enter the realm of secrecy. The poet cannot name that which he desires and desperately needs. Thus the uttered words of the poem anticipate Writer's and Professor's refusal to enter the wish-room. They do not know their desires, and are afraid to cross the threshold. Instead they stay in the space adjacent to the wish-room while the camera does not traverse the threshold – it observes the three men from outside. The stable grounds of normality are also undermined in this liminal space: breaches in the wooden floor reveal that water is splashing underneath. The whole edifice is floating.

Stalker's interrelationship with the Zone is founded on the ultimate irrationality of action; his neurotic, bewildering guidance leads his fellow travellers to nothing but utter confusion. Their winding spiritual pilgrimage reaches a dead end, with nothing tangible having been achieved. Following a sudden outburst of violence, when Professor attempts to blow up the room, they sit together calmly near the entrance, without uttering a single word. After the bomb is dismantled, the camera withdraws to the flooded wish-room; it is the only 'body' that enters the sacred space. The identification of the filming device with the omnipresent Zone is enhanced even further – after stalking the characters in the course of the film, the camera enters the focal point of the mysterious space which remains unreachable to mortals. The camera and the viewer observe the characters while located inside the wish-room. The exhausted and overwhelmed silence of Stalker and his fellow travellers is emphasized by the play of light and the short burst of heavy rain, which also transcends common sense: it is pouring inside the building. Two carp, obscured by an oily film, swim in the shallow waters of the room. The sounds of Ravel's *Boléro* and the rattle of a moving train announce the return of the characters to normal space.

The return journey from the Zone is passed over in silence by the narrative. The image of the threshold of the wish-room fades out, and is immediately followed by a scene in the dark bar which appeared at the beginning of the film. The protagonist's wife and daughter come here to meet their husband and father. The same sequence of gazes, but with a slightly different undertone, is repeated in the bar when Writer and Professor encounter the woman. Her appearance staggers the two. After emerging from the mysterious and dangerous Zone they clearly see a phenomenon of extraordinary devotion occurring in ordinary reality. The tired and begrimed faces of the two men express a different kind of puzzlement. This time it is not detached, startled observation, but an active attempt to comprehend or even to establish contact.

The close-up in colour of the profile of Monkey, Stalker's daughter, comes as an abrupt change. Her tranquil face, wrapped in a gold-brown headscarf, has certain affinities with the Orthodox iconographic image of the Virgin. The handicapped girl appears to be walking on her own, but the illusion is revealed once the camera zooms out. Stalker, with Monkey up on his shoulders, together with his wife and the dog from the Zone, crosses a devastated industrial landscape – their familiar terrain. The family returns to the flat, where the camera once again establishes unconventional contact with a character. After an emotional outburst, Stalker, devastated and exhausted, goes to bed. His wife then delivers a monologue right into the camera lens. The direct address to the camera puts the space of the viewer and that of the character into immediate contact. The woman, surrounded by uneven and damp walls, lights a cigarette and confesses to the viewer about her life with her social outcast husband. She brings the film's discourse to a close through her emotional confession.

But the very last character to appear on the screen is Monkey – the child is the sole centre of the concluding sequence of the film. The apartment, shot in rather distressing monochrome, now emerges in full colour. The close-up of Stalker's daughter serenely reading a book has a pacifying effect. The camera gradually zooms out and the girl's inner voice reads the short poem by Fedor Tiutchev, 'I love your eyes, my dear...' ('Liubliu glaza tvoi, moi drug...'). The filmmaker introduces a confusingly simple love poem as the final point of his discourse. The irrational choice becomes a puzzle or a secret in itself. The poem leaves one perplexed: what does its presence signify?

The initial plan for the concluding episode of *Stalker* confuses things further, since it differs dramatically from the scene as it appears in the film. In the initial plan, Monkey is depicted as a wilful, blabbing child devoid of the aura of mystery surrounding the mute and discreet girl of the film:

> *And Monkey is thinking aloud, her thin face turned skywards, as though she is trying to peep out from under the bandage wrapped around her eyes.* Monkey: And I want pastries too; chocolate buns with syrup and smoked eels...and everything that's got a scent: flowers, nice perfume...mushroom soup smells nice...and also a silk dress, which rustles when you stroke it, and also my innermost wish is for a fur muff, [soft] and warm, fluffy and smooth... *The rattle of an electric train grows louder, swelling, and finally drowns her voice.*[36]

The Monkey of the script is obsessed with artefacts, and she expressively enumerates desired objects – an echo of the wish-machine trope. The child carefully describes their physical qualities, including their scent and texture. The train rattle drowns out her thinking aloud. This image dramatically differs from the Monkey of the film, who is presented as an ultimately mysterious protagonist. The serene girl silently contemplates the beauty of the poem whose content is not completely suitable for children of her age. There is not a single hint of incontinent chattering; on the contrary, Monkey is surrounded with an aura of transcendental mystery. At the end of the episode the train also arrives, but this time what it drowns out is complete silence.

The first shot of Monkey presents her in an iconographic manner; the viewer is shown only her profile. The mute girl gains a voice in this sequence, and the power of the seemingly simple lines of the poem is thus enhanced. They are read aloud, though the child reads them to herself. The voice-over allows the viewer to overhear the poem and to enter the secluded world of Stalker's daughter.

> I love your eyes, my dear,
> Their splendid, sparkling fire,
> When suddenly you raise them so
> To cast a swift embracing glance
> Like lightning flashing in the sky…
>
> But there's a charm that is greater still:
> When my love's eyes are lowered
> When all is fired by passion's kiss,
> And through the downcast lashes
> I see the dull flame of desire.

Tiutchev is a poet of contrapositions, and was keen to explore the menace of mutability, formlessness, flux, or dissolution. The poem in *Stalker* is no exception: the first stanza considers the notion of wholeness, and the gaze plays a more cognitive role while the second stanza deals with some kind of disintegration, which springs from the internal chaos of passion. There is a substantial change in the point of view of the poem: from a neutral position in the first stanza to an overtly subjective and lyrical empathy in the second. Tiutchev counterpoises cognition with passion; carnal desire is always connected with something utterly irrational, like chaos.

However, the carnal pathos of 'I love your eyes, my dear…' is undermined by the fact that the poem is recited by the child: the detached, asexual Monkey emerges as an incongruous transmitter of the love poem. The pathos is undermined even further when the girl performs an act of telekinesis which becomes the final point of the film. The enigmatic reading of the poem is followed by a no less enigmatic telekinetic act. The child's gaze propels objects around the table: a glass of tea; a jar containing eggshells; and a tall, empty glass, which falls off the table on to the floor (Figure 5.4). The relatively straightforward content of the poem is counterpoised by the highly mysterious and metaphorically dense visual sequence. Monkey's supernatural eyes altogether transcend both Tiutchev's eyes with '[t]heir splendid, sparkling fire' and the lowered eyes infused with 'the dull flame of desire'.

The feeling of secrecy reaches its apogee in this sequence. The girl seems to occupy a different world; her calm detachment is intensified visually by means of the hovering fluff and the steaming cup of tea. Gently drifting bits of fluff create a sense of movement, while the overall image remains very static. It may also be contended that her supernatural gift is directly connected with the Zone – her invalid state derives from the trade of her father, that is, stalking. The unearthly power to move objects and to overcome physical laws differs dramatically from the powers of cognition and desire. The piercing gaze of Monkey becomes the ultimate riddle of the film. Tarkovsky twists the semantic directions of the poetic text by concentrating the camera, and hence the viewer's attention, on Monkey's eyes. Verbal arts can never convey a similar power to the gaze.

* * *

On 29 December 1974 Tarkovsky makes a very interesting note regarding his then-forthcoming film *Stalker*. It in some sense corresponds to the vision of the film, quoted above, as having a coherent narrative flow devoid of any digressions and leaps in space and time. He perceives *Stalker* as having 'a perfectly harmonious form: *uninterrupted* and detailed action, which is made equal to a religious act, that is, semi-transcendental, absurd and absolute'.[37] Thus, for the director, the recondite religious action (the three epithets used to refer to it are totally discrepant) 'balances' the formal harmony of the narrative. Tarkovsky juxtaposes the two: the chaos of religious experience and the continuity of the narration, that is, of the film's fabula.

This diary entry, very important to *Stalker*'s general discourse, is concluded with an intriguing reference to a canonical literary text: 'Beckett's *Molloy*. A diagram of the life of someone who is seeking (actively) to understand the meaning of life'.[38] *Molloy* is the story of two quests: one of a vagrant (Molloy) looking for his mother's house,

Figure 5.4

and the other of a sanctimonious detective (Moron) in search of him. The two characters provide accounts of their abortive pursuits by means of anxious and even neurotic monologues. They wander in woods and fields with clearly articulated purposes, but fail to reach their respective goals. The reader is presented with the process of their gradual disintegration, which culminates in ultimate failure.

The general circular structure of Beckett's novel also insinuates some kind of deferred *metaphysical* resolution. *Molloy* appears to conform to an underlying pattern – banishment followed by gradual disintegration, homecoming, and potential metamorphosis. Likewise, Tarkovsky's film leaves the viewer with a certain dimly articulated promise of hope, by means of the sequence in which Stalker is reunited with his family and returns home. The protagonist of the film, like Molloy and Moron, wanders in the Zone's 'woods' and guides his companions towards a certain wish-fulfilling place. The place is reached, but no one enters it. Instead, the men return, both literally and metaphorically, to the point of their departure – the bar – with nothing tangible being achieved.

This return exposes the circular composition of the film: Stalker's flat – the bar – the Zone – the bar – Stalker's flat. The circle is a perfectly harmonious and continuous shape, which gives the viewer an impression that 'the whole film [has] been made in a single shot'.[39] However, the non-linear wandering in space without any resolution is still accompanied by unmotivated spatio-temporal leaps. These disruptive narrative discontinuities – the stone falling in the dark well, or the tracking shot of the shallow, tiled pool of the Revelation sequence – carry unambiguously religious messages. The quotations from Laozi's *Tao-te Ching* and the New Testament, however, are a complex rhetorical move, which reflects the ambivalent nature of the sequences. The two texts recognize the interdependence of opposites and try to transcend them altogether. Tao manifests itself in antinomies and it embraces opposites, while Revelation attempts to reveal spiritual knowledge by withholding certain truths, and by means of obscure imagery which tries to conceal them. A similar move forms the kernel of *Stalker*'s aesthetic strategy: the film, which appears to observe 'the three unities of time, space and action',[40] in fact attempts to transcend the terrestrial realm altogether, and the concluding act of telekinesis is a transcendental performance per se.

6

RECOLLECTIONS OF *NOSTALGHIA*

Nostalghia (1983), the first of Tarkovsky's films to be shot outside the Soviet Union, directly addresses the idea of foreignness and the discomfort of being away from one's homeland – it is an exploration of spatial and temporal dislocation per se.[1] Parallels have frequently been drawn between developments in the director's private life (his emigration, followed by a feeling of alienation from the West) and issues raised in it. Nevertheless, the film is evidently more than a mere projection of Tarkovsky's cultural dislocation and personal anxieties. As in *Mirror*, the real–fictional amalgam in *Nostalghia* enriches the film's discourse. The film begins with an exploration of the phenomenon of *nostalgia* as a sentimental and 'acute longing for familiar surroundings' (*OED*) and develops, through the trope of *translation*, into an ostensibly universal contrast of foreignness and at-homeness.

The protagonist of the film, Andrei Gorchakov, allegedly Tarkovsky's own alter ego, is a Russian poet on a visit to Italy. He writes a biography of a compatriot – a serf-composer who came to Bologna to study music in the eighteenth century. The composer's real life prototype is Maxim Berezovsky, who longed for Russia during his stay in Italy but is believed to have committed suicide in 1777 as a result of depression upon his return to St Petersburg. The fate of the film's protagonist is different from that of Berezovsky: the contact with foreign lands proves to be fatal without a return home. Gorchakov's ennui prevents him from relating to his Italian surroundings, makes him incapable of rational action and, in a paradoxical manner, prevents him from going back. His yearning for home, an abstract absence, develops into a desperate, personal and tangible need to move away from his current location and enter an imaginary, comforting topos.

Nostalgia as a phenomenon is a type of longing for a reunion with one's homeland; it is a desperate attempt to achieve an imagined topographic wholeness. It stems from the alienation experienced in one's current surroundings. The feeling of nostalgia derives from the gap between the idealized home and the alien reality that is confronted. Moreover, as the film-maker suggests in *Sculpting in Time*,[2] nostalgia is as much a state of alienation from the self as it is from the world. It is an exercise in distancing oneself from perceiving the present by escaping into existence in an idealized imagined space. Nostalgia, in all of its connotations, permeates *Nostalghia*.

Paradoxically – or rather, fittingly – the film, inspired by Tarkovsky's journey through Italy together with Tonino Guerra in 1979, opens with a hazy monochromatic shot which is supposed to represent his Russian home. The house featured in the shot resembles the director's own country house in Miasnoe village. The uneven and hilly Central Russian landscape is scattered before the viewer. It is punctuated with lone figures: the protagonist's family members, his Alsatian dog, and a horse. This tranquil and melancholic reflection of the homeland is accompanied by the credits, and functions as a preamble to the protagonist's journey through the foreign land. At one point, while the credits are still running, the picture freezes; its immobility turns it into a snapshot of the motherland. Later on, in the course of the film, memorable images of Russia will intrude on the Italian topography and, as a consequence, will undermine its would-be stability. The desperate attempt to reconcile the two distant and utterly divergent places finds its fulfilment in the very first seconds of the film.

The hazy Russian sequence is followed by foggy images of Tuscany, the region to which Gorchakov and his translator Eugenia have travelled in order to see Piero della Francesca's *Madonna del Parto*. The veiling haze unites the two places and forebodes an improbable amalgam of the two, which will manifest itself vividly at the end of the film. Indeed, Eugenia notes to Gorchakov that the light in Tuscany reminds her of twilight in Moscow. The film starts with a similarity and, at the same time, an immediate contrast between the two spaces (Russia and Italy) and a quarrel between the main characters – speakers of the two different languages. Gorchakov refuses to leave the car and to enter the church that houses the painting. His irritation, stemming from a feeling of alienation, is overpowering, and it prevents him from enjoying the aesthetic pleasures the foreign country has to offer: he rejects 'the spatial sense of Italy'.[3]

Gorchakov repeatedly goes off into reveries, dreaming of distant places and times. As a consequence, the memory of Russia displaces him. The protagonist's constantly recurring leaps to alternative spaces destabilize the narrative flow, but more importantly they help to create a sense of the painful impossibility of bringing the two places and the two languages together. Immediately after Eugenia's visit to the church, concluded with a close-up of the *Madonna del Parto*, the viewer sees the lone figure of Gorchakov standing at some distance from his Russian home. The monochromatic slow-motion shot shows him picking up a large white feather from the ground, on which lie a lace curtain and a glass covered in dirt; the former will appear in Domenico's house, while the latter is associated with Gorchakov's memory of his wife (Figure 6.1). The protagonist's current imaginary reality is infiltrated by the former present and by the future yet to come. Gorchakov looks towards the house and notices an angel, the bearer of the feather he picked up, slowly approaching the entrance of the building. The next cut brings the narrative back to 'normal' reality.

However, Gorchakov's recollections of Russia, such as the one at the beginning of the film, do not merely constitute a former present: they are more real than his present reality. He carries keys to his Moscow apartment in his overcoat, and constantly fiddles with them as if trying to erase the knowledge that the door that they open is thousands of miles away. In addition to his spatial dislocation, the protagonist is apparently lost in time: he confuses morning with afternoon, and falls asleep during the daytime. Only Eugenia always knows what time of day it is. Recurrent recollections do not allow Gorchakov to define precisely his current spatial and temporal coordinates. At the same time, the word 'recollection', as an 'action of recalling something to memory' (*OED*), has a strong sense of gathering, re-collecting objects and people dispersed in space and time. Thus Gorchakov's recollections of Russia are not mere memories – they comprise an attempt to retrieve his motherland, to translate Italy into Russia. Gorchakov's nostalgia makes him recollect.[4]

Translation of Nostalgia

The transformation of the film's Italian and international title, from the customary 'Nostalgia' into 'Nostalgh̀ia', illuminates the central discourse of the film – the impossible possibility of translation. 'H' is a mute sound, but it hardens the preceding 'g', which

Figure 6.1

is consequently pronounced not as [dʒ(i)ə] (as in Italian and in English) but as [giːjæ], thus making it sound 'Russian', or rather Greek. Tarkovsky's insistence on his film's title being spelt with an 'h', *Nostalghia*, requires the word to be pronounced in the Russian manner. It is thus an almost violent attempt to Russianize foreign languages: a consciously utopian project.[5]

Gorchakov's very first utterance in the film – 'Parla italiano, per favore' – is another rather aggressive gesture. He foils Eugenia's attempt to speak his own language, and thus to establish an intimate link with him. The translator apologizes, and from this point on continues to communicate with Gorchakov in Italian, despite the fact that her Russian is probably more fluent than his Italian. This uneasiness at hearing his native language spoken by an 'alien' interlocutor is an early indication of the protagonist's reluctance to allow anything or anyone foreign to infiltrate his nostalgia. His complete detachment from his Italian surroundings will gradually transform itself into the idea of complete untranslatability. Gorchakov, unable to relate to his spatial surroundings, or to translate himself into the Tuscan landscape, chooses to yearn for another place: distant Russia.

Translation, as an abstract category, is based on a steadfast binary pair – native versus foreign – and Tarkovsky appears to elaborate its function on several philosophic and aesthetic levels of the film. Binary oppositions, such as male and female, dream/vision and present reality, Russia and Italy, sanity and madness, life and death, together with the phenomenon of doubling, are omnipresent in *Nostalghia*. The manner in which they emerge is similar to the clash between two foreign languages that try to find reconciliation through the act of translation. Gorchakov yearns for a place devoid of painful linguistic and metaphysical binarism, and appears to reach his goal, albeit in a tragic manner – that is, by means of a mortal 'exploit'.

The main trope that is used to express the yearned-for impossibility of complete wholeness is *translation* – an act that is, by definition, approximate and, according to some views, inevitably destined to failure.[6] While the idea of translation proceeds from the assumption that texts have a stable meaning, which can be discovered and then transmitted into another language, it also has to negotiate between a multiplicity of choices for transmission. Translation treats every word as a synonym. Translation is therefore doomed to inevitable failure because, according to Roman Jakobson, 'synonymy [...] is not complete equivalence'.[7] Since full correspondence between linguistic units is not achievable, translation is a process of constantly negotiating differences. It involves two equivalent messages in two distinct codes. As Jakobson points out, 'equivalence in difference is the cardinal problem of language'.[8] The seemingly oxymoronic expression 'equivalence in difference' is a central problem of translation studies, and various debates have developed around the resolution of this paradox.

Walter Benjamin approaches the issue from a more abstract, poetic angle. Translation, in his opinion, is a domain where a 'suprahistorical kinship between languages'[9] is established through their otherness and difference. Translation 'ultimately serves the purpose of expressing the innermost relationship of languages'[10] by turning one foreign language towards another. It should not reduce itself to mere imitation, but instead 'must lovingly and in detail incorporate the original's way of meaning, thus making both the original and the translation recognizable as fragments of a greater language, just as fragments are [a broken] part of a vessel'.[11] A 'broken part of a vessel' is an eloquent metaphor; it suggests a certain degree of wholeness without implying completeness. Gorchakov's situation resonates with this metaphor: he attempts to create topographic wholeness from two incompatible spaces: Italy and Russia.

Tarkovsky's film highlights the theoretical paradoxes of translation elaborated by Jakobson and Benjamin. For its protagonist, Gorchakov, the thesis of untranslatability becomes a condition of essential incompletion – an infinite task. Thus, despite the fact that the film includes only two direct quotations, both poems by Arseni Tarkovsky, *Nostalghia* is one of the most literary films in the director's oeuvre, since it deals primarily with the notion of translation, and linguistic translation in particular. The two poems, one in the original Russian and the other in an Italian translation, illustrate Gorchakov's confused discourse on untranslatability. Translation, or rather its impossibility, becomes the main discursive thread of the film.

Tensions between the two main characters are not solely a result of any gender power struggle; the leitmotif of translation is also at work. Gorchakov believes that Eugenia, a professional translator, is deluded in her belief that an artistic artefact or a human emotion can be transplanted from one cultural tradition into another. Ironically, he adheres to the Italian rhyming epigram – 'Traduttore, traditore' or 'A translator is a traitor'.[12] Gorchakov cannot share his anxiety over the impossibility of translation with Eugenia, whose professional *raison d'être* is to translate. She, by contrast, fully believes in the feasibility of translation. The woman carries around a volume of Arseni Tarkovsky's poems translated into Italian, and at one point even exclaims: 'I'm not just an interpreter [...] sometimes I try to improve the words of those who use my services!' Eugenia is irritated by Gorchakov's strong accent, since she appears to believe in the possibility of an unaccented confluence of two cultures. The following scene, which takes place in a hotel lobby, is illustrative of the conflict of opinion between the two:

> 'What are you reading?' Gorchakov asks, unexpectedly.
> 'Tarkovsky…Poems by Arseni Tarkovsky.' Eugenia looks a little taken aback, as though caught red-handed.
> 'In Russian?'
> 'No, it's a translation…A pretty good one…'

'Chuck them out.'
'What for?...Actually, the person who translated them, he's an amazing poet, in his own right...' she says, as though trying to justify herself.
'Poetry can't be translated...Art in general is untranslatable...'
'I can agree with you about poetry...but music? Music, for example?'
Gorchakov sings a Russian song.
'What's that?' *asks Eugenia, not comprehending.*
'It's a Russian song.'
'Right...but how would we ever have known Tolstoy, Pushkin. How could we even begin to understand Russia,' Eugenia says testily, 'if...'
Gorchakov interrupts her: 'But you don't understand Russia at all.'
'And Dante, Petrarch, Machiavelli? So Russians don't know Italy!'
'Of course not,' Gorchakov agrees, wearily. 'How could we, poor devils?'
'Then what should we do, do you think, to know each other better?'
'Abolish borders.'
'Which borders?'
'National borders...'[13]

Gorchakov refers here to a spatial category, whose cancellation, he asserts, would help to overcome the translational trauma. The complete removal of national frontiers – by definition a utopian project – would, in Gorchakov's opinion, make space into a homogeneous entity and solve the problem of translating one culture into another. The opposition between bordered and unbordered space becomes one of the most important translation-related tropes employed in *Nostalghia*. Indeed, translation is interpreted as a sort of movement in space, and this interpretation corresponds to one of the definitions of the word: translation is '[t]ransference; removal or conveyance from one person, place, or condition to another' (*OED*). Gorchakov's exclamation is followed by the very erasure of state borders he has just imagined: the viewer is suddenly presented with an image of his wife back in Russia wiping a glass. This shift is not motivated diegetically in a straightforward manner, and after a few seconds the camera returns the viewer to 'normal' reality, with a close-up of Eugenia that also suggests a connection between the two women. The rapid succession of close-up shots signifies that the protagonist transcends the spatio-temporal boundaries that separate him from his home and family; he collapses, though only mentally, the frontiers between the object of his affection and his current alienation and nostalgia.

One minute later the director once again employs the shot/reverse-shot technique to overcome the linearity of space and time. At the end of the hotel lobby episode, Gorchakov approaches the camera and looks straight into its lens. The shot of the protagonist has a symmetrical response, located in a different space and time: the intended off-screen addressee of his gaze is his wife, who inhabits distant Russia in a distant time. The woman looks 'back', smiles, and then turns away. The monochrome slow-motion shot, accompanied by a soundtrack of dripping water, captures the two children and the dog running towards the viewer. The girl plays fetch with the dog and throws a stick into a large puddle. Suddenly, the voices of a hotel receptionist and Eugenia enter the soundtrack. The implausible amalgam – the image of the past combined with the voices of the present – once again merges Russia and Italy into a single improbable topos. The sound of splashing water, produced by the dog, brings the viewer fully back to the hotel. The national border is once again violated in the protagonist's imagination.

Gorchakov, dreaming of a world without borders, appears to long for Babylon – the city that united humanity with a single language. He must also be aware that, after divine intervention, Babylon became a symbol of the impossibility of reaching the realm of the unknowable, and of the consequent damnation to the sphere of translation. The fall or relegation to the state in which translation is possible, indeed even essential, occurred, according to the Old Testament, as a result of an unsuccessful attempt to build a superstructure – the Tower of Babel, 'whose top may reach unto heaven' (Genesis 11: 4). At the centre of the story is the spatial conflict, which is provoked by linguistic unity: 'Behold, the people is one, and they have all one language; and this they begin to do' (Genesis 11: 6). God imposes a certain spatial limit beyond which humans cannot ascend; everything that lies above this point in space is destined to be beyond human reason and knowledge. Damnation is brought about by means of a confusion and dissipation of languages: 'So the Lord scattered them *abroad* from thence upon the face of all the earth: and they left off to build the city' (Genesis 11: 8, my italics).

'Abroad' is a key word that is related to the verb 'to scatter' in the King James Version, and means in this case a state of being 'widely asunder'; in its modern usage, however, it tends to signify 'any region outside one's homeland' (*OED*). *Abroad* is the condition of Gorchakov, since it describes his estrangement: the protagonist is disconnected from his current surroundings (language, people and landscape), he finds himself *abroad* in the two senses – both 'widely asunder', and outside his homeland. Language and topography operate as agents of alienation, and the film's aesthetic strategy is to resolve somehow the divergence between the character's inner aspirations and his outer surroundings.

Derrida, in his essay 'Des Tours de Babel',[14] explores the linguistic and spatial aspects of the story of Babel, which are strongly echoed in *Nostalghia*. The critic begins by enquiring whether the proper name, Babel, belongs to just one language. Proper names are by definition strictly applicable, accurate, correct, literal, non-metaphorical and untranslatable; they designate something that is unconditionally singular. The Old Testament story exemplifies the struggle for the proper and strictly singular name:

> In seeking to 'make a name for themselves', to found at the same time a universal tongue and a unique genealogy, the Semites want to bring the world to reason, and this reason can signify simultaneously a colonial violence (since they would thus universalize their idiom) and a peaceful transparency of the human community. Inversely, when God imposes and opposes his name, he ruptures the rational transparency but interrupts also the colonial violence or the linguistic imperialism. He destines them to translation, he subjects them to the law of a translation both necessary and impossible...[15]

Gorchakov seems to be acutely aware of this divine damnation. His longing for impossible monolithic singularity and cultural imperialism is the source of his constant anxiety throughout the film, and can also be understood as one of the causes of his premature death. Gorchakov perishes in his attempt to defy the dominant ideology of separatism. His task, the completion of which is both necessary and impossible, is such that it has to be carried out at the very brink of human spiritual strength.

In several episodes the protagonist tries to overcome linguistic division in the same manner as Benjamin, who envisages translation as a process in which two languages attempt to overcome their essential separation, as 'fragments of a greater language'.[16] Towards the end of the film, he tells an Italian girl called Angela a joke in Russian, which she, of course, does not understand. An important feature of this short episode is that it takes place between the recitation of two poems: in Russian by Gorchakov, and in Italian by Domenico. The fruitless act of communication (the girl utterly fails to understand) is located on the frontier between the Russian and Italian languages. The script describes the ending of the scene in the following way: 'Gorchakov laughs out loud with glee. "But of course you don't understand a thing...", and he continues in his wretched Italian: "What's your name?"'[17] Communication, in this case, is more important than the information it attempts to transmit.

In the same way, Gorchakov's poor Italian proves no obstacle to Domenico, who understands his new Russian friend without any difficulty. The men establish verbal contact and immerse themselves in linguistic and spiritual labyrinths only after Eugenia – the mediator, fluent in both languages – leaves them. The interaction between Gorchakov and Domenico is both an abortive and a successful act of communication. Gorchakov clearly experiences some problems with his limited Italian vocabulary, but nevertheless he understands Domenico. Only once, during their first meeting, does he not understand a word. It is notable that this word is *fede* ('faith'). Eugenia translates it for him, and Domenico will later teach him its real meaning.

In general, however, Gorchakov is not preoccupied with linguistic translation as such; he is concerned with the possibility of translating and relating *experiences*. Experience, or what Willard Van Orman Quine calls 'empirical meaning',[18] is what unifies people who do not speak the same language. Quine maintains that 'empirical meaning is what remains when, given discourse together with all its stimulatory conditions, we peel away the verbiage. It is what the sentences of one language and their firm translations in a completely alien language have in common.'[19] Thus Gorchakov succeeds in relating his spiritual anxieties to Domenico; or, in other words, he is able to translate his empirical knowledge into an intelligible 'language' to which Domenico has access.

Only once does there appear to be a misunderstanding between the two men: Domenico gives Gorchakov the mission 'to save the world', to which the latter replies, and then repeats several times, in Italian, 'va bene' meaning 'all right' – a standard expression of consent. However, Domenico is irritated by the phrase, and retorts: 'va male!' ('all is wrong'). The madman performs an act of linguistic reflection, and a habitual expression – 'all right' – becomes a statement concerning the human condition. Later, the understanding that 'all is wrong' will serve as a bridge between the two men, and will bring them to mirror each other's acts of self-immolation by fire. Gorchakov, however, repeatedly immerses himself in the oneiric domain before this dramatic resolution; the protagonist desperately tries to reach a spiritual ideal, a certain topographic wholeness, through various dreams and visions.

Oneiric Displacements

Nostalghia is the first of Tarkovsky's projects which is set entirely in a time contemporaneous with that in the life of the director. The present time comprises the subject-matter of the film. In fact, it partially actualizes the idea of making a film consisting only of several episodes solely about time or its passing.[20] One of the hotel scenes presents us with a pure representation of the passage of time. When Gorchakov enters his room for the first time, he switches the light on and off and then lies down. Natural light enters the room from two windows. There is almost no movement, let alone action, registered in the space. The fluctuating sound of rain and the movements of the light make the viewer aware of the movement of time. The mesmerizing sequence is interrupted by a spatial abnormality – Domenico's dog enters the room from the bathroom and lies down by Gorchakov's side.

The director's sensitivity to the present moment, manifested in his trademark meditative long takes such as the mentioned shot in Gorchakov's hotel room, receives a rather contradictory treatment in a diary entry towards the end of his career: 'The present doesn't exist. There are only the past and the future, which, practically speaking, are a cipher in terms of temporal state, and only connect with a person through the assertion of his will, through his action, which allows the future to filter through it, leaving the past.'[21] This stance, which justifies the overall spatio-temporal instability of Tarkovsky's cinema, reveals the ambiguous interplay between the given reality and the amorphous past and future in *Nostalghia*. As Domenico puts it: 'Where am I, if not in reality and in my own imagination?' Indeed, imagination and, by extension, memories of the past and atemporal dreams constantly infiltrate the film's present.

Nostalghia's improbable doubling and dream sequences, and its constantly altering topography and chronology, undermine its narrative unity. The highest level of implausibility is achieved by distorting the conventional material of everyday life: people and inanimate objects appear in abnormal circumstances. Doubling, for instance, violates the comforting notion of human singularity. Once multiplied, identity, together with physicality, acquires an uncanny quality. Moreover, one can argue that doubling is a perverse form of an 'ideal' translation: something is replicated without losing anything of the original, though this replication creates a sense of uneasiness.

There are two notable scenes in the film in which characters are duplicated. The first takes place in Domenico's house in a *mise-en-scène* which, at first glance, does not appear to be intended to introduce any uncanny dream-like effects. Gorchakov leans against a wall near a mirror and looks in someone's direction. The tracking shot reveals that this someone is another Gorchakov. The scene is infused with a nostalgic aura – the protagonist 'is already torn asunder'.²² This spatial dislocation, however, is preceded by a temporal leap: Gorchakov discovers a miniature landscape housed in one of the rooms immediately after he enters Domenico's domain. The improbability of the encounter is underlined by the sudden switch to monochrome. The protagonist sees a hilly landscape with a curved river, punctuated with electricity poles: an echo of distant Russia. The artificiality of the construction is immediately revealed, since the camera captures the whole room with its tiled floor, a window and a torn lace curtain, and only then zooms in to reveal the materials used to make the miniature landscape: moss, water and small sticks. For Tarkovsky the delimited space of this 'micro-world' reflects eternity – that is, time.²³

The second duplication occurs in an explicitly dream-like or recollection-inspired sequence-shot in sepia. Gorchakov lies on a sofa in the hotel corridor, his nose bleeding after the argument with Eugenia. The switch to monochrome announces a leap to another space and time. The protagonist imagines his wife back in Russia getting up from her bed. The woman goes outside to join the rest of the family – two of her children and her mother. The four disperse in a hazy landscape near their country house, and are observed by the tracking camera as if it were an omnipotent external observer. In both cases, the uninterrupted tracking shots present an impossible reality: the characters are presented in two incompatible spaces at once (Figure 6.2). A cut back to Gorchakov in the hotel room is accompanied by his wife calling him by name. The imaginary plane literally infiltrates the real domain.²⁴

The reverse – the real domain infiltrating the imaginary plane – takes place in the dreams in *Nostalghia*. Instead of duplication, however, the viewer is presented with the no less disturbing phenomenon of displacement. In the first dream Gorchakov imagines a 'reconciliation' between his wife and Eugenia. It is most unlikely that the two women have ever seen each other, but they are brought together by Gorchakov's anxious mind. The episode reconciles the two foreign languages and two distant spaces, Russia and Italy. Time and topography are never stable in the dream sequence; their rigidity and stability are loosened. Distant and dissimilar entities are brought together in an improbable and artificial manner: the women express a remarkable tenderness towards one another, which transforms into an almost homosexual attraction. Their embrace is followed by a shot of Eugenia on top of the sleeping Gorchakov: the woman's dirty hands grasp the bed sheets. The protagonist's erotic desire is completely displaced, for the scene is followed by the image

Figure 6.2

of his wife comforting the crying Eugenia. The dream concludes with Gorchakov leaving his bed, which is now occupied, to the viewer's surprise, by his pregnant wife.

The second dream presents a displacement which is not only improbable, but also unsettling. This time, Gorchakov has a vision in which he finds himself on a narrow Italian cobbled street. He is alone, and everywhere there are signs of devastation, as if the Apocalypse proclaimed by Domenico has already taken place. Gorchakov notices an abandoned wardrobe with a mirror and opens its door, trying to catch his reflection. However, instead of his own reflection, he sees

Domenico's. What makes the episode more unsettling is the fact that Domenico looks like Gorchakov – he wears the same coat and scarf, and his face is clean-shaven like that of his Russian friend.[25]

Doubling and substitution undermine any uniform notions of space and time. The impossibility of remaining within his current spatial and temporal context (Italy) is, for Gorchakov, the catalyst for these leaps into other spaces and temporal frameworks (imaginary Russia or illusory, non-existent places). These leaps do not sit comfortably with the conventional notions of singularity and homogeneity, while the imaginary spaces are able to accommodate their non-linear spatio-temporal essence. Thus Gorchakov overcomes the unbearable fact that he is located in an alien land by undermining the stability of his own location in space and time.

(Im)possible Translation

Doubling and substitution are also inherent qualities of translation. The idea of the uncanny – something that is both homely and intolerably alien at the same time – is analogous to the otherness produced by translation, which, by definition, deals with ideas of the familiar and the foreign. In this sense, the two poems of Arseni Tarkovsky can also be included in the realm of doubles. It is no coincidence that it is Gorchakov and Domenico who recite the poems in the film. The surroundings in which the poetic texts are read, together with the fact that one of them is an Italian translation of the original Russian, are crucial factors that inevitably overshadow the actual content of the poems.

Arseni Tarkovsky's poems 'As a child I once fell ill...' ('Ia v detstve zabolel...') and 'Si oscura la vista – la mia forza...' ('Merknet zrenie – sila moia...' / 'My sight, my strength, dims...') prominently enter the narrative of the film in the second half. The first poem is recited by Gorchakov on his way to and inside the flooded church. The protagonist walks through a stream of crystal clear water with swaying grass; he is clearly drunk, and mumbles the text of the poem almost absent-mindedly. His recitation is not very skilful and is clearly not addressed to an external audience. The viewer overhears the following lines:

As a child I once fell ill	Я в детстве заболел
From fear and hunger. I'd scratched off the scab	От голода и страха. Корку с губ
From my lips and licked my lips; I remembered	Сдеру – и губы облизну; запомнил
The cool and salty taste.	Прохладный и солоноватый вкус.

But still I go, but still I go, I go, I sit on the front stairs and warm myself, Delirious, I wander as though to follow The tune of the pied piper to the river, I warm myself on the stairs, consumed by fever. But mother stands and beckons, she seems Not far away but unapproachable: I approach a little, it's only seven steps, She beckons, I approach but she still stands Only seven steps away, she beckons.	А все иду, а все иду, иду, Сижу на лестнице в парадном, греюсь, Иду себе в бреду, как под дуду За крысоловом в реку, сяду – греюсь На лестнице; и так знобит и эдак. А мать стоит, рукою манит, будто Невдалеке, а подойти нельзя: Чуть подойду – стоит в семи шагах, Рукою манит; подойду – стоит В семи шагах, рукою манит.
Heat Gripped me, I undid my collar and lay down – And trumpets started trumpeting, my eyelids Were struck by light, and horses galloped, mother Is flying above the cobblestones, she beckons – And vanished…	Жарко Мне стало, расстегнул я ворот, лег, – Тут затрубили трубы, свет по векам Ударил, кони поскакали, мать Над мостовой летит, рукою манит – И улетела…
And now I dream Beneath the apple trees, a white ward, And the white bed-sheet beneath my throat, And the white doctor looks down at me, And the white nurse stands beside my feet Ruffling her wings. And they remained. But mother came and beckoned – And vanished…	И теперь мне снится Под яблонями белая больница, И белая под горлом простыня, И белый доктор смотрит на меня, И белая в ногах стоит сестрица И крыльями поводит. И остались. А мать пришла, рукою поманила – И улетела…

The spatio-temporal position of the poem's protagonist, presumably a small boy, is extremely unstable. Movement intermingles with stillness in a highly impulsive and improbable manner. The following five lines, for example, describe the protagonist in four successive states – movement-rest-movement-rest: 'But still I go, but still I go, I go, / I sit on the front stairs and warm myself, / Delirious, I wander as though to follow / The tune of the pied piper to the river, / I warm myself on the stairs, consumed by fever.' This volatility leads to yet more instability; the hero enters the domain of hallucinations and dreams: 'But mother stands and beckons, she seems / Not far away but unapproachable', or 'And now I dream / Beneath the apple trees, a white ward'. All spatio-temporal coordinates in the poem are subjective and volatile. As a consequence of this unsteadiness, the text seems to represent a delirious dream dominated by images of presence and absence. The narrator relates his present reality to his imaginary world. One can argue that Gorchakov's disorientation in Italy is intensified by this poem, which can also be read as a chronotopic hallucination. Moreover, the poem relates a longing for a mother who beckons but vanishes; the text ends with a non-pacifying 'And vanished….' The impossibility of reunion with something homely and cherished is another trope that can be naturally related to Gorchakov's situation.

Apart from these thematic associations, the poem has an important function as part of the translation discourse. The name of Arseni Tarkovsky is already familiar to the viewer from Eugenia's book of translations, which appears at the beginning of the film. This same book is now seized by Gorchakov and brought with him to the flooded church. Here the character recites the Russian version of the poem to himself. By reciting the poem in the language in which it was originally written, the proponent of untranslatability performs an act of self-affirmation. The book is not open in the sequence, and Gorchakov makes audible the very words that it has 'repressed'. His intentions are clearly antagonistic, and the water and fire inside the church seem to imply that the book is threatened as a material object. This sequence is a complex enactment of the idea propounded by Tarkovsky that nationality is a defining feature of artistic production.[26] However, Goethe's dictum 'Wer den Dichter will verstehen, muss in Dichters Lande gehen' ('Who wishes to understand the poet must go to the poet's land'), which found its way into Tarkovsky's 1978 diary,[27] receives different inflections in *Nostalghia*. Russian Gorchakov recites the lines of the Russian poem while exploring the extraordinary Italian topos: the flooded church.

The allegation of the impossibility of translation is further undermined a few minutes after the recitation of 'As a child I once fell ill....' Domenico, who is Gorchakov's only spiritual contact in Italy, reappears on the scene. However, the character achieves both presence and absence at the same time: Domenico's voice is heard while his physical body is not present in the sequence. The voice-over is not diegetically motivated; it interrupts the linearity and coherence of the narration. The madman does not utter a single word except for lines from another poem by Arseni Tarkovsky: 'Si oscura la vista – la mia forza....' Despite Tarkovsky's obstinate personal convictions against translation as a literary phenomenon, the poem materializes in the form of an Italian translation:

Si oscura la vista – la mia forza,	My sight, my strength, dims,
Sono due occulti dardi adamantine;	Two invisible adamant spears;
Si confonde l'udito per il tuono lontano	My hearing deafens, full of distant thunder
Della casa paterna che respire;	And the breathing of home;
Dei duri muscoli i gambi si infiacchiscono,	The knots of my tensed muscles have weakened,
Come bovi canuti all'aratura;	Like grey oxen on a ploughed field;
E non più quando è notte	Two wings at the back of my shoulders
Alle mie spalle splendono due ali.	Don't shine anymore in the night.
Nella festa, candela, mi sono consumato.	I am a candle, I burned out at a feast.
All'alba raccogliete la mia disciolta cera,	Gather my wax in the morning,

E lì leggete	And this page will prompt you
Chi piangere, di cosa andar superbi,	How to cry and what to be proud of,
Come, donando l'ultima porzione di letizia	How to give away the last third
Morire in levità,	Of joy and die easily,
E al riparo d'un tetto di fortuna	And under the shade of an inadvertent home
Accendersi postumi, come una parola.	How to burn as posthumously as a word.

The two poems appear to be quite diverse in terms of subject-matter. The hallucinatory 'As a child I once fell ill...' differs substantially from the nostalgic 'Si oscura la vista – la mia forza....' However, the idea of levitation connects the two texts. The fleeting mother and the nurse 'ruffling wings' in the first poem are counterbalanced by the two dulled wings behind the poet's shoulders in the second. More important, however, is the fact that both poems are recited while an Italian girl called Angela is present in the building. She is in fact the third 'angel' to appear in *Nostalghia*. The previous two were a human-sized angel standing by the side of Gorchakov's Russian house at the beginning of the film, and the sunken marble statue of an angel (possibly taken from a representation of the Annunciation, since the figure's hand is raised in a manner characteristic of the scene) found near the entrance to the flooded church.

In general, the structure of the visual sequence accompanying 'Si oscura la vista – la mia forza...' mirrors that of the preceding poem. The recitation takes place in the same flooded church near the bonfire that Gorchakov has made. However, the poem's appearance in the film is accompanied by several developments, none of which corresponds with the preceding sequence. First, the poem is read not by Gorchakov, but by Domenico, whose native language is Italian. The madman's presence is not diegetically motivated, and his voice-over appears as if from nowhere. Second, the recitation is followed by an *auto-da-fé* – the book is burned towards the end of the poem. Uncannily, it is only in this episode that the book is seen open for the first time, and this occurs only when it is being destroyed. The visual sequence seems to contradict the soundtrack: while Domenico's recitation reaffirms the validity of the translation, Gorchakov burns the book and makes its physical existence impossible without uttering a single word.

The recited poem deals with nostalgia for a time in the past. The process of ageing is metaphorized through various images, from the inanimate 'Two invisible adamant spears' to the animate 'Like grey oxen on a ploughed field'. The metaphorization of bodily functions leads to the statement where the poet asserts: 'Two wings at the back of my shoulders / Don't shine anymore in the night'. The idealization of the figure of the artist continues with Andrei Tarkovsky's favourite line, 'I am a candle, I burned out at a feast', in the second stanza, which functions more as a spiritual testament. The sense of finality dominates and reaches its zenith in the last line, 'How to burn as posthumously as a word', which appears to be illustrated visually: the book containing the poem's words is being burned.

The first and last lines of the second stanza can be linked with one of the most memorable sequences in *Nostalghia*, which takes place after the poems are recited: Gorchakov carrying a candle in the pool in Bagno Vignoni. This sequence is filmed in one continuous take and lasts almost nine minutes. Gorchakov accomplishes the task Domenico demands of him by carrying the candle from one end of the pool to the other without letting it go out. The world will be saved if the Russian accomplishes the task – that is, the spatial traversal of the pond gives the future (time) to mankind. The absurd task becomes a spiritual quest. Gorchakov burns himself out (he literally dies, following Domenico's example) while accomplishing the mission, like a burnt down and eventually extinguished candle. The crossing of the space of the pool culminates in the protagonist's temporal end. However, his self-sacrifice is not in vain, and through it he seeks to abide by the last line of the poem, glorifying the posthumous burning *word*.

In the moments before the tragic resolution occurs, Gorchakov has a heightened awareness of time. The task given to the actor was to enter the domain of time and to 'display an entire human life in one shot, without any editing, from beginning to end, from birth to the very moment of death'.[28] The reservoir where the character wanders is no longer filled with water – it contains pure time. Water, as a metaphor for time, evaporates and allows time to emerge as a real, almost palpable entity. At the same time, the marker of temporal progression is spatial: the burning candle, which goes out twice in the airstreams, functions as a yardstick for Gorchakov's temporal advancement. The passage of time reveals itself in the space of the empty pool in which time is enveloped.

Gorchakov reaches the end of the pool and of his life without uttering a single word. Domenico's self-immolation, in contrast, is preceded by a long, overbearing speech, delivered from the replica of the equestrian statue of Marcus Aurelius in Piazza del Campidoglio, on the top of the Capitoline Hill. The madman urges the dispersed audience, apparently made up of the patients of mental institutions who are uninterested in the speech, to regain an ability to listen to nature – to hear the 'buzzing of insects'. He advocates a more authentic and spiritual life: 'We must go back to the foundations of life, without dirtying the water.' His nonsensical and rather theatrical death also clearly echoes several lines of 'Si oscura la vista – la mia forza...': 'Gather my wax in the morning, / And this page will prompt you / How to cry and what to be proud of, / How to give away the last third / Of joy and die easily'. Domenico indeed dies easily, and the poem evolves into a spiritual testament of the two characters: the melancholic Russian and the Italian madman.

Babylonian Ruins

The reading of the two poems marks a sort of resolution to the trope of nostalgia, and to the anxiety of untranslability, which the film has explored up to this point. The setting in which the poems are delivered is itself significant: Gorchakov declaims 'As a child I once fell ill...' on his way to the ruined and flooded church, while Domenico recites the Italian version of 'Si oscura la vista – la mia forza...' inside it. The building itself embodies the impossible possibility, or possible impossibility, of translation. It is a defective construction, which, thanks to its leaking roof (a trope recognizable from other Tarkovsky films), is filled with water and rendered uninhabitable. The idea of a building as a shelter that protects humans from nature's elements is thus undermined: the inside–outside binary is dismantled.

In *Nostalghia* the viewer witnesses, in Hamid Naficy's words, 'the action of water and time on the physical world as they gradually decay, erode, and transform it from a structure into a ruin, from culture into nature'.[29] Gorchakov, who in the planning stages of the film was an architect, is an explorer of ruins, while Domenico inhabits them. The ruined edifice is a symbol of decay, but it also contains within it the possibility of future revival. The building where the two poems are recited therefore presents us with an explicitly theological narrative of decay and revival. In a certain sense, it follows the convention set by the Pantheon in Rome, which has a round opening oculus (or Great Eye) in the top of its dome. In the Pantheon, the oculus has always remained open, allowing rain to enter and fall to the floor, from where it is carried away through various drains. It also admits the only natural light into the interior of the structure. The Roman church and the ruined construction in *Nostalghia* are thus both exposed to natural phenomena, and are capable of bringing together the terrestrial and celestial strata.[30]

However, unlike the Pantheon, the flooded church, together with other buildings within the film (such as Domenico's house and the ruins of San Galgano Abbey that appear right at the end), has ceased to perform its original function – to provide a space for worship or shelter. The deficiency of these structures, seen through a mythical prism, leads to a deficiency of translation. In *Nostalghia*'s flawed buildings, constructional failure leads to linguistic failure; this twofold failure is exemplified by the Tower of Babel phenomenon. The ancient builders hoped that their project would bring into existence a place of ultimate unity: the monolithic Tower. However, the demolition of the as-yet-unfinished edifice left these hopes unfulfilled: 'The "tower of Babel" does not merely figure the irreducible multiplicity of tongues; it exhibits an incompletion, the impossibility of finishing, of totalising, of saturating, of completing something on the order of edification, architectural construction, system and architectonics.'[31]

Tarkovsky's buildings are manifestations of what Derrida calls the 'incompleteness of the structure'. These buildings are destined to remain in a state of incompleteness, open to natural meteorological phenomena, simultaneously enclosing and disclosing their inhabitants and visitors. Their 'deficiency' does not seem to bother the characters. On the contrary, Gorchakov appears to seek seclusion in the ruined churches – places that retain a trace of divine worship but are nevertheless abandoned by their congregations. Domenico, by contrast, is content with the confines of his apartment, which is known locally as the 'End of the World'. Despite the lack of partitions, he still follows habitual conventions, 'using' doors that are no longer attached to walls – like his double, the old man in *Ivan's Childhood*. Indeed, he retains his usual behavioural habits within a house that in fact no longer exists. The recurring motif of the flawed building reflects the characters' yearning to regain home, in both a spiritual and physical sense (Figure 6.3).

Domenico and Gorchakov apparently have two obsessions: reclaiming ruined buildings and striving towards the necessity, and at the same time the impossibility, of communication (translation). Both obsessions are doomed to failure: the deformity and disrepair of architectural constructions in *Nostalghia* signify the ultimate impossibility of translation. Deformed buildings are mere flawed semblances of the completed ideal of a house or other structure. Domenico's house, the flooded church in the middle of the film, and the ruins of San Galgano Abbey at the end all undermine the concept of a building as some kind of a shelter that provides refuge for human beings. Their deficiency – their dilapidated or

Figure 6.3

non-existent roofs – decreases the possibility for these buildings to hide or conceal; indeed, their openness grants a direct link with the celestial stratum. In a similar way, translation discloses a tension between two foreign linguistic systems, although full reconciliation is never possible, remaining only within the realm of hope. Furthermore, the *translational* Tower of Babel can never be built, which means, according to Derrida, that 'translation is devoted to ruin, to that form of memory or commemoration that is called a ruin; ruin is perhaps its vocation and a destiny that it accepts from the very outset'.[32]

The centrality to the film's discourse of the tropes of the impossibility of translation and of constructional unity is emphasized by the diegetic importance of the Cistercian abbey in San Galgano, Tuscany – 'a skeleton of memory, a sheer melancholy presence'.[33] Translation is a spatial incompleteness which longs for a time of wholeness. Benjamin's broken vessel and Derrida's remains of the Tower of Babel, as well as the abbey in *Nostalghia*, yearn for the time of totality and unity. The ruined gothic building appears for the first time in Gorchakov's dream in the flooded church. The protagonist wanders inside, and the image is accompanied by a voice-over exchange between Eugenia and Domenico as an angel and God: 'Lord, why have you no pity for him? Say something to him…' says the former, to which the latter replies, 'Could you imagine the consequences if he were to hear my voice?'

San Galgano in the dream – a deformed sanctuary – is clearly aestheticized, and emerges in an unobstructed state; its interior is empty: 'Remains the heavy lacework of walls, arches, columns, and window frames missing any glass. A packed earth floor has reverted to its grass covering; the grey structure stretches up from this surface of green straight into Tuscany's sky.'[34] The imposing, desolate skeleton of the Cistercian abbey is extremely photogenic. As the camera explores its picturesque aisles, breathtaking perspectives are revealed through sparse ornamentation and the sober gothic style.

But the most memorable images of the abbey come in the closing sequence of the film. Spatio-temporal lapses in *Nostalghia* are manifestations of spiritual angst – longing for another space and time, which are granted at the end. Italy remains in Gorchakov's mind a distant destination, which is never reached in its spatial completeness. The spectre of Russia haunts the Italian present. The two are conflated to form an explicitly unreal spatio-temporal entity in the somewhat literal finale. The film culminates in an impossible reunion between the dead protagonist and his Russian homeland through the Italian landscape. The two antagonistic spaces are finally merged together, though posthumously, in abstract time.[35] The architectural ghosts – the ruined church and the replica of a Russian hut – shelter the phantom of the already dead Gorchakov.

The first shot of the closing sequence hints at the Russian countryside. The topography of Gorchakov's homeland is directly linked with his native tongue and general system of values. The country house is more than a familiar and cherished space. Its image, contained within the medieval Italian church, signifies a successful failure or failed success of communication by means of translation. The hero must be reunited with his native land in order to relate to the

Italian landscape. Quine stresses that 'most talk of meaning requires tacit reference to a home language in much the way that talk of truth involves tacit reference to one's own system of the world'.[36] References to already familiar things and places are unavoidable in one's interactions with the external world.

Nevertheless, the image of Gorchakov's house already contains a hint of improbability – a reflection in a puddle of one of the two triplets of arched windows on the east end wall of San Galgano. This reflection signifies that there is something irregular about the surroundings of the house, since the puddle should reflect the open sky. The elaborately crafted illusion is revealed through this reflection. The camera gradually zooms out and discloses the side walls of the abbey together with the east end wall. In the true Cistercian tradition, the east end is square with two triplets of windows surmounted by one small and one large oculus. The eastern wall is orientated towards Gorchakov's homeland, and at the same time serves as a background for his imaginary home.

The spatial organization of Benjamin's metaphor for translation as 'a royal robe with ample folds'[37] makes it a highly apposite reference point for this sequence. The fact that the language of translation always remains unsuited, overpowering, and alien to its newly acquired content creates a disjunction which 'prevents translation'.[38] In the same manner, the Cistercian church envelops the Russian house in more than just ample folds. As the camera zooms out, it appears to consume the house completely. Artificiality and extreme stylization are the principal qualities of this final sequence.

The translation of the Russian landscape into the Italian church, or vice versa, is the climactic episode of the film, and is also its end. From this perspective, it is interesting to note the double meaning of the Greek word *nostos*, which simultaneously stands for a homecoming or homeward journey (for example, the return of Odysseus and the other Greek heroes of the Trojan War) and, in a more general sense, signifies the conclusion of a literary work (*OED*). While nostalgia is a painful longing for home (*algia* means 'pain'), the end of *Nostalghia* is a *mortal* (more than painful) homecoming, which also functions as an ultimate conclusion to the film.

Finally, the concluding sequence, shot in one continuous long take, echoes Pier Paolo Pasolini's discussion of the phenomenon of the long take through the prism of death. For the Italian filmmaker, cinema is 'an endless long take, as is reality to our senses for as long as we are able to see and feel (a long take that ends with the end of our lives)'.[39] Death completes a human life: it converts the obscure and indefinite present time into the clear and definite past, while montage 'accomplishes for the material of film [...] what death accomplishes for life'.[40] Death is always already present in the cinematic cut. The final long take of *Nostalghia* extends the life of its protagonist for another moment, then to be consummated by the final cut – the end of the film (Figure 6.4).

* * *

The impossibility of the structural unity of the Tower of Babel haunts *Nostalghia*. The Old Testament story of the ultimate failure to reach a dominant singularity culminates in damnation to the sphere of translation: a sphere of negotiating differences and multiplicities that always fails to produce satisfactory results. Gorchakov openly declares his ideological and aesthetical belief in the untranslatability of cultures. The aborted romantic encounter with his personal translator Eugenia is countered by his meeting with the local madman, Domenico. The impossible possibility of contact between the two alien cultures is easily attained by the two men, and reaches its climax in the declamation of the two poems by Arseni Tarkovsky, which are read by Gorchakov in Russian and by Domenico in the Italian translation.

The encounter between the characters represents a repeated familiarization with their native languages in the manner described by Barbara Johnson: 'Through the foreign language we renew our love–hate intimacy with our mother tongue. We tear at her syntactic joints and semantic flesh and resent her for not providing all the words we need.'[41] Once linguistic intimacy is restored, Domenico and Gorchakov recognize a mystical bond uniting them – a recognition that eventually culminates in their mortal self-sacrifices. The urge towards self-destruction is not conveyed only through language. Domenico's place of residence and the places that attract Gorchakov also inform the discourse of disintegration. The characters occupy and visit ruined edifices – annexes to the remainders of the Tower of Babel. Their incompleteness relates their failure to arrive at a monumental completion.

At the same time, the deformed churches and Domenico's house are not only symbols of the impossibility of achieving structural singularity; the extremely photogenic ruins are aestheticized by the camera, and their presence shapes the texture of the film. *Nostalghia* thus becomes a beautified longing for unity, which is aware of its own impossibility. The ruined building is always a symbol of sentimental

Figure 6.4

nostalgia for something that has perished and is painfully absent – the desired object or space is always removed. Nostalgia, according to Tarkovsky, 'is not the same as longing for past time. Nostalgia is a longing for the space of time, which has passed in vain.'[42] Gorchakov's nostalgia evolves into an entity at once spiritual and tangible: it becomes a *temporal space*.

All the aforementioned semantic possibilities are interwoven in the last sequence of the film. The final, posthumous, imaginary, or even false, homecoming of Gorchakov brings his nostalgia to an end (he overcomes the imposed distance between himself and his homeland); the sequence is also the end of *Nostalghia*, the film. The open space of the Cistercian church accommodates Gorchakov's Russian house. The concluding cinematic image is a superimposition of various incongruous concepts and phenomena which desperately attempts to reconcile its inherent dichotomies.

7

ILLUSIONS OF *SACRIFICE*

The apocalyptic motif re-enters Tarkovsky's oeuvre in his last film, *Sacrifice* (*Offret: Sacrificatio*, 1986). It not only becomes its principal theme, but also performs a clear diegetic function: nuclear apocalypse instigates the main character's 'sacrificial offering' – the climax of the film's narrative. Alexander, haunted by apocalyptic dreams and visions, is an exact copy of Domenico in *Nostalghia* (both roles were played by Erland Josephson): 'saving' the world by a violent act, the consummation by fire of something very precious (one's own life or most cherished possessions) is what unites them.[1] However, there is a substantial difference between the films' general discourses: Gorchakov's longing for a familiar land and home evolves into Alexander's violent rejection of the conventions of human dwelling.

The film opens with the 'Erbarme Dich' aria from J. S. Bach's *St Matthew Passion* and a static image of *The Adoration of the Magi* by Leonardo, with the credits appearing over it. The camera captures one of the Magi, who offers the Christ child a gift of frankincense, and then moves upward to explore Christ himself, the figures surrounding him and the holly tree above them. Seagull cries can be heard after the aria fades away, and the image of the painting is followed by an outdoor scene, which depicts Alexander with his son, nicknamed Little Man, planting a dead tree on the seashore. A verbose monologue accompanies this seemingly absurd act: Alexander tells his son (the boy has been rendered temporarily mute by a recent operation on his tonsils) an edifying story about a monk who, to test his obedience, was given the task of watering a dead plant every day until it bore fruit.² The entire scene is shot in a single, sustained camera movement. The two are soon joined by the local postman, Otto, and the camera continues tracking the characters.

The postman delivers a birthday telegram, and a rather mundane exchange immediately evolves into a somewhat pretentious dialogue with philosophical inclinations. Unexpectedly, Otto asks Alexander about his relationship with God, and then accuses him of yearning and waiting for something. This vague and abstract accusation is highly significant for the film's discourse; it soon develops into the major diegetic drive of the film. The postman's speech, loaded with references to Nietzsche, completely bewilders his interlocutor. The viewer, however, is immediately given an indication that a religious aura surrounds the characters. The reference to John's canonical 'In the beginning was the Word' intensifies this feeling – the film's double title *Offret: Sacrificatio* unambiguously stands for a sacrificial offering in the Christian sense.

After the postman cycles away, Alexander and Little Man enter a small grove, but their seclusion is once again invaded. Adelaide and Victor – Alexander's wife and friend – arrive by car, exchange a few remarks and then also leave. The protagonist and his son continue their 'conversation'. Suddenly a herding call (*kulning* – a domestic Scandinavian music form), resembling a sad chant, enters the soundtrack, and its eerie sound texture is a clear premonition of some extraordinary event. The premonition is realized in a few seconds: Little Man crawls away from his father while the latter tells him how he discovered the house they now live in. The edifice prominently enters the film's discourse as an ideal topos of human dwelling, but its ideality is undermined by the forthcoming vision of apocalyptic space and time. Alexander emerges from his lengthy monologue and realizes, with great alarm, that the boy is missing. Suddenly, Little Man jumps on his father from behind and the man involuntarily hits him. Alexander turns around to find his son with a bleeding nose, realizes that he has committed an act of violence against him, and passes out.

The first spatio-temporal leap in *Sacrifice* occurs immediately after the protagonist falls to the ground. Alexander loses consciousness and enters an alternative spatio-temporal framework. A black-and-white sequence follows: the camera slowly descends to reveal a courtyard with two sets of stairs and with the pavement covered in ashes and litter. The elevated camera continues its improbable, sublime movement and slides in parallel to the pavement. It explores an overturned car with missing parts, broken chairs, newspapers, various boxes, and items of clothing, all of which are scattered on the flooded street. A haunting herding call, accompanied by the sound of flowing water, dominates the soundtrack. Suddenly a glass platform, which appears to be hovering unnaturally in the air, enters the camera's field of vision. Its reflecting surface disorientates the viewer, since it 'confuses' two visual planes: the reflection of surrounding buildings and the sky merges with the littered pavement. Traces of blood on the glass surface indicate that the platform is a sacrificial altar, which perhaps alludes to the Abraham and Isaac story (Figure 7.1).

The sudden apocalyptic vision-premonition displaces the narrative. The hallucinatory status of the spatio-temporal leap heralds Alexander's persistent failure to distinguish between real entities and their mere images or phantasmal appearances. The notion of *illusion* thus shapes his mental state and governs the general discourse of *Sacrifice*. Illusion, defined as the 'fact or condition of being deceived or deluded by appearances', 'a mental state involving the attribution of reality to what is unreal; a false conception or idea; a deception, delusion, fancy' (*OED*), reveals its multiple semantic facets throughout the film. Alexander is torn between the real and illusionary domains, and his constant oscillations between the two prove to have tragic consequences. The amalgam of appearances and alternative realities reigns supreme in *Sacrifice*.

'In My End is My Beginning'

The illusion–reality confusion manifests itself above all in the prevailing uncertainty over whether the nuclear apocalypse actually takes place in *Sacrifice*. The answer to the question is forever deferred. We are never sure whether the war has happened, or whether it is a product of the protagonist's imagination. The viewer finds contradictory evidence in the film, and the ending delivers no definite resolution. The element that would provide the crucial clarification is always missing. The theological concept of apocalypse, as discussed in the chapter on *Stalker*, is itself deeply paradoxical: it comprises a set of vivid and unreal images which strive to determine reality as such, or rather, its end in the future. Furthermore, the end, which the apocalypse inflicts on the everyday world, is supposed to be the beginning of another, higher reality.

The tragic sense of ending and the promise of beginning interweave in *Sacrifice*, just as reality merges with illusion. The apocalyptic end of the biblical Revelation, which is a clear source of inspiration for Tarkovsky, always holds the promise of renewal. The end is never

Figure 7.1

a definitive finalization or violent rejection, but is – usually – the demolition of an old, obsolete order so that a new one may emerge. The same ambivalence is present in the very idea of sacrifice, which is an act of destruction for the sake of regaining something of a higher order; sacrifice is never a mere rejection (for instance, the slaughter of an animal for its own sake – that is, an elimination of its life) but always a confirmation (such as the surrender to God or a deity).

The end–beginning concurrence manifests itself on many levels of the film. For example, it is conveyed by the most prominent visual intertextual reference – *The Adoration of the Magi* – the image with which the film opens. The reproduction of the painting appears six times in the film and surfaces at the most critical moments of the storyline. For example, the television broadcast announcing the start of the nuclear war is shown while Alexander contemplates the painting. Immediately afterwards, Otto says that he has always been terrified by Leonardo. When Alexander comes down to find out what is happening, he sees his family members and friends sitting silently around a table and staring at the flickering screen of a television set. The audibly distressed voice of the country's leader announces with dramatic pauses the start of the war, in which there will be 'no victors and no vanquished', before crackling interference interrupts his speech and the television screen switches off.

The Adoration of the Magi's dark appearances are intensified by the soundtrack, which is dominated by haunting, melancholic *kulning* and *shakuhachi* (a Japanese end-blown flute which produces a highly meditative and mystifying tone). One of these two types of sound accompanies several of the painting's appearances in the film, and they merge together to form a single, disturbing sound texture when they annunciate the appearance of Leonardo's work in Alexander's dream. However, *kulning* is of particular importance to *Sacrifice*'s apocalyptic discourse because of its function of gathering cattle together: the protagonist is haunted by its calling to some obscure action. At several fateful moments, *kulning* enters the aural landscape and appears to encourage the characters to act. It follows the general pattern of Tarkovsky's work with sound effects: sound in general does not merely accompany images; it is often discontinuous or incongruous with them, and thus produces a disorientating effect. As Andrea Truppin suggests, 'the use of ambiguous sound plunges the audience into a never fully resolved struggle to believe in the diegesis, much as the films' characters struggle with their own ability to have faith'.[3]

The Italian master's unfinished altarpiece, like a discontinuous soundtrack, disorientates the viewer. It depicts the Virgin Mary seated with the Christ child in the centre of the composition, surrounded by a large number of figures whose identity remains unclear (it is uncertain which figure is Joseph, for instance). In the foreground, the three kings who followed the Star of Bethlehem on their journey from the East kneel to pay divine honour to the Christ child. The background shows the ruins of a palace, which emphasizes the building of the new from the ruins of the old, and figures on horseback engaged in violent combat, which may stand for the chaos of the world prior to the coming of Christ.

Martin Kemp highlights the fact that Leonardo has depicted 'the arrival of Christ's physical presence on earth as unsettling at the profoundest level'.[4] Indeed, the painting emerges as a 'dark' theme in the film – Otto, for instance, complains about its power to terrify. The colour scheme of the painting, dominated by dark brown, primarily due to the painting's unfinished nature, also adds to the creation of the disquieting aura. *The Adoration of the Magi* mystifies even further what are already unintelligible character interrelationships – Otto and Alexander seem unnaturally transfixed by this inanimate object. Towards the end of the film the canvas reappears unexpectedly, and without obvious diegetic motivation, in Alexander's disturbing dream where his family members and acquaintances appear in uncanny and unusual guises. Generally, Leonardo's work is the most enigmatic point of reference in the film; it profoundly disturbs and at the same time excites its characters.

One of the causes of anxiety may be the central narrative point of the painting: the offering of one of the kings, which is shown at the very opening of the film. A gift of frankincense – a symbol of the Eucharist – is presented to and willingly received by the Christ child. This gesture becomes a symbolic acceptance of his fate. The very beginning (conveyed in the idea of adoration) alludes to the very end: Christ's passion. Thus the altarpiece represents the celebration of birth which already contains the trace of future lamentation of death.

The opening sequence of the film, in which the painting is explored, is a clear confirmation that the semantic essence of Leonardo's canvas is central to the discourse of *Sacrifice*. The camera concentrates its attention solely on two artefacts depicted in the painting: the frankincense offered by one of the kings, which appears in the very first frame of the film, and the holly tree which concludes the sequence. On its way upwards, the camera passes the Christ child, an anguished old man, two female figures (one of them pointing up towards heaven) and horsemen, before coming to rest at the level of the crown of the tree. The viewer is taken upwards on a slow vertical trip, and is able to examine the most intricate details of the holly from its roots to its top. The whole sequence is a kind of overture to the film, but this introductory sequence already contains the trace of an epilogue.

This amalgamation of temporal segments (the present adoration of Christ and his future passion) is not accidental: indeed, it embodies the essence of Leonardo's vision of painting. Vasili Zubov suggests that '[p]ainting includes various moments simultaneously and does not snatch one moment from the stream of life'.[5] Furthermore, the art historian claims that the aesthetics of 'simultaneity' or of 'at once' are characteristic of Leonardo's paintings: '"simultaneity" [...] is not a moment of existence snatched from the stream of time, but presumes a "before" and an "after"; it presumes time to be a form of comprehension of animate, flowing life'.[6] Thus the fusion of the present and future tenses in *The Adoration of the Magi* is not a matter of individual interpretation, but part of Leonardo's broad aesthetic vision. This ontological ambivalence is of the utmost importance to the film's general aesthetic strategy. *Sacrifice* is permeated by the sense of generational continuity: the relationship between the father (the past and the present) and the son (the future) unfolds against an apocalyptic background – the ultimate end of space and time.

The prominent presence of the tree above the Virgin on the right side is another allusion to the premonition of Christ's passion in the painting. The holly possesses some precise symbolism, for it may allude to the legend that 'Christ's cross was manufactured from that tree – or it may make a more general allusion to Isaiah's famous prophecy as recited at Christmas and Epiphany: "And there shall come forth a rod [*virga*] out of the tree of Jesse and a Branch shall grow out of its roots".'[7] The two possible interpretations can also be blended into the ambivalent birth–death pair. The emerging branch of life is 'counterbalanced' by the cross of death, and both are reunited by the idea of the Christian salvation. Leonardo's tree of life and death, an 'artificial' image explored at the beginning of *Sacrifice*, finds a real counterpart at the end: the dead tree planted on the seashore by Alexander and his son, which clearly has the potential to come back to life.[8]

The predominant theme of the film – the beginning which already encompasses the end – finds its verbal manifestation in the biblical reference, which deals with the myth of the absolute beginning, and is prominently present at the beginning and the end of the film: 'In the beginning was the Word' (John 1: 1). The biblical passages that appeared in earlier films, such as those from Revelation (in *Stalker*) and Ecclesiastes (in *Andrei Rublev*), dealt with the 'negative' notions of finality and vanity. The affirmative and undeviating quotation from John's Gospel, on the other hand, glorifies the idea of creation and delivers the promise of salvation.

The first line of John's Gospel functions as the main semantic gateway to the multiplicity of meanings in the film. The director's diaries provide evidence that the quotation was already present in the very first idea for the plot of *Sacrifice*. As early as 12 February

1979, Tarkovsky writes an entry in his diary which refers to his discussion of the future film with Tonino Guerra:

> A writer, a man of great spiritual depths, prepared for death, an honest, virtuous, solitary man who despises success and the fuss that goes with it, glances one day at the mirror and sees on his face signs of a terrible illness – leprosy. For a year he waits, expecting the stark effects of the disease to manifest themselves at any moment. And at the end of the year he is told by doctors or experts that he has recovered. He returns home, where everything is covered in dust.
>
> There is a pad of mildewed paper and his pencil goes right through it when he tries to write something down. 'Never mind!' he says huskily. 'Never mind!' he repeats aloud to his living reflection in the mirror, as he affirms that he is indeed alive. But he is empty. As empty as a chrysalis from which the butterfly has emerged.
>
> And he realizes that the greatest sin of all is pride. For he had imagined, at one time, that he had attained great spiritual stature, whereas now he is nothing: through his illness the knowledge of death has laid him waste. He opens the Bible and reads:
>
> 'And out of the ground the Lord God formed every beast of the field, and every fowl of the air; and he brought them unto Adam to see what he would call them...'
>
> 'At the beginning was the word,' said the unhappy man.[9]

The traces of *Sacrifice* are easily identifiable in this passage: the 'writer', the 'man of great spiritual depths' becomes the character of Alexander – a distinguished professor of aesthetics, a literary critic, and formerly a successful actor. The passage also echoes one of the intermediate drafts produced under the title *The Witch*.[10] According to these sketches, and to the recently published draft-scenario by the Strugatsky brothers,[11] the protagonist suffers from a fatal illness (cancer). He is told that he can be cured by a certain witch if he lies with her. Eventually, the man leaves his beloved family home and abandons everything he cherishes for the sake of being reunited with the witch. All of these plot elements confirm that the 1979 entry evolved into the film *Sacrifice*, finished in 1986, and that from the beginning the opening sentence of John's Gospel haunted the director's vision of the film.

The line from the New Testament appears in the very first scene with Alexander, Little Man and Otto.[12] When the postman departs, his bicycle is caught in a lasso which the boy has tied to a bush. Otto throws the rope back to the boy after making a grotesque and exaggeratedly frightening gesture. Little Man picks it up and hurries to his father while mumbling something incomprehensible, to which Alexander says: 'What are you mumbling about? "In the beginning was the Word." But you are mute, mute as a fish.' The father emphasizes the son's inability to utter a single word, let alone a meaningful and creative Word.

In the film, *silence* – the antonym of *speech* – serves as an intermediary stage between an excess of words and necessary action. The John 1: 1 reference is embedded in various remarks on silence: apart from Little Man's manifest muteness and Alexander's reference to the boy's inability to speak, there is a brief discussion of speech and silence. When Victor – a family friend and the doctor who operated on the child – enters the scene, the first question he asks Little Man is about his muteness: 'Isn't it hard to keep silent? But it is good for you. Sociability is a burden. Not all of us can bear it.'[13] Victor develops this idea, and this time asks Alexander: 'Did you know that Gandhi had one day in the week when he spoke to no one? It was his system...He was probably tired of people.' Finally, in his desperate sacrificial act later in the film, Alexander confines himself to a silent existence, and this decision is accompanied by the renunciation of his son and the rest of the family.

Alexander follows a conventional pattern of the sacrificial act as in essence an economic transaction: after the (imaginary) start of the nuclear war, he pleads with God to return everything to how it was before the disaster and promises that, if this request is fulfilled, he will sacrifice everything precious he possesses – his reason, his family and the familial home: 'I will give Thee all I have.' More importantly, Alexander promises to abandon words altogether: 'I'll be mute and will never speak another word to anyone. I will relinquish everything that binds me to life...' Thus, he seeks a reunion with the divine life-generating Word by means of sacrificing the human capacity to speak – that is, to produce words.

The literary allusion which follows John 1: 1 reconfirms the thesis that Tarkovsky relies heavily on the discourse inspired by the binary pair of the spoken, creative word and the written, mundane word. Hamlet's '[w]ords, words, words'[14] is one of the most famous references to the word as a profane and disingenuous means of communication.[15] When asked by Polonius what he reads, Hamlet refers not to an *abstract* word but to a *written* (printed) word, which in the given case appears to be a manifestation of intellectual debasement. The inscribed words that Hamlet's eyes contemplate do not possess the divine, creative potential of the Word at the beginning according to John. These words, in their multiplicity, dissent from the singularity of the primordial Word of the New Testament.

Hamlet's introspective reasoning, which finds its culmination in the 'To be or not to be' soliloquy, leads to the conclusion that all actions are doomed to end in vanity. Thus his indecision reigns throughout the play. Shakespeare's character drowns himself in words and postpones the accomplishment of the required action. Whether as a negative or positive sign, his procrastination results in a series of very sophisticated comments on the function of words and on language in general. His '[w]ords, words, words', written or printed abundant words, form some deviant form of silence; they fail to signify anything meaningful.

Alexander in *Sacrifice* resolves his spiritual dilemma in the opposite way. Unlike Hamlet, he confines himself to silence and acts immediately when the situation 'requires' him to do so. Action is a means for Alexander to get closer to the primordial Word of the beginning. His first words after he learns about the start of the nuclear war reveal his determination: 'I've waited for this all my life. My whole life has been one long wait for this!' These words echo Otto's remark at the beginning of the film: 'We all are...waiting for something.' Though they show a certain degree of determination, Alexander's 'wait for *this*' and Otto's 'waiting for *something*' are utterly vague statements. What do the characters mean by the demonstrative pronoun 'this' and by the unspecified and indeterminate 'something'?[16]

'This'

While desperately trying to be reunited with the primordial presence (the divine, creative Word), Alexander is unable to differentiate between reality and illusion, or, more generally, presence and absence. The overall narrative uncertainty manifests itself in a number of inexplicable occurrences scattered throughout the film. For instance, several strange comments are made, and minor but unsettling events take place, just before the characters become aware of the nuclear catastrophe. Fighter jets fly over the island where Alexander and his family live, and they create havoc inside the house: glasses start trembling, a jug of milk falls and breaks, Julia and Marta start running in a rather theatrical manner from one window to another. At this disconcerting moment the camera finds Alexander outside the house – in the open space of the island of Gotland. The scene is shot with a grey-blue filter, a notable change from the warm colours of the interior. The protagonist discovers an artefact that appears to disturb him profoundly: an exact small-scale model of the house, which even replicates the original's position in space.

Claude Lévi-Strauss suggests that the miniature is 'the universal type of the work of art'.[17] Reduction of scale is a process of aestheticization per se; graphic or plastic transposition requires deformations of certain dimensions of the object. Moreover, the 'quantitative transposition extends and diversifies our power over a homologue of the thing, and by means of it the latter can be grasped, assessed and apprehended at a glance'.[18] But the miniature house in *Sacrifice* performs the opposite function – instead of delivering a positive cognitive-aesthetic effect, it utterly confuses the character. Its appearance resonates with Bachelard's suggestion that '[v]alues become engulfed in miniature, and miniature causes men to dream'.[19] The temporal point when Alexander encounters the miniature replica of the house is extremely significant, since from that point on the distinction between reality and illusion is blurred. It may even be suggested that this is the moment at which the protagonist starts to dream.

Alexander carefully observes the model, raises his head, and pronounces in an affected manner the following line from the fourth scene of the third act of *Macbeth* in the original English: 'Which of you have done this... the Lords?'[20] The small replica of his soon-to-be-sacrificed house utterly bewilders Alexander, and he is unable to decide whether this is a real object or a mere apparition. The quotation thus functions as a significant threshold, the division between the real and unreal domains in *Sacrifice*. What is remarkable about this literary allusion is a mistake the director (who also wrote the script for the film) appears to make by including a reference to 'The Lords' from the stage directions in the dialogue itself, turning it into a direct address: 'Which of you have done this, *the Lords*?' The quoted line comes from Macbeth's question upon the appearance of the ghost of Banquo, which takes the usurper's place at the feast table. 'The Lords' does not belong to the text of the play as such – it merely identifies the next speakers (the Lords) who in turn reply to Macbeth: 'What, my good lord?' The inscription 'The Lords' in Shakespeare's text belongs exclusively to the realm of the written text. It comprises a stage direction which is never uttered or heard when the play is performed. The written presence of 'The Lords' should find its natural fulfilment in its absence in the speech.

The central issue the quoted passage raises, if one is to ignore the unfortunate 'The Lords' slip, is: what does Macbeth mean by 'this' in his question and, by extension, what does Alexander mean by 'this', and by quoting the line from *Macbeth*? A Shakespeare commentator suggests two possible explanations for the passage in the play: 'Macbeth may assume a practical joke (someone is pretending to be Banquo), or he may ask who has made Banquo a ghost.'[21] Neither of these reasons seems to be persuasive, and the quintessence of the 'this' remains obscure. 'This' is an indefinable and mysterious referent which is surrounded by uncanny, unexpected appearances (the ghost of Banquo in *Macbeth*, and in a similar fashion the model-house in *Sacrifice*) and the protagonists' horror-struck reactions to them.

Alexander appears to make use of Shakespeare's play precisely as a reservoir of the uncanny elements that have started entering his own life, while *Macbeth* is preoccupied with supernatural phenomena: ghosts and witches are active agents that dramatically influence the course of the narrative. The quoted line, which is one of the most frightening moments of the drama, brings into the film the awe and disturbance of the character of Macbeth. Alexander claims a certain kinship with the intractable warrior and victim of fate: he encounters the replica of his own house, which is soon to be destroyed and sacrificed. The fact that fighter jets have started to fly over the island just prior to this episode provides a loose narrative connection between the coming nuclear apocalypse and the house – a symbol of the familial happiness and the future offering which will redeem the catastrophe.

The impossibility of providing an answer to the question of whether Shakespeare meant the ghost to be real or a mere hallucination encourages one to conclude that the play does not provide a clear-cut distinction between the two poles. Imagination, whether intensified by real phenomena or by a disturbed mind, becomes a predominant motif of the play, which is referred to by Harold Bloom as 'a tragedy of the imagination'.[22] The film's central theme – the co-existence of end and beginning – is intensified by a representational ambiguity between reality and illusion in the filmic narrative. The principal question of whether the nuclear war and subsequent visit to the 'witch' took place or not cannot be resolved in definite terms. The semantic vagueness of the referent 'this' belongs to the same domain of uncertainty.

The nuclear apocalypse – the final crisis – is interpreted by Alexander as a time to act. It becomes the most significant diegetic point of the film, and motivates the occurrence of the actual sacrifice. However, for the viewer its presence/absence develops into a narrative anxiety – the inability to separate dream from reality or the actual from a fantasy of the protagonist's disturbed mind. The 'real' linear succession of events becomes impossible to reinstate.[23] Both Macbeth and Alexander appear to be on the verge of madness, or have already entered the domain of insanity – their dreams and visionary hallucinations fuelled by real events lead them to their respective catastrophes. Their failure to distinguish reality from fantasy is absolutely central to the plots of both *Macbeth* and *Sacrifice*. It is no coincidence that the role of sleep is extremely prominent and ambiguously presented in the two stories.

After Alexander concludes his pact with God – 'I will give Thee all I have. I'll give up my family, whom I love. I'll destroy my home and give up Little Man. I'll be mute and never speak another word to anyone. […] If only Thou dost restore everything as it was before … as it was this morning and yesterday' – he crawls on all fours to a sofa and lies down in a completely devastated state. A herding call accompanies a disturbing dream. After Alexander wakes up, the sofa, to the attentive viewer's surprise, is transformed – it is now covered with a white sheet, and there is a white pillow on it. Alexander, who does not know how long he has slept, does not notice that the sofa has undergone a transformation. A lapse in time manifests itself by spatial means: the white sheet and the pillow on the sofa stand for a temporal slip. The protagonist of *Sacrifice* deals with the apocalyptic end of conventional space and time by displacing himself in a spatio-temporal sense.

The phenomenon of temporal confusion also lies at the heart of *Macbeth*'s opening, with the three 'weird' sisters. For Frank Kermode, Banquo and Macbeth's encounter with the three old women 'is a figure for the seemingly atemporal agony of a moment when times cross; when our usual apprehension of successive past and future is translated into another order of time'.[24] Macbeth experiences out-of-joint time when he wanders onto a heath – an uncanny topos. While Shakespeare's character faces the supernatural in the guise of the three witches and of Banquo's ghost, Alexander encounters the model-house as a bizarre phenomenon, almost as a spectral apparition; but its nature is immediately clarified and relieved of any mysticism: the miniature house turns out to be a gift from his son made by the boy and Otto. However, it is extremely significant that the person who supplies the clarification and whom Alexander meets outside is Maria – a local 'witch', according to Otto, who is himself a collector of mysterious phenomena, which by their nature place pressure on the human understanding of reality.[25]

The character of Maria corresponds to the stereotypes which fuelled witch-hunts across Europe. Poverty and isolation were common signs used to identify a woman as a witch. Old women without familial or communal support were typical 'witches'. Maria, who is profoundly other because of her Icelandic origins, unmarried status and humble mode of existence (she lives in a semi-demolished building outside the village centre), makes for a perfect 'witch'. The dark nuclear tragedy is explicitly connected with the 'demonic' figure of Maria in the filmic narrative, and a loose connection between the two is suggested. The episode of the coming apocalypse manifested in the fighter jets is surrounded by scenes featuring the 'witch'. The sound of trembling glass that betokens the jets enters the soundtrack of the film before the actual indoor scene is shown. The sound enters the soundtrack while the viewer is presented with the image of Maria walking in the direction of the house. The beginning of the end commences while the lone woman is present on the screen: the 'witch' is the herald of the nuclear apocalypse, and at the same time its future redeemer. Her ambivalent nature is in keeping with the self-contradictory essence of the film, formed of divergences and digressions.

Alexander's decisive contact with Maria, which in his and Otto's mind saves the world from the nuclear disaster, is sexual. He lies with Maria (both are shown levitating), and the nature of his relationship with her conforms to prevailing stereotypes of witchcraft. The Dominican authors of the most famous witchcraft manual, the notorious *Malleus maleficarum* (1487), claimed that 'witchcraft is spread, and its power augmented, through the venereal act'.[26] They regarded sexual intercourse as the fundamental source of evil. Tarkovsky, however, reverses the function of sexual intercourse with a witch; his protagonist does not multiply evil but, on the contrary, 'saves the world'.[27] In the same manner in which the frail distinction between reality and dream is enacted in the film, the role of the witch in *Sacrifice* is thoroughly ambiguous. A traditional companion of evil forces becomes the saviour of the world.

The film's discursive ambivalences – the illusion–reality confluence, the beginning which already encloses the end, and the dark forces of witchcraft that 'save' the world – have a visual counterpart. *Sacrifice* is permeated with various images of semi-reflective glass surfaces, which allow the viewer to observe two planes simultaneously: one behind the glass and another reflected by it. The platform with the traces of blood superimposed on the pavement and the sky, which appears during Alexander's first apocalyptic vision; the protective glass covering the reproduction of Leonardo's *The Adoration of the Magi*, which constantly reflects the interior and outside trees;

and the window panes in Alexander's upstairs room through which he talks to Otto – all superimpose two visual planes (Figure 7.2). They all destroy the singularity of reality. The dual function of glass, both to transmit light and to reflect it, is vigorously employed by the director. The mystifying amalgam of the half-reflections can be read as a visual metaphor for Alexander's inability to distinguish reality from illusion. It is not possible to discern individual planes; instead one has to deal with the confluence of images and, by extension, realities.

Spectral Apocalypse
Sacrifice, as we learn from Tarkovsky's notes, was structurally conceived as early as 5 September 1982. The film-maker divides the film into six distinct parts in his diary:

1. *Stroll.*
2. *Declaration of war.*
3. *Prayer.* Vow. Conversation with God (Monologue).
4. *The world again.*
5. *Fire.* (He burns his house down.)
6. *In hospital.* (Have I gone insane or not?) The war has been declared, hasn't it?[28]

From the very beginning, Tarkovsky intended the ordering of events in *Sacrifice* to be ambivalent, and the narrative relied on incompatible diegetic elements. In fact, this ambivalence lies at the core of the film – the end culminates in the protagonist's uncertainty over whether the war has been declared or not. Actuality and hallucination merge into a single narrative line. Although one can claim that there is a differentiating colour code (black and white for dream and colour for reality), in the film as made, the sound code does not follow this pattern. Herding calls, which accompany two explicitly dream-like sequences with rapidly alternating scenes with different characters, constantly infiltrate ordinary reality; Otto and Alexander repeatedly hear them while engaged in everyday activities. Moreover, abnormal spatial manifestations such as the miniature model of the house or the implausibly transformed sofa signify that reality is not always what it seems to be; Alexander dwells in a space of indeterminacy.

Tarkovsky employs a rather conventional dream trope to undermine the homogenous linear progression of space and time. Dream, which functions as a core structural element in *Ivan's Childhood* and is prominently counterpoised with reality, reaches a qualitatively

Figure 7.2

different plane in *Sacrifice*: the ephemeral dream is not countered with supposedly stable reality, for the latter is no less ephemeral. The diegetic reality of the director's final film undergoes a substantial deformation, as compared with his preceding projects: its narrative resists a straightforward split between the illusion–reality binary pair, and instead comprises a multiplicity of narrative threads.

The first apparently oneiric sequence enters the film's narrative when Alexander goes to bed after learning about the start of the nuclear war and praying earnestly to God to deliver salvation. The entry into the domain of dreams is immediately signified by a haunting and reverberating herding call. The protagonist dreams of his (step)daughter undressing in Little Man's room and calling out to

Victor. The young woman goes into the corner, and a large mirror on the opposite side of the room catches her reflection. The camera cuts from the soothing interior in warm colours to a corridor, probably in the same house, shot in black and white. The interior is transfigured this time: the house is shown in a decrepit state, with a leaking roof and small puddles all over the floor. Alexander, who is standing down the corridor, turns and runs away.

The next sequence finds the protagonist inside the dark ground-floor room of a different house with a window missing its pane of glass. The house and the surrounding area are also found in a devastated state – presumably following the nuclear catastrophe. Alexander sits in the middle of the room and looks outside. The camera follows his gaze and tracks outside to reveal his double walking on the dirty snow; the continuous movement of the camera once again undermines the character's singularity. The man bends down and pulls a wire attached to some kind of material out of the snow and dirt. A few seconds later, a panning shot with almost imperceptible slow motion finds him surrounded by trees and buildings in a deserted area.

A purely visual rendering of the apocalyptic motif in the form of self-quotation enters the film at this point. The tracking shot approaching a devastated house in *Sacrifice* emulates the famous pool sequence from *Stalker*. Both sequences unsettle the viewer and reveal places of human habitation in a devastated condition. The various 'defeated' objects lying in the shallow pool in *Stalker*, and the bowl with coins and pieces of material covered in dirt and snow in *Sacrifice*, are scrutinized by the moving camera, which is positioned almost perpendicularly to the observed surface. The meditative movement of the camera in Tarkovsky's final film, however, is disrupted by the sudden appearance of Little Man's feet – the boy stands barefoot on the snow-covered ground. Alexander calls his name, but the boy runs away. A strong wind suddenly starts 'sweeping' snow and frost across the ground. The camera slowly raises its lens to register swinging doors attached to a walled-up entrance, so that the logic of the structure's entrances and exits is unclear. The image of the walled-up entrance is accompanied by the sound of flying fighter jets. The spectral fantasy ends with Alexander waking up, and is followed by an encounter with Otto, who tells him about the possibility of saving the world by lying with Maria.

Cycling to visit Maria, Alexander falls into a puddle, hears a herding call, and decides to go back home. After a moment of indecision he turns back and sets out on the road again. At this moment the camera tracks aside to reveal an abandoned car with an open door, from which a white sheet spills. This unexpected and bizarre apparition is a phenomenon that blurs the reality–illusion border. Does it have something to do with the transformation of the sofa, when the pillow and the 'same' white sheet appear all of a sudden after Alexander's dream? Can this white sheet, upon whose whiteness anything can be projected, be the ultimate 'site' of indeterminacy of the film? While the camera's sideways tracking movement draws the viewer's attention to it, Alexander completely ignores the sheet. He continues his journey, and soon approaches an old, ramshackle building and enters Maria's domain. The woman, bewildered by such a late and unexpected visit, lets him in and washes his dirty hands. It is notable that the jug and the basin Maria is using are almost identical to those used by Chris's mother during the former's hallucinatory visit to Earth in *Solaris*.

This self-quotation is followed by a parable-like story in which time plays a crucial role. Alexander tells Maria a story about his mother's neglected and overgrown garden. The protagonist decides to clean it up, and works there for two weeks cutting grass, uprooting weeds and pruning trees. The result is quite unexpected: the interference with the natural flow of time spoils the natural beauty of the garden. Alexander disrupts the passage of time and, as a consequence, witnesses an ugly sight. A clock chimes and interrupts the story; the man gets up and says that they 'won't have *time*'. The fear of nuclear apocalypse – the ultimate end of conventional space and time – makes the protagonist act. After threatening to commit suicide, he attracts Maria's attention and rouses pity in her. Fighter jets start flying over the island again, causing the glass to tremble: the couple make love and hover in the air. Alexander starts crying, and a herding call mixes with another haunting 'call' – the sound of *shakuhachi*; the two impose themselves on the soundtrack.

After the sexual union with the 'witch', Alexander experiences his second apocalyptic dream-vision. A tracking shot explores a devastated narrow city street – the same street that appears at the beginning of the film, but which is now filled with chaotically running people. The camera again captures the glass platform superimposing two levels, but this time it tracks further down to reveal Little Man, wrapped in burned fabric, lying down with blood flowing from his head. At this point a sound – Adelaide's voice consoling Alexander and making him drink something – enters the soundtrack. This is followed by an image of Maria dressed as Adelaide, a close-up of *The Adoration of the Magi*, and a sequence depicting the naked Julia chasing chickens inside a house. The dream ends with a plain tracking shot of a half-lit Adelaide moving in slow motion towards Alexander's room. The phantasmatic wife approaches the lace curtain near the entrance, and stops there while the camera continues tracking aside. Dream literally enters reality, since the continuous movement of the camera emerges from the oneiric corridor and enters the room, which is found in its normal state with normal lighting, and is shown at a normal speed of projection (Figure 7.3). The spectral effects fade away; only the sound of *shakuhachi* remains, though its presence is later revealed to be diegetically motivated, for it has been coming from a stereo inside the room.

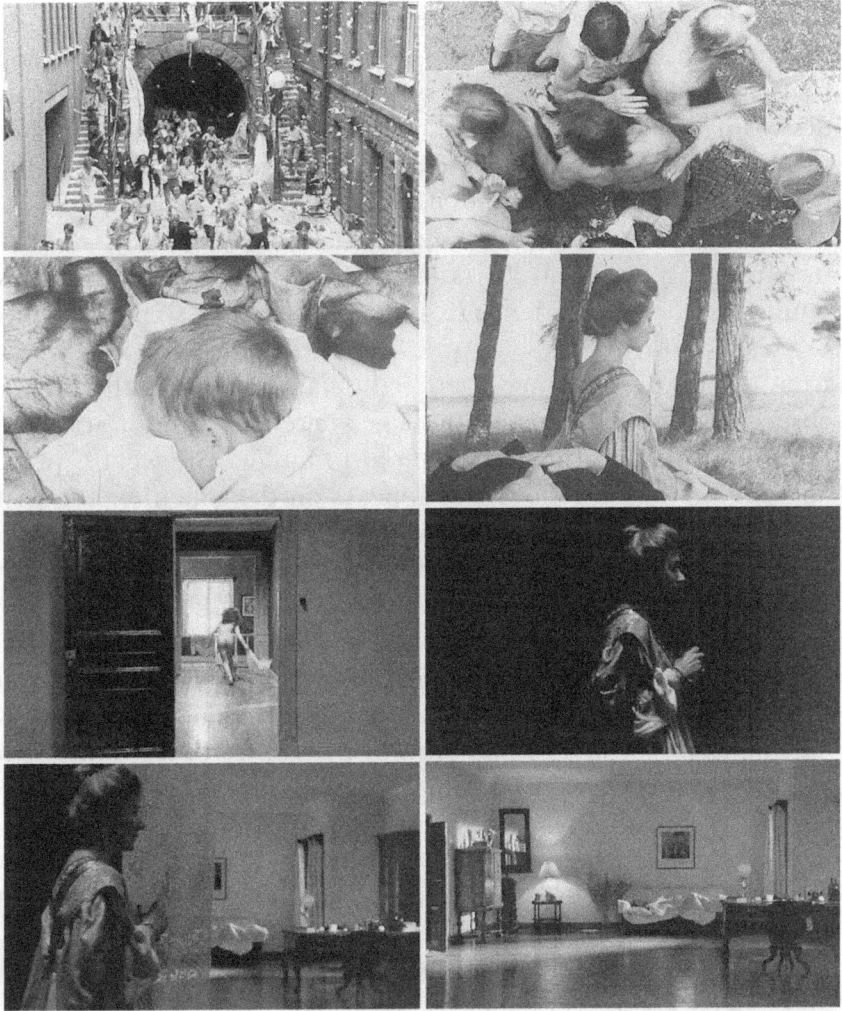

Figure 7.3

The protagonist wakes up underneath a blanket on the sofa with a white pillow and sheet in a beautifully and calmly lit room. He calls his mother, and then gets up in a visibly alarmed state. The film's narrative does not provide any clues as to how Alexander has returned here from Maria's house. Everything seems to be normal, as if there had been no nuclear disaster. The rest of the family enjoy breakfast outside. There is electricity in the house and the phone is working. The awakening thus fails to draw a clear line between reality and illusion. The question of whether or not Alexander dreamt the war announcement, the subsequent meeting with Otto and the visit to Maria cannot be resolved definitively.[29] However, the main character is sure of one thing: now is his time to act.

The climax of the film is the sacrificial act performed by Alexander. The protagonist enters the realm of nonexistence; he renounces his beloved son and the rest of the family by confining himself to silence, and dispossesses his familial home by physically destroying it. The former professor of aesthetics and a searcher after truth seems to follow Martin Heidegger's suggestion that one of the ways in which truth establishes itself lies in 'the essential sacrifice'.[30]

Alexander meticulously prepares the house for sacrificial fire by arranging a pile of chairs on a terrace, after persuading his family members and friends to go for a walk. He also puts Victor's briefcase in his friend's car and then moves the vehicle far away from the house; this small, rational detail underlines the overall absurdity of Alexander's action. The viewer may find it arresting that the protagonist uses as material to build a fire what is probably the same white sheet that appears on the sofa after the first dream-hallucination, and then in the abandoned car on his way to visit Maria. Alexander goes upstairs after the house is set on fire to turn the *shakuhachi* music on, and leaves the building by a ladder attached to the second floor. The latter fact is significant since the ladder, as an extraneous addition, also undermines the structural integrity of the soon-to-be-demolished edifice, and it is used several times by Alexander and Otto in the course of the film when they devise their 'plot' for saving the world.

The next cut finds Alexander outside, walking through puddles and watching the house in flames. This scene is the ultimate confluence of the four natural elements: the openness of the island of Gotland (air), the burning house (fire), and the surrounding muddy landscape punctuated with puddles of different sizes (earth and water). The hero surrenders completely to the divine or hallucinatory plane, and abandons the conventional place and time. His house is burned and his mind is lost. Alexander is soon joined by his distressed family members, the housemaid Julia, and Victor, who orders everyone: 'Ask nothing, say nothing'. Suddenly, a telephone rings and Alexander, limping, starts moving towards the house as if enchanted by the call. However, he digresses when he sees Maria, who suddenly appears in the scene. The man scurries to-and-fro between the 'witch' (illusion) and his family (reality). This launches a rather theatrical and pathetic sequence in which the characters run back and forth. Otto, and an ambulance, which arrives on the scene unrealistically quickly, join the others in this silly game of tag.

The finale, both tragic and absurd, invites numerous interpretations. Žižek, for instance, wonders whether there is a distance between Tarkovsky's ideological project 'of sustaining meaning, of generating new spirituality, through an act of meaningless sacrifice'[31] and his actual aesthetic vision. He suggests that one may interpret 'the Tarkovskian sacrificial gesture as a very elementary ideological operation, as a desperate strategy of beating the meaninglessness of existence by its own means, i.e. of engendering meaning – of overcoming the unbearable Otherness of meaningless cosmic contingency – through a gesture that is itself utterly meaningless.'[32] The final scene of the film 'ends with a comic ballet of men from the infirmary running after the hero to take him to the asylum – [it] is shot as a children's game',[33] and this ending emphasizes the apparent absurdity and theatricality of the situation.

However, the absurd resolution is preceded by a narrative crisis: various contradictory clues are scattered throughout the film. Thus the absurd gesture leads the character into a realm devoid of the truth–lie or illusion–reality binarism. *Sacrifice* challenges the representational order of everyday experience. Ambiguity finds its culmination in this final gesture, which is also the end of the film. Has Alexander lost his reason? Has he saved the world? Did the nuclear apocalypse take place in reality? These questions will remain open. Moreover, Alexander's 'meaningless' sacrifice is immediately followed by one of the most affirmative literary quotations – John's 'In the beginning was the Word' – and the final scene in general comprises an affirmative message per se: the son fulfilling his father's testament.

After the collapse of the house, which 'represents a time out of joint, a potential future which has been consigned back to the past, now no longer imaginable or speakable',[34] the camera cuts to Little Man carrying two buckets full of water towards the dead tree he and his father had planted the previous day. Alexander, however,

Figure 7.4

experiences temporal confusion, for in the note he leaves to his family members he does not remember when they planted the tree. A herding call again dominates the aural landscape of the film, and for the first time the viewer sees its possible source: there is a flock of cows with a shepherd nearby. Maria rides up on a bicycle, and an ambulance enters the scene. The boy and the woman see off a passing car. When the latter cycles away, Little Man waters the tree, and Bach's 'Erbarme Dich', which opened the film, re-enters the soundtrack.

The 'beginning of the end' theme unambiguously manifests itself at both the beginning and the end of *Sacrifice*, not only by means of the aria but also through the trope of the life–death tree.

The episode that follows the *Adoration of the Magi* overture shows Alexander 'planting' a withered tree – the phenomenological equivalent of Leonardo's painted holly. The same withered tree dominates the film's final sequence – this time Alexander's son lies under its 'shade' after carrying out his father's instruction to water its 'roots'. The boy pronounces: '"In the beginning was the Word." Why is that, Papa?' The creative Word, which has been inaccessible to Little Man owing to his muteness, now becomes a matter of interest to him. He voices his question-concern, thus imitating the enacting nature of the Word of John's Gospel.

The camera goes on a vertical journey, as it did at the beginning; it stops at the level of the tree's crown, and the image dissolves into the director's inscription-dedication: 'This film is dedicated to my son Andriusha – with hope and confidence.' The movement clearly echoes the very opening of the film, in which Leonardo's canvas is explored (Figure 7.4). The two trees – the Italian master's holly and Alexander's withered tree – are explicitly symbolic and artificial entities. The dead state of the latter and the highly representative presence of the former (the holly stands prominently on a rock, and this creates the illusion that the tree is hovering in the air) underline their fabricated essence. This symbolic vagueness culminates in the fact that the two trees contain both the trace of death and the promise of hope. The concluding sequence of *Sacrifice* encloses the two. Moreover, the finale of Tarkovsky's last film alludes to the beginning of the director's first feature, *Ivan's Childhood*, which opens with Ivan looking through a spider's web attached to tree branches. The camera explores a conifer tree as it moves upwards after the boy leaves the frame, and the camera in *Sacrifice* emulates this very movement. The first shot of *Ivan's Childhood* depicts Ivan (Tarkovsky's peer during the Second World War) entering the cinematic space, while the last sequence of *Sacrifice* shows Alexander (approximately the same age as Tarkovsky in 1986) exiting the same cinematic space in an ambulance. Finally, the end meets the beginning.

* * *

The concluding episode of *Sacrifice* entered the realm of legend as early as the production stage. Equipment failure meant that camera operator Sven Nyqvist and the director could not capture the scene in one continuous take. The ending of the film was aborted and deprived of its finalizing function: it had to be restaged. This unfortunate accident can be taken as a metaphor for Tarkovsky's grand cinematic project as a whole. The artistic material, in the case of *Sacrifice*, refutes the director's philosophic stance and ambition; the singular, finalizing nature of the ending is shattered, and everything has to start all over again. In the same manner, the seemingly monologic statement-affirmations, such as 'In the beginning was the Word', are undone by the inherently ambiguous visual material and by problematizing narrative ploys. The film evolves into a struggle between the discourse it fiercely pursues and the aesthetic strategies it employs.

POSTSCRIPT

The director's last film represents a man's desperate attempt to reach a certain spiritual absolute – a singular otherworldly truth. The protagonist of *Sacrifice* attempts to undermine everyday reality, symbolized by the house, and tries to attain a divine totality. Tarkovsky insisted that the final scene had to be shot in one take, continuously depicting a delimited space in a single stretch of time. As a result of this almost desperate striving towards a spatio-temporal unity, the scene had to be re-shot. In the final cut, there is no freedom of montage – that is, there is no interposition of alternative spaces and times, only the tracking movement of the camera. However, this unity contains within it a grotesque and incongruous action: the hero's act of sacrifice. The absolute meets the absurd. Further ambiguity is introduced when the ambulance carrying the protagonist drives off in an unknown direction. Alexander, who loses his sense of reality, is taken away, and the car's destination and his destiny are unknown.

The journeys of Ivan, Chris and Gorchakov end in a similar manner, on the borderline between reality and illusion, happiness and grief, life and death. Ivan's posthumous hide-and-seek, Chris's and Gorchakov's hallucinatory returns to their homes: all transcend the normality of the everyday. The finales of *Mirror* and *Stalker* – the intersecting paths of the old and young Mothers in the buckwheat field and Monkey's telekinetic performance – are no less unearthly and enigmatic. The only affirmative ending in Tarkovsky's oeuvre is that of *Andrei Rublev*: the unambiguous divine presence of the *Zvenigorod Saviour* (not its image, for icons do not represent but present a deity) concludes the film. Though it is not certain whose point of view the tracking camera represents, Christ's presence is direct and almost overbearing. Is it a coincidence that the sole unambiguous finale in Tarkovsky's oeuvre is permeated by an authoritative and singular religious message?

Hallucinatory visions are found side by side with rigid theological patterns in all of the director's seven feature films. Their protagonists – Ivan, Rublev, Chris, the narrator of *Mirror*, Stalker, Gorchakov and Alexander – are lost in spatio-temporal labyrinths comprising bewilderingly complex sets of connecting passages and pathways. It seems that there are no guides in these vagrant quests. But every labyrinth still has an unambiguous route to the centre, and all wanderings, however disorientating they are, ultimately lead to it. The phenomenon of the labyrinth in this sense resonates with Tarkovsky's aesthetics, which at once present a non-linear set of spatio-temporal relationships and try to deliver a singular, almost intolerant, spiritual message. Unlike Nietzsche's 'labyrinthine man' who 'never seeks the truth but always only his Ariadne',[1] Tarkovsky's protagonists seek always and only the truth. The lapses in space and time that they repeatedly experience lead towards the creation of some sort of spiritual totality.

However, this totality still has strong oneiric qualities. Not a single character in Tarkovsky's cinema comes to terms with reality in its ultimate and finalized glory. Dogmatism leads only to the hallucinatory domain. The term *image*, a central concept for the director's theoretical framework, has a contradictory etymology, reflecting the inherent tension of Tarkovsky's cinematic project. Image is associated with an act of imitation of reality – that is, moving towards reality ('artificial imitation or representation', *OED*) and at the same time it stands for a process of moving away from reality ('illusory apparition, phantom, hallucination, representation to the imagination', *OED*). Cinema, as a flow of images, intensifies this ambivalent quality. 'Stray cats' – the poem by the Russian-born American poet Alexei Tsvetkov – beautifully depicts the process of the transformation of real time into something more dreamlike:

> time moves in its mysterious ways beneath
> thick summer tree-crowns the oppressive heat
> has liquified its strands which now appear
> to be coalescing from all sides towards
> some hidden basin steamy in the heart
> of the impenetrable clotted woods
> the cauldron of vile dreams[2]

The current of time manifests itself through space, 'beneath thick summer tree-crowns', and splits in 'liquified' strands, which strive towards a singular yet hallucinatory 'hidden basin' – 'the cauldron of vile dreams'. In a similar manner, Tarkovsky's films reject the standard temporal topology. His cinematic time is not a single, straight, non-branching, continuous line that extends without end in each of its two directions; on the contrary, its path is forking and full of lapses and digressions, which usually manifest themselves through spatial abnormalities. These labyrinthine movements, deriving from dreams, visions, phantasies, memories, revelations, recollections and illusions, lead to nothing but unreal reality.

The same paradox is at work in the phenomenon of the continuous long take, set in opposition to the films' spatio-temporal discontinuity. The director's non-linear cinematic aesthetics cannot be defined as a succession of points and instants. On the contrary, the confusing co-existence of diverse spatio-temporal frameworks is their characteristic feature. At the same time, the long take, the most distinctive Tarkovskian device, stands for anything but a spatio-temporal discontinuity. The tracking movement of the camera in a typical long take presents a singular space with no temporal disruptions; it allows the viewer to experience an elongated dwelling in time. The incessant temporal passage is enveloped by a continuous stretch of space. Thus Tarkovsky's cinema is a cinema of contrasts: the long take manifests a spatio-temporal unity – prolonged dwelling in a single space and time – and it is contrasted with persistent leaps and irrational cuts to other spatio-temporal frameworks.

However, even the homogenous space and time of the Tarkovskian long take is infiltrated from time to time by ghostly apparitions, which undermine the seeming totality. The doubling of characters, which violates the comforting notion of human singularity and occurs in all of the director's films, is usually accomplished by means of the tracking movement of the camera. The uninterrupted continuous movement reveals an incongruous co-existence of a character and his or her tangible double. The phenomenon of character-doubling or bilocation also disrupts the narrative flow and creates identity confusion. A homogenous, stretched space is invaded by heterogeneous spectral apparitions: spatial disorientation reigns supreme.

Tarkovsky's Janus-faced aesthetic project (the continuous long take as against the general spatio-temporal discontinuity) resonates with the ontological status of cinema as a ghostly phenomenon – an incorporeal vision of life. Cinema is a visionary practice, and the cinematic image is a perfect illusion of a four-dimensional continuum. Even the most conventional of film-related places – Hollywood – is known as a 'dream factory'. The ability to transform rigid and palpable space into an amorphous and dream-like visual sequence on a rectangular screen is an essential feature of cinematic representation. The oneiric medium of cinema turns reality into an immaterial shadow. Maxim Gorky's account of watching the Lumière brothers' *The Arrival of a Train* at the Nizhny Novgorod Fair in July 1896 highlights the novel attraction's ambivalent nature. The Russian writer describes watching the film as a trip to 'the kingdom of the shadows'.[3] The world he sees is deprived of vividness and vitality – it is a mere phantom of life:

> There are no sounds, no colours. There, everything – the earth, the trees, the people, the water, the air – is tinted in a grey monotone: in a grey sky there are grey rays of sunlight; in grey faces, grey eyes, and the leaves of the trees are grey like ashes. This is not life but the shadow of life and this is not movement but the soundless shadow of movement.[4]

The world's *greyness*, in Gorky's account, soon develops into something more ominous: 'It is terrifying to watch but it is the movement of shadows, mere shadows. Curses and ghosts, evil spirits that have cast whole cities into eternal sleep come to mind and you feel as though Merlin's vicious trick is being played out before you.'[5] The tone of the descriptive narrative dramatically changes once the notion of reality, with its stable rigidity and consoling palpability, is undermined. The phenomenon of the ghost is a perturbing semblance of something which was at some point real and palpable – it is the apparition of a person or thing from another temporal framework. Jacques Derrida, almost a century after Gorky, reiterates the argument in Ken McMullen's film *Ghost Dance* (1983): 'the cinema is the art of ghosts, a battle of phantoms [or] the art of allowing ghosts to come back'. The forebear of Socialist Realism and the founding father of poststructuralism – two markedly different modes of aesthetic perception – uncannily arrive at the same conclusion.

This seemingly uncomplicated and straightforward transformation of stable reality into ghostly, unreal manifestations has significant ontological implications. Jean Epstein suggests that in cinema 'there is no movement, no flux, no life in the mosaics of light and shadow which the screen always presents as fixed'.[6] The celluloid strip that is projected on the screen is made up of separate stills – frozen photographic impressions. The illusion of continuity takes place neither in the camera nor by means of the projector, but in the viewer's mind, where 'there is an impression which, like all other sensory data, is an interpretation of the object, that is, an illusion, a phantom'.⁷ The human perception animates the film footage; a cinematic image comes to life in a virtual mental space. This transformation echoes the general process of modelling the world, for everyday reality, as perceived by an individual human consciousness, is also illusionary.

In general terms, the reality of the all-inclusive absolute is inaccessible to the human consciousness or sentient experience – all that is accessible is its fragments, its spatio-temporal chunks. As the philosopher Anthony Quinton puts it, private subjective space and time are 'a sort of ontological litter to be bundled into the wastepaper basket of the imaginary'.⁸ Plato's prisoners, if unchained and released from the famous cave, would not witness the true form of absolute reality, for it is ultimately unattainable. The cinematographic illusion is thus always deeply rooted in reality, and the unsubstantial cinematic image 'merely' imitates the human cognitive act, while confronting us 'rather brutally with the unreality of space-time'.⁹

But this condition, which may appear to be a consequence of some sort of ontological curse, has an edifying potential: the cinematic apparatus enlightens the spectator. Susan Sontag suggests that '[t]o possess the world in the form of images is, precisely, to re-experience the unreality and remoteness of the real'.¹⁰ Sitting in the darkness of a theatre in front of a flickering screen offers a self-reflexive simulation of a real-life experience. Tarkovsky's aesthetic agenda – to create an illusionary spatio-temporal framework which would expose real space and time as still more illusory – is also clearly permeated with epistemological traits. But the persistent search for the absolute truth in his films always leads to something yet more unstable than reality itself.

Cinema is ultimately an artificial 'artefact', which creates an illusion of reality but at the same time uses elements of this reality as its building blocks: as André Bazin puts it, 'what is imaginary on the screen must have the spatial density of something real'.¹¹ Tarkovsky is one of the pioneers who explored this inherent feature of cinematic language. His strategy consists of a refusal to differentiate between reality and its phantasmagorical appearances. The characters of his films enter an intermediary domain of abstract illusion and concrete reality, and face situations where the boundaries between nominally real and nominally illusionary events are unstable, or at times even completely effaced. Their temporally anomalous and spatially abnormal journeys do not lead them to greater clarity, but into uncertainty wrapped in a sense of cosmic homelessness.

NOTES

On Space(s) and Time(s)

1. A. Tarkovsky, *Time Within Time: The Diaries 1970–1986*, transl. K. Hunter-Blair, London, 1994, p. 53.
2. O. Mandelstam, *The Noise of Time: Selected Prose*, transl. C. Brown, Evanston, IL, 2002, p. 143.
3. A. Tarkovsky, *Sculpting in Time: Reflections on the Cinema*, transl. K. Hunter-Blair, Austin, 2006, p. 139.
4. Tarkovsky, *Time Within Time*, p. 343.
5. Tarkovsky, *Sculpting in Time*, pp. 63–4.
6. A. Tarkovskii, 'Edinomyshlennik prezhde vsego', *Sovetskie khudozhniki teatra i kino*, Moscow, 1977, p. 181.
7. Tarkovsky, *Sculpting in Time*, pp. 64–5.
8. A. Bazin, 'The Evolution of the Language of Cinema', in *What is Cinema? Volume 1*, transl. H. Gray, Berkeley, CA, 2005, p. 25.
9. Tarkovsky, *Sculpting in Time*, p. 121.
10. A. Tarkovskii, *Uroki rezhissury*, Moscow, 1993, p. 59.
11. Ibid., p. 60.
12. For instance, Maiia Turovskaia considers the category of time as a gateway to the cinema of Tarkovsky (M. Turovskaia, *7 s ½ ili fil'my Andreia Tarkovskogo*, Moscow, 1991, p. 229), while Slavoj Žižek notes that one of the key features of Tarkovsky's cinema is an effect of temporal anamorphosis (S. Žižek, *The Fright of Real Tears: Krzysztof Kieślowski Between Theory and Post-Theory*, London, 2001, p. 102).
13. G. Deleuze, *Cinema 2: The Time-Image*, transl. H. Tomlinson and R. Galeta, London, 2005, p. xi.
14. Cf. Tarkovsky's suggestion that all 'artistic work relies on memory, and is a means of crystallizing it' (C. Devarrieux, 'The Artist Lives Off His Childhood like a Parasite: An Interview with the Author of *The Mirror* [1978]', in J. Gianvito (ed.), *Andrei Tarkovsky: Interviews*, Jackson, MS, 2006, p. 45).
15. Deleuze, *Cinema 2*, pp. 125–6.
16. It should be noted that the notion of *juncture* is crucial to Eisenstein – it is a gateway to his theory of montage (see S. Eisenstein, 'An Unexpected Juncture', in *S. M. Eisenstein: Selected Works: Volume 1, Writings, 1922–34*, ed. and transl. R. Taylor, London, 1988, pp. 115–22).

17. M. Foucault, 'Of Other Spaces', transl. J. Miskowiec, *Diacritics*, vol. 16, no. 1 (1986), p. 22.
18. Deleuze also refers to the story to illustrate the problem of future contingents (G. Deleuze, *The Fold: Leibniz and the Baroque*, transl. T. Conley, London, 2006, p. 71).
19. J. L. Borges, *Labyrinths: Selected Stories and Other Writings*, New York, 2007, pp. 27–8.
20. E. Rohmer, *The Taste for Beauty*, transl. C. Volk, Cambridge, 1989, p. 21.
21. A. Tarkovskii, *Martirolog. Dnevniki 1970–1986*, Florence, 2009, p. 309.
22. In this sense, the phenomenon of slow motion can be defined as a certain type of long take where the conventional flow of time is manipulated.
23. Deleuze, *Cinema 2*, p. 1.
24. Tarkovsky, *Sculpting in Time*, p. 104.
25. *Béla Balázs: Early Film Theory. Visible Man and The Spirit of Film*, transl. R. Livingstone, New York, 2010, pp. 137–8.
26. J. Aumont, A. Bergala, M. Marie and M. Vernet, *Aesthetics of Film*, transl. and revised by R. Neupert, Austin, TX, 1992, pp. 214–5.
27. W. Benjamin, 'On Some Motifs in Baudelaire', in *Selected Writings: Volume 4, 1938–1940*, transl. by E. Jephcott, Cambridge, MA, 2003, p. 335.
28. Anthony McCall's film project *Line Describing a Cone* (1973) is arguably an ideal sculpture in time, which complicates even further Tarkovsky's discussion of the art of cinema and challenges cinematic conventions in general. McCall's film does not focus the viewer's attention on an image projected onto a screen; instead it makes the viewer aware of the projector beam itself. The beam of light emerges as a gradually growing cone and makes visible various particles in the air. It invites the viewer to interact with the 'film'. The resulting three-dimensional light sculpture elevates cinematic experience to a different plane where real space and time, not their illusions, play the key role.
29. Bazin, 'The Ontology of the Photographic Image', in *What is Cinema? Volume 1*, p. 15. Bazin also suggests that photographic technology 'embalms time, rescuing it simply from its proper corruption' (ibid., p. 14). Cf. Tarkovsky's assertion that 'cinema stands out as giving time *visible, real form*' (Tarkovsky, *Sculpting in Time*, p. 104, italics added).
30. Tarkovsky, *Sculpting in Time*, p. 63.
31. Ibid.
32. D. C. Williams, 'The Myth of Passage', *Journal of Philosophy*, vol. 48, no. 15 (1951), pp. 457–72.
33. M. Bakhtin, 'Forms of Time and Chronotope in the Novel', in *The Dialogic Imagination*, transl. C. Emerson and M. Holquist, Austin, TX, 1981, p. 208.
34. H. Bergson, *Matter and Memory*, transl. N. M. Paul and W. S. Palmer, Mineola, NY, 2004, p. 250.
35. H. Bergson, *Key Writings*, transl. K. A. Pearson and J. Mullarkey, London, 2002, p. 258.
36. Bergson, *Matter and Memory*, p. 250.

37. Ibid., p. 77.
38. H. Bergson, *Creative Evolution*, transl. A. Mitchell, New York, 1944, pp. 7, 20, 45.
39. G. Deleuze, *Bergsonism*, transl. H. Tomlinson and B. Habberjam, New York, 1991.
40. Deleuze, *Cinema 2*, p. 5.
41. R. Stam, *Reflexivity in Film and Literature: From Don Quixote to Jean-Luc Godard*, New York, 1992, p. 260.
42. C. Metz, 'Photography and Fetish', *October*, vol. 34 (1985), p. 82.
43. R. Descartes, *The Philosophical Writings of Descartes: Volume II*, Cambridge, 1984, p. 13. It should be noted that the dreaming example is put forward as part of a more fundamental sceptical hypothesis, according to which there might be no external world at all.
44. J. Brodsky, 'Spoils of War', in *On Grief and Reason: Essays*, New York, 1995, p. 13.
45. F. H. Bradley, *Appearance and Reality: A Metaphysical Essay*, London, 7th impression, 1920.
46. J. Epstein, 'Magnification and Other Writings', transl. S. Liebman, *October*, vol. 3 (1977), p. 16.
47. J. Hoberman and G. Bachmann, 'Between Two Worlds [1983]', in Gianvito, *Andrei Tarkovsky: Interviews*, pp. 92–3.
48. The book focuses on Tarkovsky's 'canon' – the seven full-length films. It excludes from the discussion the director's work in radio, theatre and opera, which deserves separate studies due to the specificity of the genres. The three short-length projects made while Tarkovsky was a student (*The Killers, There Will Be No Leave Today* and *Steamroller and Violin*) and the documentary (*Time of Travel*) are arguably of chiefly historical or biographical, rather than aesthetic, value. *Steamroller and Violin*, however, stands out against the two preceding immature films. The main character of the film – a boy named Sasha – constantly lapses into reveries in order to avoid a reality in which he is bullied by his peers. Moreover, the film is punctuated with various reflections from multiple mirroring surfaces, which undermine the homogeneity of the visual representation.

Chapter 1 Dreams of *Ivan's Childhood*

1. V. Bogomolov, 'Ivan', transl. B. Isaacs, in *The Third Flare: Three War Stories*, Moscow, 1963, p. 7.
2. The term was coined by the Russian poet Andrei Voznesensky and used by Jean-Paul Sartre in his article dedicated to *Ivan's Childhood* which was published on 9 October 1963 in *L'Unità*. J.-P. Sartre, 'Letter on the Critique of *Ivan's Childhood*', transl. J. Berenbeim, *Tarkovsky*, ed. N. Dunne, London, 2008, p. 39.
3. P. Florensky, *Iconostasis*, transl. D. Sheehan and O. Andrejev, New York, 2000, p. 44.
4. Tarkovskii, *Martirolog*, p. 583.
5. Tarkovsky, *Sculpting in Time*, p. 30.

6. E. Montale, *Satura: 1962–1970*, transl. W. Arrowsmith, New York, 1998, p. 25.
7. Sartre, 'Letter on the Critique of *Ivan's Childhood*', p. 39.
8. Ibid., p. 38.
9. Tarkovsky, *Time Within Time*, p. 154.
10. However, there is a failed romantic encounter in the film – Kholin's abortive relationship with the nurse Masha. The young woman comes in the middle of the song to bid farewell to Kholin and Galtsev.
11. G. Bachelard, *Water and Dreams: An Essay on the Imagination of Matter*, transl. E. R. Farrell, Dallas, TX, 1983, p. 55.
12. Ibid., p. 6.
13. Deleuze, *Cinema 2*, p. xi.
14. Tarkovsky, *Sculpting in Time*, p. 58.
15. Ibid., pp. 30–1.
16. S. Sontag, *On Photography*, New York, 1977, p. 15.
17. R. Barthes, *Camera Lucida: Reflections on Photography*, transl. R. Howard, New York, 1981, p. 49.
18. Ibid.
19. Foucault, 'Of Other Spaces', p. 23.
20. Arseni Tarkovskii, *Poems/Stikhi*, transl. P. Norman, London, 1998, p. 9.
21. Tarkovsky, *Time Within Time*, p. 280.
22. Bakhtin, 'Forms of Time and Chronotope in the Novel', p. 154.

Chapter 2   Visions of *Andrei Rublev*

1. There are three DVD versions of the film available (175 minutes [Krupnyi plan], 175 minutes [Artificial Eye], and 205 minutes [*The Passion According to Andrei*, The Criterion Collection]). In an interview Tarkovsky maintains that the shorter version is 'the most accomplished' (M. Ciment, L. Schnitzer and J. Schnitzer, 'The Artist in Ancient Russia and in the New USSR [1969]', in Gianvito, *Andrei Tarkovsky: Interviews*, p. 29). The director goes on to claim that the 'cuts don't change anything as regards subject-matter, the things we wanted to accentuate, and important dialogues. In short, we changed the timing, which had been badly calculated at the beginning'. All stills and dialogue lines used in this chapter are drawn from the shorter version unless otherwise stated.
2. For instance, Rublev's Zvenigorod icons were recovered in 1918 from an old barn where they had been stored under firewood.
3. The titles of the chapters and chronology in the 205-minute edition are slightly different from the standard 175-minute edition. In addition, the 'Passion According to Andrei' chapter is not highlighted in the longer version, probably because of the fact that the 205-minute film has the identical title.
4. There is evidence that the director also considered a non-chronological order for the 'novellas' (A. Tarkovskii, 'Iskat' i dobivat'sia', *Sovetskii ekran*, 1962, no. 17, p. 9). However, several years after making the film he claimed: 'the structure of *Andrey Rublyov* strikes me today as disjointed and incoherent' (Tarkovsky, *Sculpting in Time*, p. 204).
5. Tarkovskii, 'Iskat' i dobivat'sia', p. 20.

6. According to the script (A. Tarkovsky, *Andrei Rublëv*, transl. K. Hunter-Blair, London, 1991, p. 180), Daniil reappears in the 'Bell' novella when Andrei breaks his vow of silence while comforting Boriska.
7. Tarkovsky, *Sculpting in Time*, p. 34–5.
8. L. Ouspensky and V. Lossky, *The Meaning of Icons*, ed. U. Graf-Verlag, Olten, 1952, p. 28, italics added.
9. Ibid., italics added.
10. V. N. Lazarev, *Andrei Rublev*, Moscow, 1960, p. 5.
11. V. N. Lazarev, *Andrei Rublev i ego shkola*, Moscow, 1966, p. 32.
12. Ibid., p. 50.
13. K. Lindsay and B. Huppé, 'Meaning and Method in Brueghel's Painting', *Journal of Aesthetics and Art Criticism*, vol. 14, no. 3 (1956), p. 376.
14. Compare Tarkovsky's puzzling and contradictory comment during a discussion about *Andrei Rublev*: 'I have never understood [...] attempts to construct *mise-en-scène* from a painting' (Tarkovsky, *Sculpting in Time*, p. 78).
15. Tarkovsky, *Andrei Rublëv*, p. 73.
16. There is a detailed description of a flight in the script: the swan flock leader 'saw the earth from high above when the flock was in flight, through breaks in the clouds he saw cloud shadows running over yellow and green fields; dense, dark woods and sparse, light ones, with black, scorched patches from great fires, and little circles, bright as the sky – the lakes for which they longed' (Ibid., p. 49).
17. Ibid., p. 71.
18. Ouspensky and Lossky, *The Meaning of Icons*, p. 41.
19. For instance, N. Demina, *'Troitsa' Andreiia Rubleva*, Moscow, 1963, p. 29, or Lazarev, *Andrei Rublev*, p. 15.
20. As is evident from an interview given in 1969 (Ciment et al., 'The Artist in Ancient Russia', pp. 21–2).
21. S. Žižek, 'The Thing from Inner Space: On Tarkovsky', *Angelaki: Journal of Theoretical Humanities*, vol. 4, no. 3 (1999), p. 229.
22. Ouspensky and Lossky, *The Meaning of Icons*, pp. 44–5.
23. A. Konchalovskii and A. Tarkovskii, 'Andrei Rublev (Chast' I)', *Iskusstvo kino*, 1964, no. 4, p. 188.
24. Tarkovsky, *Sculpting in Time*, p. 45.
25. J. Barclay, 'I Corinthians', in *The Oxford Bible Commentary*, ed. J. Barton and J. Muddiman, Oxford, 2001, p. 1128.
26. Tarkovsky, *Andrei Rublëv*, p. 111.
27. The 205-minute version includes an additional flashback scene in the middle of the sacking of Vladimir. The duke remembers a scene of public physical humiliation by his elder brother who, apparently after a public fight, steps on his face. What is important is that the scene takes place near the cathedral.
28. Florensky, *Iconostasis*, p. 62.
29. Ibid.
30. R. Bird, *Andrei Tarkovsky: Elements of Cinema*, London, 2008, p. 97.
31. Bachelard, *Water and Dreams*, p. 16.
32. Ibid., p. 97.

33. Ibid.
34. M. A. Doane, *The Emergence of Cinematic Time: Modernity, Contingency, the Archive*, Cambridge, MA, 2002, p. 30.
35. K. Marker [C. Marker], 'Sem' pechatei', *Kinovedcheskie zapiski*, no. 57 (2002), p. 283.
36. N. Misler in A. Dalle Vacche, *Cinema and Painting: How Art is Used in Film*, London, 1996, p. 148.
37. P. Florensky, 'Reverse Perspective', in *Beyond Vision: Essays on the Perception of Art*, transl. W. Salmond, London, 2002, pp. 197–272.
38. B. Uspenskii, 'Semiotika ikony', in *Semiotika iskusstva*, Moscow, 1995, pp. 219–94.
39. L. F. Zhegin, *Iazyk zhivopisnogo proizvedeniia (Uslovnost' drevnego iskusstva)*, Moscow, 1970.
40. C. Antonova and M. Kemp, '"Reverse Perspective": Historical Fallacies and an Alternative View', in *Visual Mind II*, ed. M. Emmer, Cambridge, MA, 2005, pp. 399–431; D. Likhachev, *Razvitie russkoi literatury X-XVII vekov: Epokhi i stili*, Leningrad, 1973, p. 313.
41. Ciment et al., 'The Artist in Ancient Russia and in the New USSR [1969]', p. 24.
42. Ibid.
43. Tarkovsky, *Andrei Rublëv*, p. 187, italics added.
44. A. Tarkovskii, 'Beseda o tsvete', *Kinovedcheskie zapiski*, no. 1 (1988), p. 148.
45. Ibid., p. 150.
46. Antonova and Kemp, '"Reverse Perspective"', p. 426.
47. M. Alpatov, *Andrei Rublev: Okolo 1370–1430*, Moscow, 1972, p. 99.
48. Ouspensky and Lossky, *The Meaning of Icons*, p. 29.
49. Ciment et al., 'The Artist in Ancient Russia and in the New USSR [1969]', p. 24.

Chapter 3 Phantasies of *Solaris*

1. S. Lem, *Solaris*, transl. J. Kilmartin and S. Cox, London, 1970, p. 1.
2. Bakhtin, 'Forms of Time and Chronotope in the Novel', p. 147.
3. S. Lem, 'The Profession of Science Fiction: XV: Answers to a Questionnaire', transl. M. Jakubowski and D. Jakubowski, in *Foundation: The Review of Science Fiction*, no. 15 (1979), pp. 45–6.
4. Lem, *Solaris*, p. 75.
5. Ciment et al., 'The Artist in Ancient Russia', p. 21.
6. Žižek, The Fright of Real Tears, p. 102.
7. Lem, *Solaris*, p. 92.
8. Ibid., p. 205.
9. Ibid., p. 43.
10. S. Sontag, *Against Interpretation*, London, 1994, p. 225.
11. M. Purcell, 'Tarkovsky's Film *Solaris* (1972): A Freudian Slip?', *Extrapolation*, vol. 19, no. 2 (1978), p. 126.
12. Tarkovsky, *Time Within Time*, p. 37.
13. Tarkovsky, *Sculpting in Time*, p. 92.

14. Ibid., p. 66.
15. Ibid.
16. M. de Cervantes, *Don Quixote*, transl. J. Ormsby, New York, 1981, p. 469.
17. Ibid., p. 185.
18. S. Freud, 'The Uncanny', in *The Pelican Freud Library, Volume 14: Art and Literature*, transl. J. Strachey, ed. A. Dickson, Harmondsworth, 1985, p. 367.
19. Lem, *Solaris*, p. 105.
20. Cervantes, *Don Quixote*, p. 801.
21. Ibid.
22. J. Lacan, *Écrits: A Selection*, transl. A. Sheridan, London, 1977, p. 166.
23. Deleuze, *Cinema 2*, p. 73.
24. Tarkovsky filmed a whole episode in the mirror room, but subsequently cut its presence to this brief moment.
25. T. Todorov, *The Fantastic: A Structural Approach to a Literary Genre*, transl. R. Howard, New York, 1973, p. 120.
26. Deleuze, *The Fold: Leibniz and the Baroque*, p. 143.
27. Žižek, 'The Thing from Inner Space: On Tarkovsky', p. 223.
28. Lem, *Solaris*, p. 212.
29. This image will be explored to a greater extent in *Mirror* – Tarkovsky's next project: the same reunion will take place when the father returns home to embrace his children.
30. Tarkovskii, *Martirolog*, p. 34.
31. J. Baudrillard, *Simulacra and Simulation*, transl. S. F. Glaser, Ann Arbor, MI, 1994 pp. 123–4.
32. A. Tarkovskii, 'Poiasneniia rezhissera k fil'mu 'Soliaris'', *Kinovedcheskie zapiski*, no. 14 (1992), p. 53.

Chapter 4   Memories of *Mirror*

1. M. Proust, *In Search of Lost Time, Volume I: Swann's Way*, transl. S. Moncrieff and T. Kilmartin, New York, 2003, p. 64.
2. G. Bachelard, *The Poetics of Space*, transl. E. Gilson, Boston, MA, 1969, p. 9.
3. Tarkovsky, *Time Within Time*, p. 300.
4. A. Tarkovskii, '"Vstat' na put'", beseda s Ezhi Illgom i Leonardom Noigerom', *Iskusstvo kino*, 1989, no. 2, p. 109.
5. Tarkovsky, *Sculpting in Time*, p. 117.
6. K. Mets (C. Metz), 'Zerkala v kino', *Kinovedcheskie zapiski*, no. 13 (1992), p. 29.
7. Foucault, 'Of Other Spaces', p. 24.
8. Ibid.
9. Dmitri Salynsky (in his book *Kinogermenevtika Tarkovskogo*, Moscow, 2009, p. 206) notes that there is an 'accidental' appearance of the director in the film in the doctor's house. When someone turns the mirrored door of a wardrobe, one can see Tarkovsky for less than a second in its reflection before the camera focuses its attention on the redhead girl

sitting by a fire. Tarkovsky turns for a moment, and then walks away. This 'cameo' appearance fits the overall discourse found in *Mirror*: the real–autobiographical domain enters the film as a reflection.
10. *The Norton Shakespeare*, ed. S. Greenblatt, New York, 1997, p. 1944.
11. M. Sheringham, *French Autobiography: Devices and Desires: Rousseau to Perec*, Oxford, 1993, p. 8.
12. Devarrieux, 'The Artist Lives Off His Childhood Like a Parasite', p. 45.
13. Deleuze, *Cinema 2*, p. 73.
14. Tarkovskii, 'Edinomyshlennik prezhde vsego', p. 182.
15. F. Ermash, et al., 'Glavnaia tema – sovremennost'', *Iskusstvo kino*, 1975, no. 3, p. 14.
16. A. Tarkovskii, 'Belyi den'', *Iskusstvo kino*, 1970, no. 6, pp. 109–14.
17. M. A. Doane, 'The Voice in the Cinema: The Articulation of Body and Space', *Yale French Studies*, no. 60, 1980, p. 35.
18. For instance S. Sandler ('On Grief and Reason, On Poetry and Film: Elena Shvarts, Joseph Brodsky, Andrei Tarkovsky', *Russian Review*, vol. 66 [2007]) and A. Smith ('Andrei Tarkovsky as Reader of Arseni Tarkovsky's Poetry in the Film *Mirror*', *Russian Studies in Literature*, vol. 40, no. 3 [2004]) follow this interpretative line.
19. L. Renza, 'The Veto of the Imagination: A Theory of Autobiography', *New Literary History*, vol. 9, no. 1 (1977), p. 2.
20. N. Synessios, *Mirror*, London, 2001, p. 92.
21. Renza, 'The Veto of the Imagination: A Theory of Autobiography', p. 22.
22. Tarkovsky's second wife and stepdaughter also appear as actors in *Mirror*. However, their presence does not seem to derive from the autobiographical intentions of the film.
23. All translations of Arseni Tarkovsky are by Alexander Nemser and Nariman Skakov unless otherwise indicated.
24. A. Misharin and A. Tarkovskii, 'Zerkalo', *Kinostsenarii*, 1988, no. 2, p. 132.
25. Doane, 'Voice in the Cinema', p. 45.
26. Bachelard, *Poetics of Space*, p. 6. Compare Martin Heidegger's discussion of the phenomenon of the house/building in his analysis of a line from Hölderlin's 'Poetically man dwells' (M. Heidegger, *Poetry, Language, Thought*, transl. A. Hofstadter, New York, 1971). The German philosopher brings together the notions of poetry and human dwelling: 'poetry first causes dwelling to be dwelling. Poetry is what really lets us dwell. But through what do we attain to a dwelling place? Through building. Poetic creation, which lets us dwell, is a kind of building' (p. 213). Furthermore, the possibility of raising a building comes from the domain of poetry: 'Man is capable of such building only if he already builds in the sense of the poetic taking of measure. Authentic building occurs so far as there are poets, such poets as take the measure for architecture, the structure of dwelling' (p. 225).
27. Tarkovsky, *Sculpting in Time*, p. 58, italics added.

28. A. Tarkovsky, *Collected Screenplays*, transl. N. Synessios and W. Powell, London, 1999, p. 298.
29. Bachelard, *Poetics of Space*, p. 7.
30. The only irregularity occurs in the line 'And the rain, and the especially late hour' of the original Russian text, where the rhythmical pattern is broken. The resulting shortening creates an impression of an emphasis on this particular line (that is, on the significance of the rain).
31. The film is also marked by the presence–absence of Leonardo's *Treatise on Painting*. Several extensive passages detailing instructions for painting battle scenes were in fact supposed to appear as a voice-over accompanying a sequence depicting the destruction of a local church in Iurevets (Misharin and Tarkovskii, 'Zerkalo', pp. 133–5, 145), but the idea was abandoned during the shooting process.
32. Tarkovskii, 'Edinomyshlennik prezhde vsego', p. 182.
33. Tarkovskii, 'Vstat' na put" p. 112.
34. T. Nelson, 'Sculpting the End of Time: The Anamorphosis of History and Memory in Andrei Tarkovsky's *Mirror* (1975)', *Cinémas*, vol. 13, no. 3 (2003), p. 129.
35. The following lines exemplify this point: 1) 'I run from neither slander / Nor poison'; 2) 'When immortality swims by like a shoal'; 3) 'I will summon any of the centuries, / I will enter it and build a house in it'; 4) 'I measured time with a surveying chain, / And passed through it, as if through the Urals'; 5) 'Going south, we held dust over the steppe'; 6) 'Whenever its flying needle / Would lead me, like a thread, around the world'.
36. Žižek, *Fright of Real Tears*, p. 77.
37. Ibid. Deleuze also provides an intriguing reflection on the interaction between movement- and time-images in the light of the opposition between the actual and the virtual. The actuality of the movement-image is challenged by the time-image's inclinations towards the virtual. However, 'if virtual is opposed to actual, it is not opposed to real' (Deleuze, *Cinema 2*, p. 40). Therefore, according to the French critic, documentary chronicle possesses a potential to instigate direct time-images in spite of its overtly realistic nature.
38. G. W. F. Hegel, *Aesthetics: Lectures on Fine Art: Volume I*, transl. T. M. Knox, Oxford, 1975, p. 363.
39. Ibid.
40. F. Kermode, *The Sense of an Ending: Studies in the Theory of Fiction*, London, 1967, p. 81.
41. Deleuze, *Cinema 2*, p. xii.
42. P. Lejeune, *On Autobiography*, transl. K. Leary, Minneapolis, MN, 1989, p. 113.
43. J. Brodsky, 'In the Shadow of Dante', in *Less Than One: Selected Essays*, New York, 1986, p. 100.
44. Ibid., p. 104.
45. Sheringham, *French Autobiography*, p. 14.
46. Dante, *Inferno*, transl. C. Singleton, Princeton, NJ, 1970, p. 3.
47. O. Mandelstam, *The Complete Critical Prose*, transl. J. G. Harris and C. Link, Dana Point, CA, 1979, p. 254.

48. E. Auerbach, *Dante: Poet of the Secular World*, transl. R. Manheim, Chicago, IL, 1961, p. 175.
49. Dante, *Paradiso*, transl. C. Singleton, Princeton, NJ, 1977, p. 349.
50. A. Steiner, 'St Jerome and the First Terzina of the *Divine Comedy*', *Modern Language Notes*, vol. 52, no. 4 (1937), p. 260.

Chapter 5   Revelations of *Stalker*

1. B. Strugatsky, 'Working for Tarkovsky', transl. E. Simon, *Science Fiction Studies*, vol. 31, no. 3 (2004), *Soviet Science Fiction: The Thaw and After*, p. 419.
2. The script that has been translated into English (Tarkovsky, *Collected Screenplays*, pp. 381–416) is not the final version, but is based on one of the intermediate versions – the only version that has been published in Russian.
3. Tarkovsky, *Sculpting in Time*, pp. 193–4.
4. Strugatsky, 'Working for Tarkovsky', p. 419.
5. A. Tarkovskii, 'Slovo ob Apokalipsise', *Iskusstvo kino*, 1989, no. 2, p. 96.
6. Tarkovsky, *Sculpting in Time*, p. 57.
7. F. Jameson, *The Geopolitical Aesthetic: Cinema and Space in the World System*, London, 1992, p. 91.
8. The miniature landscape device finds its further development in *Nostalghia* and *Sacrifice*.
9. Žižek, *Fright of Real Tears*, p. 104.
10. *The Classic of the Way and Virtue: A New Translation of the Tao-te Ching of Laozi as Interpreted by Wang Bi*, transl. R. J. Lynn, New York, 1999, p. 187. However, Tarkovsky extracts only one of the numerous facets of *Tao-te Ching* in the quoted passage – the idea that pliable matter always takes over unyielding matter. The quotation, which is taken out of its authentic context, functions as an exotic intellectual decoration in the film – the film-maker declines to pursue the semantic depths of the text. On the surface level it propounds some kind of binary conflict: hard and stiff versus soft and pliable. However, the ultimate aim of the Taoist Way, according to one of its contemporary commentators, is to 'move from relativism to dialectics, recognizing the interdependence of opposites and using this recognition as a basis to equalize and transcend them' (L. Kohn and M. LaFargue, eds, *Lao-tzu and the Tao-te-ching*, Albany, NY, 1998, p. 14). While pliability is an inherent quality of Tao, it also possesses an aptitude to transmute itself into its complete opposite. Thus the apparent binarism should be overcome, and this is what actually happens throughout the classical Chinese text.
11. The allusion to the text of Revelation in *Stalker* is not found in the film script, so it can be assumed that it was added at some later stage. This fact suggests that there was no initially planned schema of superimposing the text with images, and that the episode was a result of some kind of improvisation on a particular theme.
12. Tarkovskii, 'Slovo ob Apokalipsise', pp. 96–7.
13. D. H. Lawrence, *Apocalypse and the Writings on Revelation*, Cambridge, 1980, pp. 59, 62.

14. P. Green, *Andrei Tarkovsky: The Winding Quest*, London, 1993, p. 96.
15. Bird, *Andrei Tarkovsky*, p. 9.
16. J. Kovacs and C. Rowland, *Revelation: The Apocalypse of Jesus Christ*, Oxford, 2004, p. 40.
17. Ibid., p. 248.
18. Deleuze, *Cinema 2*, p. xii.
19. Kovacs and Rowland, *Revelation*, pp. 81, 83.
20. E. Dhanens, *Van Eyck: The Ghent Altarpiece*, London, 1973, p. 76.
21. Tarkovskii, 'Slovo ob Apokalipsise', p. 100.
22. J. Derrida, *The Gift of Death*, transl. D. Wills, Chicago, IL, 1995, p. 59.
23. This could also be explained in pragmatic terms – reference to the figure of Jesus Christ and to the Bible in general was to be avoided in the Soviet Union.
24. This ambiguity also allows *anyone* or *any place* to be substituted, thus fulfilling the universal appeal of Christianity.
25. If one does not count a minor character – the bartender, called Liuker.
26. N. Boldyrev, *Zhertvoprinoshenie Andreia Tarkovskogo*, Moscow, 2004, p. 315.
27. Tarkovsky, *Time Within Time*, p. 169.
28. C. Castaneda, *Journey to Ixtlan: The Lessons of Don Juan*, London, 1974.
29. Ibid., p. 9.
30. Castaneda has authored another concept called *stalking*. *Stalking* is a way to perceive another reality in a more harmonious way. When seers 'steadily behave in ways not customary for them, [...] their assemblage points [i.e. imagined points that 'stabilize' the multiple realities, which are then perceived] shift' (C. Castaneda, *The Fire from Within*, London, 1998, pp. 168–9). This ability to move an assemblage point steadily between realities is called *stalking*, because the word 'entailed a specific kind of behaviour with people [who force a seer to act in a way that is unusual to him or her – for example, by tyrannizing them, thus creating a boundary-situation], behaviour that could be categorized as surreptitious' (ibid., p. 169). It would be farfetched to apply Castaneda's concept systematically, but the idea of alternating realities is a powerful metaphor for a discourse concerned with the notion of secrecy, as opposed to calculating economy in relation to the unknown. Moreover, Stalker's profession (stalking) is to behave in *non-customary ways*, akin to a seer practising stalking, since the Zone's laws are beyond rationality. Finally, it should be mentioned that there is a reference to Stalker's visionary abilities in the Strugatskys' novel *The Roadside Picnic* – the source text for the film. The science-fiction writers even describe one of the visions where the protagonist perceives his given reality differently, in the manner of Castaneda's seers (A. Strugatskii and B. Strugatskii, *Zona*, New York, 1983, p. 70).
31. The reflection is likely to be a result of the negligence of the set-designer, who, according to the credits, was Andrei Tarkovsky himself. However, since the unintended reflection is already part of the final cut of the film, its semantic potential should be considered.

32. *Norton Shakespeare*, p. 1708.
33. G. Deleuze, *Cinema 1: The Movement-Image*, transl. H. Tomlinson and B. Habberjam, London, 2005, p. 21.
34. The artist's presence in this painting is not only visual – he also inscribed in Latin on the back wall above the convex mirror: 'Jan van Eyck was here, 1434'.
35. Borges, *Labyrinths*, p. 196.
36. Tarkovsky, *Collected Screenplays*, p. 416.
37. Tarkovskii, *Martirolog*, p. 129.
38. Tarkovsky, *Time Within Time*, p. 101.
39. Tarkovsky, *Sculpting in Time*, p. 194.
40. Ibid., p. 193.

Chapter 6   Recollections of *Nostalghia*

1. This chapter is a substantially reworked version of a previously published article: N. Skakov, 'The (Im)Possible Translation of *Nostalgia*', *Studies in Russian and Soviet Cinema*, vol. 3, no. 3 (2009), pp. 309–33.
2. Tarkovsky, *Sculpting in Time*, pp. 204–5.
3. J. Macgillivray, 'Andrei Tarkovsky's Madonna del Parto', in N. Dunne, ed., *Tarkovsky*, London, 2008, p. 163.
4. 'Recollection' is also defined as 'serious concentration of thought, esp. religious meditation' (*OED*), and this definition reveals the film's rather transparent and overbearing religious message.
5. Cf. another 'nationalist' appropriation of the concept of *ennui* by Orhan Pamuk. He claims that Turkish *ennui* (*hüzün*) is a particular form of melancholy denoting a feeling of deep spiritual loss, but also a hopeful way of looking at life: 'a state of mind that is ultimately as life affirming as it is negating' (O. Pamuk, *Istanbul: Memories and the City*, transl. M. Freely, London, 2005, p. 82). In addition, the Portuguese word *saudade*, which is also alleged to be difficult to translate, describes a deep emotional state of nostalgic longing for something or someone.
6. Ironically, in order to avoid additional costs, Tarkovsky had to reassure the Italian side of the co-production team that the film would not need dubbing or subtitles for any dialogue spoken in Russian. As a result, the 'impossibility' of translation as a discourse finds its way into the film as an economically motivated necessity.
7. R. Jakobson, 'On Linguistic Aspects of Translation', in *Selected Writings II: Word and Language*, The Hague, 1971, p. 261.
8. Ibid., p. 262.
9. W. Benjamin, 'The Task of the Translator', *Selected Writings, Volume 1: 1913–1926*, ed. M. Bullock and M. Jennings, Cambridge, MA, 1996, p. 257.
10. Ibid., p. 255.
11. Ibid., p. 260. Paul de Man (in his *The Resistance to Theory*, Minneapolis, MN, 1986, p. 91) points out that Harry Zohn's English translation of Benjamin's text is inaccurate in some places. For example, in the quoted passage the crucial word 'broken' is missed out. As a result, the

reader is presented with a substantially distorted translation of the text, which puts translation into the realm of essential incompletion.
12. Interestingly, Jakobson translates this phrase into English as 'The translator is a betrayer'. This variation of the translation, *betrayer*, instead of the seemingly more appropriate *traitor*, deprives the rhyming aphorism of all its paronomastic qualities. In spite of, or even thanks to, this 'mistranslation', Jakobson is able to make the following astute observations: 'a cognitive attitude would compel us to change this aphorism into a more explicit statement and to answer the questions: translator of what messages? betrayer of what values?' (Jakobson, 'On Linguistic Aspects of Translation', p. 266).
13. Tarkovsky, *Collected Screenplays*, pp. 475–6, my italics. The lines and actions in italics appear in the film but differ from those in the script.
14. J. Derrida, 'Des Tours de Babel', transl. J. Graham, in *Difference in Translation*, ed. J. Graham, Ithaca, NY, 1985, pp. 165–207. The title itself is an 'untranslatable' pun. *Des* may mean 'some', 'of the', 'from the' or 'about the', while *tours* can designate 'towers', 'twists', 'tricks' or 'turns'. *Des tours* is also pronounced the same as *détour* ('detour'). The translator of the article into English left the title as it was in order to preserve the ambiguity.
15. Ibid., pp. 174–5.
16. Benjamin, 'The Task of the Translator', p. 260.
17. Tarkovsky, *Collected Screenplays*, p. 495.
18. W. V. Quine, 'Meaning and Translation', *On Translation*, ed. R. Brower, New York, 1966, p. 148.
19. Ibid.
20. There is a note made in 1979 which reflects the idea in relation to *Nostalghia*: 'Panorama of the *town*? At different times – through time (weather, time of day, precipitations, light).' (Tarkovsky, *Time Within Time*, p. 188).
21. Tarkovsky, *Time Within Time*, p. 307.
22. Z. Samardzija, '1+1=1: Impossible Translations in Andrey Tarkovsky's *Nostalghia*', *Literature / Film Quarterly*, vol. 32, no. 4 (2004), p. 303.
23. A. Tarkovskii, 'Dlia tselei lichnosti vysokikh', *Iskusstvo kino*, 1992, no. 4, p. 120.
24. The fact that the voice belongs to the director's own wife, Larisa, again reveals the complex interaction between reality and fiction in Tarkovsky's oeuvre.
25. The sequence where Gorchakov sees Domenico's reflection in a mirror instead of his own has clear affinities with an episode conceived for another of Tarkovsky's projects – *Hoffmanniana*. The film was supposed to be an imagined biography of E. T. A. Hoffmann mixed with episodes from the German writer's novellas and short stories. Tarkovsky describes one of the episodes in which a mirrored wardrobe functions as an uncanny object: '[Hoffmann] rises from the bed, walks up to the mirror to comb his hair, but he cannot see himself as a young man; the only thing reflected in it is the sunlit room and the wardrobe with the half-open door. He does not see his face. He is drawn by a quiet rustle

inside the wardrobe. He walks up to it. Listens. Then he quietly opens the wardrobe doors wide. It seems to him that the wardrobe has no back' (Tarkovsky, *Collected Screenplays*, p. 367). The two sequences invite a psychoanalytic interpretation. The episodes can be read as a dividing and interchanging of the self in the Freudian sense or, if one is to follow Otto Rank (O. Rank, *The Double: A Psychoanalytic Study*, transl. and ed. H. Tucker, Chapel Hill, NC, 1971), as a means of avoiding the total destruction of the ego through death (that is, doubling functions as a defence against physical extinction). One may also employ the Lacanian model and describe the sequence as an operation of the mirror apparatus, which accommodates images 'of the double, in which psychical realities, however heterogeneous, are manifested' (Lacan, *Écrits: A Selection*, p. 3).

26. For instance, in T. Mitchell, 'Tarkovsky in Italy [1982]' and J. Gianvito, *Andrei Tarkovsky: Interviews*, p. 74. The idea of untranslatability, however, does not interest just Tarkovsky. In *Time of Travel*, a documentary shot by the Russian film-maker prior to *Nostalghia*, his co-writer Tonino Guerra clearly addresses the same issue: 'I don't believe in painting reproductions. I don't believe in poem translations. Art is very jealous. Very jealous.'
27. Tarkovsky, *Time Within Time*, p. 183.
28. G. Loughlin, 'The Long Take: Messianic Time in Andrei Tarkovsky's *Nostalghia*', *Journal for Cultural Research*, vol. 13, nos 3 and 4 (2009), p. 376.
29. H. Naficy, *An Accented Cinema: Exilic and Diasporic Filmmaking*, Princeton, NJ, 2001, p. 177.
30. Cf. Joseph Brodsky's fascination with the same phenomenon in 'A Halt in the Desert' ('Ostanovka v pustyne') – a ruined Greek church which suddenly reveals something unsettling: 'And night itself / yawned widely in the altar's gaping holes. / And I – through these same altar's holes – looked out / upon the trams that ran off in the distance, / upon the row of streetlights that were dim. / And what you'd never see inside a church / I now saw clearly through the church's prism' (Translation taken from M. Wachtel, *The Development of Russian Verse: Meter and its Meanings*, Cambridge, 2006, p. 106).
31. Derrida, 'Des Tours de Babel', p. 165.
32. J. Derrida, 'What Is a "Relevant" Translation?', transl. L. Venuti, in L. Venuti, ed., *The Translation Studies Reader*, New York, 2004, p. 429.
33. J. Pallasmaa, 'Space and Image in Andrei Tarkovsky's *Nostalgia*: Notes on a Phenomenology of Architecture', in A. Pérez-Gómez and S. Parcell, eds, *Chora 1: Intervals in the Philosophy of Architecture*, Montreal, 1994, p. 156.
34. P. Kamuf, 'A Post Card from San Galgano', *Assemblage*, no. 20, *Violence, Space* (1993), p. 46.
35. It is interesting that the concept of a building housing another building was inspired by a sight Tarkovsky encountered in Italy during his trip as an alienated tourist: 'In Loreto there is a famous cathedral [...] in the middle of which stands Mary's house in which Jesus was

born, transported here from Nazareth.' (Tarkovsky, *Time Within Time*, p. 274).
36. Quine, 'Meaning and Translation', p. 171.
37. Benjamin, 'The Task of the Translator', p. 258.
38. Ibid.
39. P. P. Pasolini, 'Observations on the Long Take', transl. N. MacAfee and C. Owens, *October*, vol. 13 (1980), p. 5.
40. Ibid., p. 6.
41. B. Johnson, 'Taking Fidelity Philosophically', in J. Graham, ed., *Difference in Translation*, Ithaca, NY, 1985, pp. 143–4.
42. A. Tarkovskii, 'O prirode nostal'gii [Interview with Gideon Bachmann]', *Iskusstvo kino*, 1989, no. 2, p. 136.

Chapter 7   Illusions of *Sacrifice*

1. Žižek claims that the actions of the two characters played by Josephson are mere consequences of a neurotic disorder: 'To this gesture of senseless sacrifice, one should give all the weight of an obsessional-neurotic compulsive act: if I accomplish *this* (sacrificial gesture), the catastrophe (in *Sacrifice*, literally the end of the world in an atomic war) will not occur or will be undone – the well-known compulsive gesture of "If I do not do this (jump twice over that stone, cross my hands in this way, etc., etc.) something bad will occur." (The childish nature of this compulsion to sacrifice is clear in *Nostalghia* where the hero, following the injunction of the dead Domenico, crosses the pool with the burning candle in order to save the world...) As we know from psychoanalysis, this catastrophic X whose outbreak we fear is none other than *jouissance* itself' (Žižek, 'The Thing from Inner Space', p. 228).
2. Tarkovsky registers the Christian source of this legend (*Lives of the Fathers*) in his diary (Tarkovskii, *Martirolog*, p. 391). However, as several critics have shown (for example, N. Zorkaia, 'Konets', in A. Sandler, ed., *Mir i fil'my Andreia Tarkovskogo: Razmyshleniia, issledovaniia, vospominaniia, pis'ma*, Moscow, 1991, p. 182, and V. Mikhalkovich, 'Energiia obraza', in ibid., p. 241), there are many alternative renderings of the story. Among others is a Buddhist tale used by Kim Ki-duk for his 2003 feature *Spring, Summer, Fall, Winter... and Spring* (*Bom yeoreum gaeul gyeoul geurigo bom*).
3. A. Truppin, 'And Then There Was Sound: The Films of Andrei Tarkovsky', in R. Altman, ed., *Sound Theory/Sound Practice*, New York, 1992, p. 235.
4. M. Kemp, *Leonardo da Vinci: The Marvellous Works of Nature and Man*, Oxford, 2006, p. 52.
5. V. P. Zubov, *Leonardo da Vinci*, transl. D. Kraus, Cambridge, MA, 1962, p. 262.
6. Ibid., p. 263.
7. Kemp, *Leonardo da Vinci*, p. 54.
8. Death is an overcoming of everyday reality – of its space and time. The visual theme of the life–death tree is supplemented by the rejection of

death, as the definitive end of a human life, on the level of discourse in *Sacrifice*. During his long monologue, Alexander alludes to Lev Tolstoy's *The Death of Ivan Il'ich*: his sentiment that 'there is no death, only the fear of death' paraphrases the crucial idea delivered right at the end of Tolstoy's short novel (L. Tolstoy, *The Death of Ivan Ilyich and Other Stories*, transl. R. Pevear and L. Volokhonsky, New York, 2009, p. 91). The desperate attempt to eliminate all-eliminating death knits together the characters of Ivan Il'ich and Alexander in *Sacrifice*. Moreover, the idea of death – the most profound liminal experience in every person's life – is also a salient feature of Seneca's letters, one of which is unambiguously mentioned as a source of inspiration for the film at earlier stages of its development. On 3 September 1981, while still in Russia and before shooting *Nostalghia*, Tarkovsky recorded the following diary entry: 'Seneca, *Letters to Lucilius*. Letter XXX could be the basis on which to build the character of the Philosopher at the beginning of the screenplay, The Witch' (Tarkovsky, *Time Within Time*, p. 292). The 'Letter XXX' is an encomium to a certain Aufidius Bassus, an ageing and dying philosopher who is not anguished by his mortal destiny: 'he contemplates his own end with the courage and countenance which you would regard as undue indifference in a man who so contemplated another's' (L. A. Seneca, *Epistulae Morales, Volume I*, transl. R. Gummere, London, 1917, p. 213). The philosopher offers the rational argument that one cannot be afraid of something which brings the absence of suffering – an eternal anaesthesia. This train of thought allows Seneca to arrive at the same conclusion as Ivan Il'ich: 'We do not fear death; we fear the thought of death. For death itself is always the same distance from us; wherefore, if it is to be feared at all, it is to be feared always. For what season of our life is exempt from death?' (ibid., p. 221).
9. Tarkovsky, *Time Within Time*, pp. 174, 176.
10. Tarkovsky, *Collected Screenplays*, p. 507.
11. A. Strugatskii and B. Strugatskii, 'Ved'ma: stsenarii', *Iskusstvo kino*, 2008, no. 2, p. 133.
12. In addition, Otto cites the famous line from Revelation 8: 1 – the text depicting the ultimate end – which provides one of the most memorable references to silence in the script: 'there was silence in heaven about the space of half an hour' (Tarkovsky, *Collected Screenplays*, p. 514).
13. The line may be inspired by Nietzsche's Zarathustra, who puts forward the following maxim: 'It is difficult to live among men because keeping silent is so difficult. Especially for a babbler' (F. Nietzsche, *Thus Spoke Zarathustra*, transl. R. J. Hollingdale, London, 2003, p. 163).
14. *Norton Shakespeare*, p. 1695.
15. Tarkovsky adapted *Hamlet* for the stage – his only experience as a theatrical director – in the Soviet Union, and the play remained one of the literary texts he regarded most highly.
16. When the two meet in the upstairs room of the house, the postman tells his friend that 'all of this will be over' if he sleeps with Maria. Alexander clearly does not understand what is meant by 'this', and in the forthcoming 'clarification' Otto simply reiterates: 'all of this'.

17. C. Lévi-Strauss, *The Savage Mind*, Chicago, IL, 1966, p. 23.
18. Ibid.
19. Bachelard, *The Poetics of Space*, p. 152.
20. Enter the Ghost of Banquo, and sits in Macbeth's place.

    MACBETH   Sweet remembrancer. Now good digestion wait on appetite, And health on both.
    LENNOX   May't please your highness sit.
    MACBETH   Here had we now our country's honour roofed, Were the graced person of our Banquo present, Who may I rather challenge for unkindness Than pity for mischance.
    ROSS   His absence, sir, Lays blame upon his promise. Please't your highness To grace us with your royal company?
    MACBETH   The table's full.
    LENNOX   Here is a place reserved, sir.
    MACBETH   Where?
    LENNOX   Here, my good lord. What is't that moves your highness?
    MACBETH   Which of you have done this?
    THE LORDS   What, my good lord?
    MACBETH   [to the Ghost] Thou canst not say I did it, never shake Thy glory locks at me!
    ROSS   [*rising*] Gentlemen, rise, his highness is not well.

    Norton Shakespeare, p. 2591.
21. W. Shakespeare, *Macbeth*, ed. A. R. Braunmuller, Cambridge, 1997, p. 178.
22. H. Bloom, *Shakespeare: The Invention of the Human*, London, 1999, p. 517.
23. The real–unreal confusion appears to be part of Tarkovsky's general aesthetic strategy in *Sacrifice*. However, it has raised some puzzlement in critical texts that deal with the film. Johnson and Petrie, for instance, write: 'Unfortunately, the merging of the original and new story lines produces disharmony and confusion on the level of plot: an unexplained double sacrifice is created when Alexander both sleeps with the witch as encouraged by a new soothsayer, the postman Otto, and burns down his house and becomes mute, thus fulfilling his vow to God. This results in a frustrating absence of thematic and philosophical coherence that ultimately damages the film' (V. Johnson and G. Petrie, *The Films of Andrei Tarkovsky: A Visual Fugue*, Bloomington, IN, 1994, p. 172). However, at a later point the critics come to the conclusion that 'we have to believe and not believe simultaneously rather than attempt to place a logical structure on events which are ultimately, and perhaps deliberately, incompatible with one another and suit neither a "realistic" nor an "it was all – or mostly – a dream" explanation' (ibid., p. 178). Green, in his turn, proposes a straightforward differentiation between dream and reality (Green, *Andrei Tarkovsky*, p. 133). Multiple references to sleep, and more importantly a differentiating colour code, according to the critic, imply that the nuclear apocalypse is a dream: 'The entire central, nocturnal section of the film – from the time Alexander goes out into the garden to seek Little Man and finds Maria and the model

of the house, to the time he wakes on the couch in the morning – is cast in the form of a dream and is photographed in darkly lit sequences virtually devoid of colour. The everyday waking reality of beginning and end is painted in the pale, natural colours of a northern summer, framing the interior world of the dream. There is also a third level of photography: the black and white or sepia sequences of the visions, or the scenes from other times, past or future, inset into the coloured reality and into the sombre central section' (ibid., p. 134).

24. Kermode, *Sense of an Ending*, p. 84.
25. At one point in the film Otto collapses after a herding call enters the soundtrack. He lies down on the floor without moving for a few seconds and then gets up, claiming that an evil angel's wing pushed him. It is noteworthy that the character immediately checks to see if his pocket watch is still functioning, as if realizing that time will soon be out of joint.
26. S. Anglo, 'Evident Authority and Authoritative Evidence: *The Malleus Maleficarum*', in S. Anglo, ed., *The Damned Art: Essays in the Literature of Witchcraft*, London, 1977, p. 17.
27. Lars von Trier's *Antichrist* (2009), which is dedicated to Andrei Tarkovsky, also explores the phenomenon of witchcraft. Moreover, *Antichrist* emulates the structure of *Sacrifice*: it opens and ends with parable-like episodes accompanied by Handel's aria 'Lascia ch'io pianga'.
28. Tarkovskii, *Martirolog*, p. 453.
29. There are several indications in the script of the film that the dramatic events are products of Alexander's imagination. The nuclear war episode ends with Adelaide comforting the dreaming protagonist: 'That's it, all gone...Now...Now it'll pass...It's a bad dream, that's all...it'll pass now...That's it, all over' (Tarkovsky, *Collected Screenplays*, p. 545). Moreover, before seeing Otto climbing up to his room, Alexander is described as regarding 'his surroundings as though they are an extension of his dream' (ibid.), and when he sees Otto he is 'completely dazed by his dream' (ibid., p. 546).
30. M. Heidegger, 'The Origin of the Work of Art', in D. F. Krell, ed., *Basic Writings From* Being and Time *(1927) to* The Task of Thinking *(1964)*, London, 1993, p. 187.
31. Žižek, *Fright of Real Tears*, p. 107.
32. Ibid.
33. Žižek, 'The Thing from Inner Space', pp. 228–9.
34. J. Beasley-Murray, 'Whatever Happened to Neorealism? Bazin, Deleuze, and Tarkovsky's Long Take', *Iris*, no. 23 (1997), p. 48.

Postscript

1. K. Jaspers, *Nietzsche: An Introduction to the Understanding of His Philosophical Activity*, transl. C. Wallraff and F. Schmitz, Baltimore, MD, 1997, p. 226.
2. <http://aptsvet.livejournal.com/660360.html>, accessed 1 January 2011.

3. R. Taylor, ed. and trans., and I. Christie, ed., *The Film Factory: Russian and Soviet Cinema in Documents, 1896–1939*, London, 1988, p. 25.
4. Ibid.
5. Ibid.
6. Epstein, 'Magnification and Other Writings', p. 23.
7. Ibid.
8. A. Quinton, 'Spaces and Times', *Philosophy*, vol. 37, no. 140 (1962), p. 138.
9. Epstein, 'Magnification and Other Writings', p. 20.
10. Sontag, *On Photography*, p. 164.
11. Bazin, *What is Cinema? Volume 1*, p. 48.

FILMOGRAPHY AND CREDITS

The Killers (*Ubiitsy*), 1956, 19 minutes. Black and white
Production Company: VGIK (All-Union State Institute of Cinematography)
Directors: Marika Beiku, Aleksandr Gordon, Andrei Tarkovskii
Screenplay: Aleksandr Gordon, Andrei Tarkovskii, based on the story 'The Killers' by Ernest Hemingway
Cinematography: Aleksandr Rybin, Alfred Alvares
Cast: Iulii Fait (Nick Adams), Aleksandr Gordon (George), Iurii Dubrovin (first customer), Valentin Vinogradov (Al), Vadim Novikov (Max), Andrei Tarkovskii (second customer), Vasilii Shukshin (Ole Andreson)

There Will Be No Leave Today (*Segodnia uvol'neniia ne budet*), 1958, 47 minutes. Black and white
Production Company: The Training Studio of VGIK and the Central Television Studio
Producer: A. Kotoshev
Directors: Aleksandr Gordon, Andrei Tarkovskii, under the supervision of I. Zhigalko and E. Foss in the course of Mikhail Romm
Assistant Director: A. Kuptsova
Screenplay: Aleksandr Gordon, Inna Makhova, Andrei Tarkovskii
Cinematography: Lev Bunin, Ernst Iakovlev, under the supervision of K. Vents
Assistant to cameramen: V. Ponomarev
Art Director: Semen Peterson
Music: Iurii Matskevich
Sound: O. Polisonov
Military consultant: Lieutenant-Colonel I. I. Sklifus
Cast: Oleg Borisov (Captain Galich), Aleksei Alekseev (Colonel Gvelesiani), Petr Liubeshkin (Vershinin), Oleg Moshkantsev (Vishniakov), Vladimir Marenkov (Vasin), Igor' Kosukhin (Tsignadze), Leonid Kuravlev (Morozov), Stanislav Liubshin (Sadovnikov), A. Smirnov (man in a cowboy shirt), Aleksei Dobronravov (Dr. Kuz'min), Nina Golovina (Galich's wife)

Steamroller and Violin (*Katok i skripka*), 1961, 46 minutes. Colour (Sovcolour)
Production Company: Mosfil'm (Creative Unit for the Production of Children's films)
Producer: A. Karetin
Director: Andrei Tarkovskii
Assistant Director: O. Gerts
Screenplay: Andron Konchalovskii, Andrei Tarkovskii
Screenplay Editor: S. Bakhmet'eva
Cinematography: Vadim Iusov
Editor: Liubov' Butuzova
Art Director: Savet Agoian
Special effects cinematography: B. Pluzhnikov, Vasilii Sevost'ianov
Special effects design: Al'bert Rudachenko
Music: Viacheslav Ovchinnikov
Conductor: Emin Khachaturian
Sound: Vladimir Krachkovskii
Costumes: A. Martinson
Make-up: Anna Makashova
Cast: Igor' Fomchenko (Sasha), Vladimir Zamanskii (Sergei), Natal'ia Arkhangel'skaia (girl), Marina Adzhubei (mother)
Supporting cast: Iurii Brusser, Viacheslav Borisov, Aleksandr Vitoslavskii, Aleksandr Il'in, Nikolai Kozyrev, Gennadii Kliachkovskii, Igor' Korovikov, Evgenii Fedchenko, Tat'iana Prokhorova, Antonina Maksimova, Liudmila Semenova, G. Zhdanova, M. Figner

Ivan's Childhood/My Name is Ivan (*Ivanovo detstvo*), 1962, 95 minutes. Black and white
Production Company: Mosfil'm (Second Creative Unit 'Time')
Producer: Gleb Kuznetsov
Director: Andrei Tarkovskii
Assistant Director: Georgii Natanson
Screenplay: Mikhail Papava, Vladimir Bogomolov, based on the story 'Ivan' by Vladimir Bogomolov
Screenplay Editor: E. Smirnov
Cinematography: Vadim Iusov
Editor: Liudmila Feiginova
Art Director: Evgenii Cherniaev
Special effects cinematography: Vasilii Sevost'ianov
Special effects design: Sergei Mukhin
Music: Viacheslav Ovchinnikov
Conductor: Emin Khachaturian
Sound: Inna Zelentsova
Make-up: Liudmila Baskakova
Military adviser: Colonel G. Goncharov
Cast: Nikolai Burliaev (Ivan), Valentin Zubkov (Captain Kholin), Evgenii Zharikov (First Lieutenant Galtsev), Stepan Krylov (Corporal Katasonych), Nikolai Grin'ko (Lieutenant-Colonel Griaznov), Valentina

Maliavina (Masha), Irma Tarkovskaia (Ivan's mother), Dmitrii Miliutenko (old man)
Supporting cast: Andrei Konchalovskii (soldier with glasses), Ivan Savkin, Vladimir Marenkov, Vera Miturich

Andrei Rublev (*Andrei Rublev*), 1964–66 (released 1969), 175 minutes. Black and white and part colour (Sovcolour), CinemaScope. Original version: *The Passion According to Andrei* (*Strasti po Andreiu*), 205 minutes. Black and white and part colour (Sovcolour), CinemaScope
Production Company: Mosfil'm (Creative Unit of Writers and Cinema Workers)
Producer: Tamara Ogorodnikova
Director: Andrei Tarkovskii
Assistant Director: I. Petrov
Intern Director: Bagrat Oganesian
Assistants to the director: A. Macheret, M. Volovich, A. Nikolaev
Screenplay: Andrei Mikhalkov-Konchalovskii, Andrei Tarkovskii
Screenplay Editors: N. Beliaeva, L. Lazarev
Cinematography: Vadim Iusov
Cameramen: Vasilii Sevost'ianov, assisted by L. Andrianov, R. Ruvinov, P. Sudilin
Editors: Liudmila Feiginova, Tat'iana Egorycheva, Ol'ga Shevkunenko
Art Director: Evgenii Cherniaev, assisted by Ippolit Novoderezhkin and Sergei Voronkov
Special effects cinematography: Vasilii Sevost'ianov
Set design: F. Korablev, assisted by T. Isaeva, L. Pertsev, Pavel Safonov
Music: Viacheslav Ovchinnikov
Sound: Inna Zelentsova
Costumes: Lidiia Novi, Maiia Abar-Baranovskaia
Make-up: Vera Rudina, M. Aliautdinov, S. Barsukov
Advisers: V. Pashuto, S. Iamshchikov, M. Mertsalova
Cast: Anatolii Solonitsyn (Andrei Rublev), Ivan Lapikov (Kirill), Nikolai Grin'ko (Daniil Chernyi), Nikolai Sergeev (Feofan Grek), Nikolai Burliaev (Boriska), Iurii Nazarov (Grand Duke, Duke), Irma Raush (the fool), Iurii Nikulin (Patrikei), Rolan Bykov (jester), Nikolai Grabbe (Stepan), Mikhail Kononov (Foma), Stepan Krylov (head bell-founder), Bolot Beishenaliev (Mongol khan)
Supporting cast: B. Matysik (Petr), Anatolii Obukhov, Vladimir Titov, Nikolai Glazkov (Efim), K. Aleksandrov, S. Bardin, I. Bykov, G. Borisovskii, Vasilii Vasil'ev, Zinaida Vorkul', Aleksandr Titov, Vladimir Volkov, Irina Miroshnichenko (Mary Magdalene), Tamara Ogorodnikova (Mary, Mother of Christ), N. Radolitskaia, Nikolai Kutuzov (old mason), Dmitrii Orlovskii, Vladimir Gus'kov, Igor' Donskoi, I. Ryskulov, P. Makarov, G. Sachevko, Nelli Snegina (Marfa), G. Pokorskii, A. Umuraliev, Viacheslav Tsarev

Solaris (*Soliaris*), 1972, 169 minutes. Colour (Sovcolour) and black and white, CinemaScope
Production Company: Mosfil'm (Creative Unit of Writers and Cinema Workers)

Producer: Viacheslav Tarasov
Director: Andrei Tarkovskii
Assistant Director: Iurii Kushnerev
Assistants to the director: A. Ides, Larisa Tarkovskaia, Mariia Chugunova
Intern Director: N. Mann
Screenplay: Fridrikh Gorenshtein, Andrei Tarkovskii, based on the novel *Solaris* by Stanisław Lem
Screenplay Editors: N. Boiarova, L. Lazarev
Cinematography: Vadim Iusov
Cameramen: Evgenii Shvedov, assisted by Iurii Nevskii, V. Shmyga
Editor: Liudmila Feiginova
Art Director: Mikhail Romadin
Special effects cinematography: Vasilii Sevost'ianov
Special effects design: A. Klimenko
Music: Eduard Artem'ev, additional music by J. S. Bach
Sound: Semen Litvinov
Set design: S. Gavrilov, V. Prokof'ev
Lighting: E. Paramonov
Costumes: Nelli Fomina
Make-up: Vera Rudina
Stills photographer: Vadim Murashko
Advisers: Dr. Lupichev, I. Shklovskii
Cast: Natal'ia Bondarchuk (Hari), Donatas Banionis (Chris Kelvin), Jüri Järvet (Snaut), Vladislav Dvorzhetskii (Berton), Nikolai Grin'ko (father), Anatolii Solonitsyn (Sartorius)
Supporting cast: Ol'ga Barnet (mother), Vitalii Kerdimun, Ol'ga Kizilova (girl), Tat'iana Malykh, Aleksandr Misharin (chairman of debriefing), Bagrat Oganesian, Tamara Ogorodnikova (Anna), Sos Sarkisian (Gibarian), Iulian Semenov, V. Statsinskii, Valentina Sumenova, Georgii Teikh

Mirror (*Zerkalo*), 1974, 108 minutes. Colour (Sovcolour) and black and white
Production Company: Mosfil'm (Fourth Creative Unit)
Producer: Erik Vaisberg
Director: Andrei Tarkovskii
Assistant Director: Iurii Kushnerev
Assistants to the director: Larisa Tarkovskaia, V. Kharchenko, Mariia Chugunova
Screenplay: Aleksandr Misharin, Andrei Tarkovskii
Screenplay Editors: N. Boiarova, L. Lazarev
Poems: Arseni Tarkovskii
Cinematography: Georgii Rerberg, assisted by V. Ivanov
Cameramen: Aleksei Nikolaev, I. Shtan'ko
Editor: Liudmila Feiginova
Art Director: Nikolai Dvigubskii

Special effects cinematography: Iurii Potapov
Music: Eduard Artem'ev, additional music by J. S. Bach, Giovanni Batista Pergolesi, Henry Purcell
Sound: Semen Litvinov
Set construction: A. Merkulov
Lighting: V. Gusev
Costumes: Nelli Fomina
Make-up: Vera Rudina
Stills photographer: V. Murashko
Cast: Margarita Terekhova (Maria, Aleksei's mother, Natal'ia, Aleksei's wife), Ignat Danil'tsev (Aleksei/Ignat, age 12), Nikolai Grin'ko (colleague at the printing house), Alla Demidova (Liza), Iurii Nazarov (military instructor), Anatolii Solonitsyn (doctor), Innokentii Smoktunovskii (voice of Aleksei, the narrator), Larisa Tarkovskaia (doctor's wife), Mariia Tarkovskaia (Aleksei's mother as an old woman)
Supporting cast: Tamara Ogorodnikova (visitor), Oleg Iankovskii (Aleksei's father), Filip Iankovskii (Aleksei, age 5), Iurii Sventikov, Tamara Reshetnikova, Ernesto del Bosque, L. Correcher, Alejandro Guttiérez, Diego García, Teresa Pames, Teresa del Bosque, Tat'iana del Bosque

Stalker (*Stalker*), 1979, 155 minutes. Colour (Sovcolour and Eastmancolor) and black and white, CinemaScope
Production Company: Mosfil'm (Second Creative Unit)
Producer: Aleksandra Demidova
Director: Andrei Tarkovskii
Assistant Director: Larisa Tarkovskaia
Intern Director: Araik Agaronian
Assistants to the director: Mariia Chugunova, Evgenii Tsymbal
Screenplay: Arkadii Strugatskii, Boris Strugatskii, based on their novel *The Roadside Picnic*
Screenplay Editor: A. Stepanov
Poems: Fedor Tiutchev, Arseni Tarkovskii
Cinematography: Aleksandr Kniazhinskii
Cameramen: N. Fudim, S. Naugol'nykh
Assistants to the director of cinematography: G. Verkhovskii, S. Zaitsev
Editor: Liudmila Feiginova
Assistants to the editor: T. Alekseeva, V. Lobkova
Art Director: Andrei Tarkovskii
Artists: Rashit Safiullin, V. Fabrikov
Music: Eduard Artem'ev
Conductor: Emin Khachaturian
Music Editor: R. Lukina
Sound: Vladimir Sharun
Set construction: A. Merkulov
Lighting: Lev Kamzin, Tat'iana Maslennikova
Costumes: Nelli Fomina

Make-up: Vitalii L'vov
Administrative support: Tamara Aleksandrovskaia, Vera Vdovina, Vladimir Mosenkov
Cast: Alisa Freindlikh (Stalker's wife), Aleksandr Kaidanovskii (Stalker), Anatolii Solonitsyn (Writer), Nikolai Grin'ko (Professor)
Supporting cast: Natal'ia Abramova (Stalker's daughter), Faime Iurna, E. Kostin, R. Rendi

Time of Travel (*Tempo di Viaggio*), 1983, 62 minutes. Colour (Technicolor)
Production Company: Genius S.r.l./RAI 2, Fono Roma
Director: Andrei Tarkovskii
Screenplay: Tonino Guerra
Cinematography: Luciano Tovoli
Cameraman: Giancarlo Pancaldi
Editor: Franco Letti
Assistant Editor: Carlo D'Alessandro
Sound: Eugenio Rondani
Mixing: Romano Checcacci
Music selection: Andrei Tarkovskii
General Organization: Franco Terilli
Interpreter: Lora Jabloskina
Voice: Andrei Tarkovskii, Gino La Monica

Nostalghia, 1983, 120 minutes. Colour (Technicolor) and black and white
Production Company: Rete 2 TV RAI in association with Sovinfil'm (USSR) for Opera Film (Rome)
Executive Producer: Renzo Rossellini, Manolo Bolognini
Producer: Francesco Casati
Director: Andrei Tarkovskii
Assistants to the director: Norman Mozzato, Larisa Tarkovskaia
Screenplay: Andrei Tarkovskii, Tonino Guerra
Italian Editor: Cesare Noia
Cinematography: Giuseppe Lanci
Cameraman: Giuseppe De Biasi
Editor: Erminia Marani, Amedeo Salfa
Assistant Editor: Roberto Puglisi
Art Director: Andrea Crisanti
Special effects cinematography: Paolo Ricci
Music: Giuseppe Verdi, Richard Wagner, Ludwig van Beethoven, Claude Debussy
Music Editor: Gino Peguri
Sound: Remo Ugolinelli
Dub mixing: Danilo Moroni
Director of dubbing: Filippo Ottoni
Dubbing assistant: Ivana Fidele
Dubbing consultant: Denis Pekarev

Sound effects: Massimo Anzellotti, Luciano Anzellotti
Set design: Mauro Passi
Costumes: Lina Nerli Taviani, Annamode 68
Make-up: Giulio Mastrantonio
Hair: Iole Cecchini
Stills photographer: Bruno Bruni
Press attache: Raffaelle Striano
Dog trainer: Massimo Perla
RAI representative: Lorenzo Ostuni
Production Supervisor: Filippo Campus, Valentino Signoretti
Production Secretary: Eutizio di Salvarore
Editorial Secretary: Ilde Muscio
Production Administrator: Nestore Baratella
Cast: Oleg Iankovskii (Andrei Gorchakov), Erland Josephson (Domenico), Domiziana Giordano (Eugenia), Patrizia Terreno (Gorchakov's wife), Laura De Marchi (woman with a towel), Delia Boccardo (Domenico's wife), Milena Vukotić (town worker), Alberto Canepa (peasant)
Supporting cast: Raffaele Di Mario, Rate Furlan, Livio Galassi, Piero Vida, Elena Magoia
Voices: Lia Tanzi (Eugenia), Sergio Fiorentini (Domenico)

Sacrifice (*Offret: Sacrificatio*), 1986, 142 minutes. Colour (Eastmancolor)
Production Company: Swedish Film Institute (Stockholm) and Argos Films (Paris) in association with Film Four International (London). Josephson & Nykvist, Sveriges Television/SVT 2, Sandrew Film and Theater. With the participation of the French Ministry of Culture
Executive Producer: Anna-Lena Wibom (Swedish Film Institute)
Producer: Katinka Faragó (Faragó Film)
Director: Andrei Tarkovskii
Assistants to the director: Kerstin Eriksdotter, Michał Leszczyłowski
Screenplay: Andrei Tarkovskii
Scriptgirl: Anne von Sydow
Cinematography: Sven Nykvist
Cameramen: Lars Karlsson, Dan Myhrman
Editor: Andrei Tarkovskii, Michał Leszczyłowski
Consulting Editors: Henri Colpi, Nils Melander (FilmTeknik)
Art Director: Anna Asp
Assistant Art Director: Cecilia Iversen
Special effects cinematography: Lars Höglund, Lars Palmqvist (Svenska Stuntgruppen)
Music: J. S. Bach, Swedish and Japanese traditional music
Sound: Owe Svensson, Bo Persson, Lars Ulander, Christin Loman, Wille Peterson-Berger
Set design: Jan Andersson
Set construction: Harry Klava, Rolf Persson, Gunilla Bandolin, Teddy Holm, Bengt Svedberg, Percy Nilsson, Jan Eriksson, Martti Malkamaa, Leif Nilsson, Håkan Nilsson

Electrical department: Daniel Bergman, Ocki Hansson, Hans Wallin, Kent Högberg, Kjell Sundquist
Costumes: Inger Pehrsson
Costumes assistant: Carina Dalunde
Hair and make-up: Kjell Gustavsson, Florence Fouquier
Props: Kicki Ilander
Stills Photographer: Arne Carlsson
Production Manager: Göran Lindberg
Production Assistant: Agneta Jansson
Casting: Priscilla John, Claire Denis, Françoise Menidrey
Interpreters: Layla Alexander, Lars Erik Blomqvist, Håkan Lövgren
Technical manager: Kaj Larsen
Catering: Puck Jansson, Sophie Lundberg, Jan Linderström, Peter Schildt, Caterina Åhlander, Stig Björkman, Harald Stjerne
Drivers: Göran Andersson, Thure Ljunggren
Cast: Erland Josephson (Alexander), Susan Fleetwood (Adelaide), Allan Edwall (Otto), Guðrún Gísladóttir (Maria), Sven Wollter (Victor), Valérie Mairesse (Julia), Filippa Franzén (Marta), Tommy Kjellqvist (Little Man), Per Källman (ambulance man), Tommy Nordahl (ambulanceman)
Voices: Tintin Andersson, Helena Brodin, Birgit Carlstén, Jane Friedmann, Martin Lindström, Jan-Olof Strandberg

BIBLIOGRAPHY

I. Published works by Andrei Tarkovsky

Screenplays
'Andrei Rublev (Chast' I)', with A. Konchalovskii, *Iskusstvo kino*, 1964, no. 4, pp. 139–200.
'Andrei Rublev (Chast' II)', with A. Konchalovskii, *Iskusstvo kino*, 1964, no. 5, pp. 125–58.
Andrei Rublëv, translated by Kitty Hunter-Blair, London, Faber & Faber, 1991.
'Antarktida, dalekaia strana. Otryvok iz stsenariia', with A. Bezukhov and O. Osetinskii, *Moskovskii komsomolets*, 31 January and 2 February, 1960.
Collected Screenplays, translated by W. Powell and N. Synessios, London, Faber & Faber, 1999.
'Gofmaniana. Stsenarii', *Iskusstvo kino*, 1976, no. 8, pp. 167–89.
'Svetlyi veter. Po motivam povesti Aleksandra Beliaeva *Ariel*': Stsenarii', with Fridrikh Gorenshtein, *Kinostsenarii*, 1995, no. 5, pp. 44–74.
'Zerkalo', with A. Misharin, *Kinostsenarii*, 1988, no. 2, pp. 122–54.

Books
Andrei Tarkovskii: Arkhivy. Dokumenty. Vospominaniia, ed. P. D. Volkova, Moscow, Eksmo-Press, 2002.
Andrei Tarkovskii: Nachalo... i puti (vospominaniia, interv'iu, lektsii, stat'i), ed. M. Rostotskaia, Moscow, VGIK, 1994.
Instant Light: Tarkovsky Polaroids, ed. G. Chiaramonte and A. Tarkovsky, London, Thames & Hudson, 2006.
Martirolog: Dnevniki 1970–1986, Florence, Mezhdunarodnyi Institut imeni Andreia Tarkovskogo, 2008.
Sculpting in Time: Reflections on the Cinema, translated by K. Hunter-Blair, Austin, TX, University of Texas Press, 2005.
Time within Time: The Diaries 1970–1986, translated K. Hunter-Blair, London, Faber & Faber, 1994.

Uroki rezhissury, Moscow, Vserossiiskii institut perepodgotovki i povysheniia kvalifikatsii rabotnikov kinematografii, 1993.

Articles

'20 vek i khudozhnik', *Iskusstvo kino*, 1989, no. 4, pp. 88–106.
'Adres neizvesten', *Komsomol'skaia pravda*, 3 June 1965.
'Belyi den'', *Iskusstvo kino*, 1970, no. 6, pp. 109–14.
'Beseda o tsvete', *Kinovedcheskie zapiski*, no. 1 (1988), pp. 147–53.
'Between Two Worlds', *American Film*, vol. 9, no. 2 (1983), pp. 75–9.
'Dlia tselei lichnosti vysokikh', *Iskusstvo kino*, 1992, no. 4, p. 120.
'Dostoianie segodniashnego dnia', *Sovetskii ekran*, 1967, no. 8, p. 9
'Edinomyshlennik prezhde vsego', *Sovetskie khudozhniki teatra i kino*, Moscow, Sovetskii khudozhnik, 1977, pp. 181–2.
'Eto ochen' vazhno', *Literaturnaia gazeta*, 20 September 1962, p. 1.
'Eto pridet na ekran', *Literaturnaia gazeta*, 1 December 1962, p. 1.
'Federiko Fellini', *Iskusstvo kino*, 1980, no. 12, pp. 158–60.
'Gorenie', *Ekran-65: Sbornik*, 1966, Moscow, pp. 154–7.
'Gor'koe chuvstvo poteri [on Grigorii Kozintsev]', *Iskusstvo kino*, 1973, no. 10, pp. 158–9.
[Introduction to Tonino Guerra], *Inostrannaia literatura*, 1979, no. 7, pp. 188–9.
'Iskat' i dobivat'sia', *Sovetskii ekran*, 1962, no. 17, pp. 9, 20
'Istoricheskii fil'm', *Vecherniaia Moskva*, 10 June 1982.
Kogda fil'm okonchen: Govoriat rezhissery 'Mosfil'ma', Moscow, 1964, pp. 137–71.
'Mezhdu dvumia fil'mami', *Iskusstvo kino*, 1962, no. 11, pp. 82–4.
'M. I. Rommu 70 let', *Sovetskii ekran*, 1971, no. 2, p. 5.
'My delaem fil'my', *Kino* [Vilnius], 1981, no. 10, pp. 16–18.
'On vyrazil vremia, kak nikto [on Vladimir Vysotsky]', *V. Vysotskii: Vse ne tak*, Moscow, Vakhazar, 1991, p. 19.
'O kinoobraze', *Iskusstvo kino*, 1979, no. 3, pp. 80–93.
'Opyt na budushchee', *Voprosy literatury*, 1973, no. 1, p. 101.
'Pered novymi zadachami', ed. O. Surkova, *Iskusstvo kino*, 1977, no. 7, pp. 116–18.
'Po doroge k fil'mu *Soliaris*', *Sovetskii ekran*, 1971, no. 3, p. 6.
'Poiasneniia rezhissera k fil'my *Soliaris*', *Kinovedcheskie zapiski*, no. 14 (1992), pp. 48–53.
'Rezhisser i zritel': problema kontakta', ed. O. Surkova, *Molodoi kommunist*, 1974, no. 6, pp. 86–91.
'Skoro nachnutsia s"emki...Rasskaz o rabote nad fil'mom *Andrei Rublev*', *Moskovskii komsomolets*, 3 June 1965.
'Slovo ob Apokalipsise', *Iskusstvo kino*, 1989, no. 2, pp. 95–100.
'Spor o geroiakh', *Komsomol'skaia pravda*, 13 September 1962, p. 4.
'Tam nas zhdet neizvestnoe', *Trud*, 9 September 1971.
[Vsesoiuznaia pereklichka kinematografistov], *Iskusstvo kino*, 1971, no. 4, pp. 51.
'Zachem proshloe vstrechaetsia s budushchim', *Iskusstvo kino*, 1971, no. 11, pp. 96–101.

'Zapechatlennoe vremia', *Voprosy kinoiskusstva. Istoriko-teoreticheskii sbornik*, no. 10, Moscow, Izdatel'stvo akademii nauk, 1967, pp. 79–102.
'Zhguchii realizm', *Luis Buniuel': Sbornik*, Moscow, 1979, pp. 69–75.

Interviews

Abramov, N., 'Dialog s A. Tarkovskim o nauchnoi fantastike na ekrane', *Ekran. 1970–1971. Obozrenie kinogoda*, Moscow, Iskusstvo, 1971, pp. 162–5.
Andrei Tarkovsky: Interviews, ed. John Gianvito, Jackson, MS, University Press of Mississippi, 2006.
'Andrei Tarkovsky on the film *Roublev*', *Young Cinema & Theatre*, 1965, no. 8, pp. 16–23.
Gibu, N., '"Zhizn' rozhdaetsia iz disgarmonii…" Interv'iu 1967 goda', *Kinovedcheskie zapiski*, no. 50 (2001), pp. 219–30.
Bakhmann, G., '"O prirode nostal'gii" interv'iu s Gideonom Bakhmannom', *Iskusstvo kino*, 1989, no. 2, pp. 131–6.
Beliavsky, O., 'The Filming of *Andrei Rublyov*', *Soviet Film*, 1966, no. 5, pp. 18–21.
Herlinghaus, H., 'V besede s Germanom Kherlingkhausom', *Kinovedcheskie zapiski*, no. 14 (1992), pp. 34–48.
'Ia nikogda ne stremilsia byt' aktual'nym', *Forum*, 1985, no. 10, pp. 227–36.
Kublanovskii, Iu., 'Inspiratsiia vdokhnoveniia: Andrei Tarkovskii pered *Zhertvoprinosheniem*', *Nezavisimaia gazeta*, 29 December 1992, p. 7.
Lipkov, A., 'Strasti po Andreiu', *Literaturnoe obozrenie*, 1988, no. 9, pp. 74–80.
Loisha, V., 'Iskusstvo sozdaetsia narodom', *Kino* [Riga], 1979, no. 11, pp. 20–2.
Lopukhin, A., 'Nel'zia verit' v budushchee, esli ne verish' v sebia', *Moskovskie novosti*, 15 February 1987, p. 11.
Nikitin, N. 'Dlia menia kino – eto sposob dostich' kakoi-to istiny', *Sovetskaia Rossiia*, 3 April 1988, p. 4.
Noiger, L., and I. Illg, 'Vstat' na put' (beseda s Izhi Illgom i Leonardom Noigerom)', *Iskusstvo kino*, 1989, no. 2, pp. 109–30.
'Stremlius' k maksimal'noi pravdivosti', *Kinostsenarii*, 2001, no. 5, p. 124.
Verina, T., 'Tarkovskii o Tarkovskom: pochti semeinyi razgovor', *Kul'tura i zhizn'*, 1979, no. 10, p. 23.
Zorkaia, N. 'Vozvrashchenie v budushchee', *Sovetskii fil'm*, 1977, no. 4, pp. 210–21.

II. Selected Studies on Andrei Tarkovsky

Alexander-Garrett, L., *Andrei Tarkovskii: sobiratel' snov*, Moscow, AST, 2009.
Artem'ev, E., 'Kak poiut derev'ia (besedu vedet i kommentiruet Oleksii-Nestor Naumenko)', *Iskusstvo kino*, 2007, no. 4, pp. 9–15.
Batkin, L., 'Ne boias' svoego golosa', *Iskusstvo kino*, 1988, no. 11, pp. 77–101.
Beasley-Murray, J., 'Whatever Happened to Neorealism? Bazin, Deleuze, and Tarkovsky's Long Take', *Iris*, no. 23 (1997), p. 48.
Bird, R., *Andrei Rublëv*, London, BFI, 2004.
—— *Andrei Tarkovsky: Elements of Cinema*, London, Reaktion Books, 2008.

Boldyrev, N., *Zhertvoprinoshenie Andreia Tarkovskogo*, Moscow, Vagrius, 2004.

Bulgakova, O., 'Motivy protivostoianiia Zapada i Vostoka', *Kinovedcheskie zapiski*, no. 14 (1992), pp. 90–4.

Chion, M., 'La maison où il pleut: sur l'esthétique de Tarkovski', *Cahiers du cinéma*, no. 358 (1984), pp. 37–43.

Dalle Vacche, A., *Cinema and Painting: How Art is Used in Film*, London, Athlone, 1996.

De Baecque, A., *Andrei Tarkovski*, Paris, Cahiers du cinéma, 1989.

Deleuze, G., *Cinema 2: The Time-Image*, transl. H. Tomlinson and R. Galeta, London, Continuum, 2005.

Deltcheva, R., and E. Vlasov, 'Back to the House II: On the Chronotopic and Ideological Reinterpretation of Lem's *Solaris* in Tarkovsky's Film', *Russian Review*, vol. 56, no. 4 (1997), pp. 532–49.

Dempsey, A., 'Lost Harmony: Tarkovsky's *The Mirror* and *The Stalker*', *Film Quarterly*, vol. 35, no. 1 (1981), pp. 12–17.

Dunne, N., ed., *Tarkovsky*, London, Black Dog Publishing, 2008.

Efird, R., '*Andrei Rublev*: Transcendental Style and the Creative Vision', *Journal of Popular Film and Television*, vol. 35, no. 2 (2007), pp. 86–93.

—— 'Dreams, Mirrors and Subjective Filtration in *Ivan's Childhood*', *Studies in Russian and Soviet Cinema*, vol. 3, no. 3 (2009), pp. 289–308.

Ermash, F., et al. 'Glavnaia tema – sovremennost'', *Iskusstvo kino*, 1975, no. 3, pp. 1–18.

Evlampiev, I., *Khudozhestvennaia filosofiia Andreia Tarkovskogo*, St Petersburg, Aleteiia, 2001.

Filippov, S., 'Teoriia i praktika Andreia Tarkovskogo', *Kinovedcheskie zapiski*, no. 56 (2002), pp. 41–74.

Foster, D., 'Where Flowers Bloom but Have No Scent: The Cinematic Space of the Zone in Andrei Tarkovsky's *Stalker*', *Studies in Russian and Soviet Cinema*, vol. 4, no. 3 (2010), pp. 307–20.

Green, P., 'Apocalypse & *Sacrifice*', *Sight and Sound*, vol. 56, no. 2 (1987), pp. 111–18.

—— *Andrei Tarkovsky: The Winding Quest*, London, Macmillan, 1993.

Herrera de la Muela, J. J., 'Ispanskie tsitaty v tvorchestve Andreia Tarkovskogo', *Kinovedcheskie zapiski*, no. 78 (2006), pp. 261–72.

Ian'pin, L., 'Simvolika Tarkovskogo i daoizma', *Kinovedcheskie zapiski*, no. 9 (1991), pp. 154–65.

Johnson, V., and G. Petrie, *The Films of Andrei Tarkovsky: A Visual Fugue*, Bloomington, IN, Indiana University Press, 1994.

Jones, D., 'Tarkovsky i feminizm: Novyi vzgliad na *Nostalgiiu*', *Iskusstvo kino*, 2007, no. 4, pp. 24–8.

Kovács, B. A., and A. Szilágyi, *Les Mondes d'Andreï Tarkovski*, transl. V. Charaire, Lausanne, L'Age d'Homme, 1987.

—— '"Zona" i "Narushiteli"', *Kinovedcheskie zapiski*, no. 3 (1989), pp. 185–91.

Kozlov, L., *Izobrazhenie i obraz: Ocherki po istoricheskoi poetike sovetskogo kino*, Moscow, Iskusstvo, 1980.

Lahusen, T., 'Decay or Endurance? The Ruins of Socialism', *Slavic Review*, vol. 65, no. 4 (2006), pp. 736–46.
Lawton, A., 'Art and Religion in the Films of Andrei Tarkovsky', in W. C. Brumfield and M. M. Velimirovic, eds, *Christianity and the Arts in Russia*, Cambridge, Cambridge University Press, 1991, pp. 151–64.
Le Fanu, M., *The Cinema of Andrei Tarkovsky*, London, BFI, 1987.
Loughlin, G., 'The Long Take: Messianic Time in Andrei Tarkovsky's *Nostalghia*', *Journal for Cultural Research*, vol. 13, no. 3 (2009), pp. 365–79.
Lövgren, H., 'Leonardo da Vinchi i *Zhertvoprinoshenie*: O roli "Pokloneniia volhvov" v poslednem fil'me Andreia Tarkovskogo', *Iskusstvo kino*, 1992, no. 6, pp. 55–60.
Marker, C., 'Sem' pechatei', *Kinovedcheskie zapiski*, no. 57 (2002), pp. 281–6.
McCormick, M., *Model of a House: An Essay on Andrei Tarkovsky's* The Sacrifice, London, Lulu Enterprises, 2006.
Mikheeva, Iu., 'Molchanie. Pauza. Tishina. Svet. (Apofatika zvuka v *Zerkale* Andreia Tarkovskogo)', *Kinovedcheskie zapiski*, no. 57 (2002), pp. 286–91.
Nelson, T., 'Sculpting the End of Time: The Anamorphosis of History and Memory in Andrei Tarkovsky's *Mirror* (1975)', *Cinémas*, vol. 13, no. 3 (2003), pp. 119–47.
Nesterova, O., 'Khristianskaia simvolika v *Andree Rubleve*', *Kinovedcheskie zapiski*, no. 14 (1992), pp. 86–9.
Odde, T., 'Time Sickness in Andrey Tarkovsky's *The Sacrifice*', *Canadian Journal of Film Studies*, vol. 18, no. 2 (2009), pp. 66–86.
Pallasmaa, J., 'Space and Image in Andrei Tarkovsky's *Nostalgia*: Notes on a Phenomenology of Architecture', in A. Pérez-Gómez and S. Parcell, eds, *Chora 1: Intervals in the Philosophy of Architecture*, Montreal, McGill-Queen's University Press, 1994, pp. 143–66.
Petrić, V., 'Tarkovsky's Dream Imagery', *Film Quarterly*, vol. 43, no. 2 (1989–90), pp. 28–34.
Petrovskii, M., 'Andrei Tarkovskii i Fedor Tiutchev', *Kinovedcheskie zapiski*, no. 9 (1991), pp. 169–82.
Pomerants, G. S., 'V poiskakh utrachennogo kruga', *Kinovedcheskie zapiski*, no. 14 (1992), pp. 65–9.
Purcell, M., 'Tarkovsky's Film *Solaris* (1972): A Freudian Slip?', *Extrapolation*, vol. 19, no. 2 (1978), pp. 126–31.
Raush, I., ed., 'Andrei Tarkovskii: Odin god zhizni', *Kinostsenarii*, 1991, no. 4, pp. 169–78.
Rosenbaum, J., *Movies as Politics*, Berkeley, CA, University of California Press, 1997.
Salvestroni, S., 'The Science-Fiction Films of Andrei Tarkovsky', *Science-Fiction Studies*, vol. 14, no. 3 (1987), pp. 294–306.
—— *Fil'my Andreia Tarkovskogo i russkaia dukhovnaia kul'tura*, Moscow, Bibleisko-bogoslovskii institut Sv. Apostola Andreia, 2007.
Salynskii, D., *Kinogermenevtika Tarkovskogo*, Moscow, Kvadriga, 2009.
Samardzija, Z., '1 + 1 = 1: Impossible Translations in Andrey Tarkovsky's *Nostalghia*', *Literature/Film Quarterly*, vol. 32, no. 4 (2004), pp. 300–4.

Sandler, A., ed., *Mir i fil'my Andreia Tarkovskogo: Razmyshleniia, issledovaniia, vospominaniia, pis'ma*, Moscow, Iskusstvo, 1991.

Sandler, S., 'On Grief and Reason, On Poetry and Film: Elena Shvarts, Joseph Brodsky, Andrei Tarkovsky', *Russian Review*, no. 66 (2007), pp. 647–70.

Sartre, J. P., 'Letter on the Critique of *Ivan's Childhood*', transl. J. Berenbeim, in N. Dunne, ed., *Tarkovsky*, London, Black Dog Publishing, 2008, pp. 34–45.

Semeniuk, V., 'Za "Zerkalom"', *Kinovedcheskie zapiski*, no. 9 (1991), pp. 183–6.

Shumakov, S., 'V poiskakh utrachennogo slova', *Kinovedcheskie zapiski*, no. 3 (1989), pp. 163–75.

Skakov, N., 'The (Im)Possible Translation of *Nostalgia*', *Studies in Russian and Soviet Cinema*, vol. 3, no. 3 (2009), pp. 309–33.

Skramtaeva, Iu., 'Postsovetskoe myshlenie i avangard', *Iskusstvo kino*, 1995, no. 9, pp. 114–21.

Slevin, T., 'Existence, Ethics and Death in Andrei Tarkovsky's Cinema: The Cultural Philosophy of *Solaris*', *Film International*, vol. 8, no. 2 (2010), pp. 49–62.

Smith, A., 'Andrei Tarkovsky as Reader of Arsenii Tarkovsky's Poetry in the Film *Mirror*', *Russian Studies in Literature*, vol. 40, no. 3 (2004), pp. 46–63.

Solov'ev, V., 'Dvoinoe tiagotenie vremeni', *Iskusstvo kino*, 1989, no. 10, pp. 40–9.

Solzhenitsyn, A., 'Fil'm o Rubleve', in *Publitsistika. V trekh tomakh. Tom 3. Stat'i, pis'ma, interv'iu, predisloviia*, Yaroslavl, Verkhniaia Volga, 1997, pp. 157–67.

Strugatskii, A., 'Kakim ia ego znal', *Ogonek*, 1987, no. 29, pp. 7–8

Strugatskii, A., and B. Strugatskii, 'Ved'ma: stsenarii', *Iskusstvo kino*, 2008, no. 2, pp. 129–46.

Strugatsky, B., 'Working for Tarkovsky', transl. E. Simon, *Science Fiction Studies*, vol. 31, no. 3 (2004), *Soviet Science Fiction: The Thaw and After*, p. 419.

Surkova, O., 'Avtobiograficheskie motivy v tvorchestve Andreia Tarkovskogo', *Kinovedcheskie zapiski*, no. 9 (1991), pp. 187–93.

—— *Kniga sopostavlenii: Tarkovsky – 79*, Moscow, Vsesoiuznoe tvorchesko-proizvodstvennoe ob"edinenie Kinotsentr, 1991.

—— *S Tarkovskim i o Tarkovskom*, Moscow, Raduga, 2005.

—— *Tarkovsky i ia: Dnevnik pionerki*, Moscow, Zebra E, 2005.

Synessios, N., *Mirror*, London, I.B.Tauris, 2001.

Tarkovskaia, M., *Oskolki zerkala*, Moscow, Vagrius, 2006.

Thomson, C., 'It's All About Snow: Limning the Post-Human Body in *Солярис/Solaris* (Tarkovsky, 1972) and *It's All about Love* (Vinterberg, 2003)', *New Cinemas: Journal of Contemporary Film*, vol. 5, no. 1 (2007), pp. 3–21.

Truppin, A., 'And Then There Was Sound: The Films of Andrei Tarkovsky', in R. Altman, ed., *Sound Theory/Sound Practice*, New York, Routledge, 1992, pp. 234–48.

—— *Tarkovsky: Cinema as Poetry*, ed. and transl. N. Ward, London, Faber & Faber, 1989.
Turovskaia, M., *7 s ½ ili fil'my Andreia Tarkovskogo*, Moscow, Iskusstvo, 1991.
Urban, A., 'V chelovecheskom kosmose', *Iskusstvo kino*, 1973, no. 5, pp. 46–59.
Yezzi, D., 'Helicon's Filmmaker', *Parnassus: Poetry in Review*, vol. 22, nos 1 & 2 (1997), pp. 184–200.
Zamiatin, D., 'Neuverennost' bytiia: Obrazy doma i dorogi v fil'me Andreia Tarkovskogo Zerkalo', *Kinovedcheskie zapiski*, no. 82 (2007), pp. 14–22.
Žižek, S., 'The Thing from Inner Space: On Tarkovsky', *Angelaki: Journal of Theoretical Humanities*, vol. 4, no. 3 (1999), pp. 221–31.
—— *The Fright of Real Tears: Krzysztof Kieślowski Between Theory and Post-Theory*, London, BFI, 2001.

III. General Bibliography

Alpatov, M., *Andrei Rublev: Okolo 1370–1430*, Moscow, Izobrazitel'noe iskusstvo, 1972.
Anglo, S., ed., *The Damned Art: Essays in the Literature of Witchcraft*, London, Routledge & Kegan Paul, 1977.
Antonova, C., and M. Kemp, '"Reverse Perspective": Historical Fallacies and an Alternative View', in M. Emmer, ed., *Visual Mind II*, Cambridge, MA, MIT Press, 2005, pp. 399–431.
Auerbach, E., *Dante: Poet of the Secular World*, transl. R. Manheim, Chicago, IL, University of Chicago Press, 1961.
Aumont, J., A. Bergala, M. Marie and M. Vernet, *Aesthetics of Film*, transl. and revised by R. Neupert, Austin, TX, University of Texas Press, 1992.
Bachelard, G., *The Poetics of Space*, transl. E. Gilson, Boston, MA, Beacon, 1969.
—— *Water and Dreams: An Essay on the Imagination of Matter*, translated by E. R. Farrell, Dallas, TX, Dallas Institute Publications, 1983.
Bakhtin, M., *The Dialogic Imagination*, transl. C. Emerson and M. Holquist, Austin, TX, University of Texas Press, 1981.
Balázs, B., *Béla Balázs: Early Film Theory. Visible Man and The Spirit of Film*, transl. R. Livingstone, New York, Berghahn, 2010.
Barthes, R., *Camera Lucida: Reflections on Photography*, transl. R. Howard, New York, Hill & Wang, 1981.
Barton, J., and J. Muddiman, eds, *The Oxford Bible Commentary*, Oxford, Oxford University Press, 2001.
Baudrillard, J., *Simulacra and Simulation*, transl. S. F. Glaser, Ann Arbor, MI, University of Michigan Press, 1994.
Bazin, A., *What is Cinema? Volume I*, transl. H. Gray, Berkeley, CA, University of California Press, 2005.
Benjamin, W., *Selected Writings, Volume 1: 1913–1926*, ed. M. Bullock and M. Jennings, Cambridge, MA, Harvard University Press, 1996.
—— *Selected Writings, Volume 4: 1938–1940*, transl. E. Jephcott, Cambridge, MA, Harvard University Press, 2003.

Bergson, H., *Creative Evolution*, transl. A. Mitchell, New York, Modern Library, 1944.
—— *Key Writings*, transl. K. A. Pearson and J. Mullarkey, London, Continuum, 2002.
—— *Matter and Memory*, transl. N. M. Paul and W. S. Palmer, Mineola, NY, Dover, 2004.
Bloom, H., *Shakespeare: The Invention of the Human*, London, Fourth Estate, 1999.
Bradley, H. F., *Appearance and Reality: A Metaphysical Essay*, 7th impression, London, Clarendon, 1920.
Brodsky, J., *Less Than One: Selected Essays*, New York, FSG, 1986.
—— *On Grief and Reason: Essays*, New York, FSG, 1995.
Bogomolov, V., *The Third Flare: Three War Stories*, Moscow, Foreign Languages Publishing House, 1963.
Borges, J.-L., *Labyrinths: Selected Stories and Other Writings*, New York, New Directions, 2007.
Castaneda, C., *Journey to Ixtlan: The Lessons of Don Juan*, Harmondsworth, Penguin, 1974.
—— *The Fire from Within*, London, Touchstone, 1998.
Cervantes, M. de, *Don Quixote*, transl. J. Ormsby, New York, Norton, 1981.
Dante Alighieri, *Inferno*, transl. C. Singleton, Princeton, NJ, Princeton University Press, 1970.
—— *Paradiso*, transl. C. Singleton, Princeton, NJ, Princeton University Press, 1977.
De Man, P., *The Resistance to Theory*, Minneapolis, MN, University of Minnesota Press, 1986.
Deleuze, G., *Bergsonism*, transl. H. Tomlinson and B. Habberjam, New York, Zone, 1991.
—— *Cinema 1: The Movement-Image*, transl. H. Tomlinson and B. Habberjam, London, Continuum, 2005.
—— *The Fold: Leibniz and the Baroque*, transl. T. Conley, London, Continuum, 2006.
Demina, N., *'Troitsa' Andreiia Rubleva*, Moscow, Iskusstvo, 1963.
Derrida, J., 'Des Tours de Babel', transl. J. Graham, in J. Graham, ed., *Difference in Translation*, Ithaca, NY, Cornell University Press, 1985, pp. 165–207.
—— *The Gift of Death*, transl. D. Wills, Chicago, IL, University of Chicago Press, 1995.
—— 'What Is a "Relevant" Translation?', transl. L. Venuti, in L. Venuti, ed., *The Translation Studies Reader*, New York, 2004, pp. 423–46.
Descartes, R., *The Philosophical Writings of Descartes, Volume II*, Cambridge, Cambridge University Press, 1984.
Dhanens, E., *Van Eyck: The Ghent Altarpiece*, London, Allen Lane, 1973.
Doane, M. A., 'The Voice in the Cinema: The Articulation of Body and Space', *Yale French Studies*, no. 60 (1980), pp. 33–50.
—— *The Emergence of Cinematic Time: Modernity, Contingency, the Archive*, Cambridge, MA, Harvard University Press, 2002.
Eisenstein, S., *S. M. Eisenstein: Selected Works, Volume 1: Writings, 1922–34*, ed. and transl. R. Taylor, London, BFI, 1988.

Epstein, J., 'Magnification and Other Writings', transl. S. Liebman, *October*, vol. 3 (1977), pp. 9–25.

Florensky, P., *Iconostasis*, transl. D. Sheehan and O. Andrejev, New York, St Vladimir's Seminary Press, 2000.

—— *Beyond Vision: Essays on the Perception of Art*, transl. W. Salmond, London, Reaktion, 2002.

Foucault, M., 'Of Other Spaces', transl. J. Miskowiec, *Diacritics*, vol. 16, no. 1 (1986), pp. 22–7.

Freud, S., *The Pelican Freud Library, Volume 14: Art and Literature*, transl. J. Strachey, ed. A. Dickson, Harmondsworth, Penguin, 1985.

Hegel, G. W. F., *Aesthetics: Lectures on Fine Art, Volume I*, transl. T. M. Knox, Oxford, Clarendon, 1975.

Heidegger, M., *Basic Writings From Being and Time (1927) to The Task of Thinking (1964)*, ed. D. F. Krell, London, Routledge, 1993.

Jakobson, R., *Selected Writings II: Word and Language*, The Hague, Mouton, 1971.

Jameson, F., *The Geopolitical Aesthetic: Cinema and Space in the World System*, London, BFI, 1992.

Jaspers, K., *Nietzsche: An Introduction to the Understanding of His Philosophical Activity*, transl. C. Wallraff and F. Schmitz, Baltimore, MD, Johns Hopkins University Press, 1997.

Johnson, B., 'Taking Fidelity Philosophically', *Difference in Translation*, ed. J. Graham, Ithaca, NY, Cornell University Press, 1985, pp. 142–8.

Kamuf, P., 'A Post Card from San Galgano', *Assemblage*, no. 20, *Violence, Space* (1993), pp. 46–7.

Kemp, M., *Leonardo da Vinci: The Marvellous Works of Nature and Man*, Oxford, Oxford University Press, 2006.

Kermode, F., *The Sense of an Ending: Studies in the Theory of Fiction*, London, Oxford University Press, 1967.

Kohn, L., and M. LaFargue, eds, *Lao-tzu and the Tao-te-ching*, Albany, NY, State University of New York Press, 1998.

Kovacs, J., and C. Rowland, *Revelation: The Apocalypse of Jesus Christ*, Oxford, Blackwell, 2004.

Lacan, J., *Écrits: A Selection*, transl. A. Sheridan, London, Routledge, 1977.

Lazarev, V. N., *Andrei Rublev*, Moscow, Sovetskii khudozhnik, 1960.

—— *Andrei Rublev i ego shkola*, Moscow, Iskusstvo, 1966.

Laozi, *The Classic of the Way and Virtue: A New Translation of the Tao-te Ching of Laozi as Interpreted by Wang Bi*, transl. R. J. Lynn, New York, Columbia University Press, 1999.

Lawrence, D. H., *Apocalypse and the Writings on Revelation*, Cambridge, Cambridge University Press, 1980.

Lejeune, P., *On Autobiography*, transl. K. Leary, Minneapolis, MN, University of Minnesota Press, 1989.

Lem, S., *Solaris*, transl. J. Kilmartin and S. Cox, London, Faber & Faber, 1970.

—— 'The Profession of Science Fiction: XV: Answers to a Questionnaire', transl. M. and D. Jakubowski, *Foundation: The Review of Science Fiction*, no. 15 (1979), pp. 41–50.

Lévi-Strauss, C., *The Savage Mind*, Chicago, IL, University of Chicago Press, 1966.
Likhachev, D., *Razvitie russkoi literatury X-XVII vekov: Epokhi i stili*, Leningrad, Nauka, 1973.
Lindsay, K., and B. Huppé, 'Meaning and Method in Brueghel's Painting', *Journal of Aesthetics and Art Criticism*, vol. 14, no. 3 (1956), pp. 376–86.
Mandelstam, O., *The Noise of Time: Selected Prose*, transl. C. Brown, Evanston, IL, Northwestern University Press, 2002.
—— *The Complete Critical Prose*, transl. J. G. Harris and C. Link, Dana Point, CA, Vintage, 1979.
Mets, K. (C. Metz), 'Zerkala v kino', *Kinovedcheskie zapiski*, no. 13 (1992), pp. 26–30.
Metz, C., 'Photography and Fetish', *October*, vol. 34 (1985), pp. 81–90.
Montale, E., *Satura: 1962–1970*, transl. W. Arrowsmith, New York, Norton, 1998.
Naficy, H., *An Accented Cinema: Exilic and Diasporic Filmmaking*, Princeton, NJ, Princeton University Press, 2001.
Nietzsche, F., *Thus Spoke Zarathustra*, transl. R. J. Hollingdale, London, Penguin, 2003.
Ouspensky, L., and V. Lossky, *The Meaning of Icons*, ed. U. Graf-Verlag, Olten, 1952.
Pamuk, O., *Istanbul: Memories and the City*, transl. M. Freely, London, Faber & Faber, 2005.
Pasolini, P. P., 'Observations on the Long Take', transl. N. MacAfee and C. Owens, *October*, vol. 13 (1980), pp. 3–6.
Proust, M., *In Search of Lost Time, Volume I: Swann's Way*, transl. S. Moncrieff and T. Kilmartin, New York, Modern Library, 2003.
Quine, W. V. O., 'Meaning and Translation', in R. Brower, ed., *On Translation*, New York, Oxford University Press, 1966, pp. 148–72.
Quinton, A., 'Spaces and Times', *Philosophy*, vol. 37, no. 140 (1962), pp. 130–47.
Rank, O., *The Double: A Psychoanalytic Study*, transl. and ed. H. Tucker, Chapel Hill, NC, University of North Carolina Press, 1971.
Renza, L., 'The Veto of the Imagination: A Theory of Autobiography', *New Literary History*, vol. 9, no. 1 (1977), pp. 1–26.
Rohmer, E., *The Taste for Beauty*, transl. C. Volk, Cambridge, Cambridge University Press, 1989.
Seneca, L. A., *Epistulae Morales, Volume I*, transl. R. Gummere, London, William Heinemann, 1917.
Shakespeare, W., *Macbeth*, ed. A. R. Braunmuller, Cambridge, Cambridge University Press, 1997.
—— *The Norton Shakespeare*, ed. S. Greenblatt, New York, Norton, 1997.
Sheringham, M., *French Autobiography: Devices and Desires: Rousseau to Perec*, Oxford, Clarendon Press, 1993.
Sontag, S., *On Photography*, New York, Picador, 1977.
—— *Against Interpretation*, London, Vintage, 1994.

Stam, R., *Reflexivity in Film and Literature: From Don Quixote to Jean-Luc Godard*, New York, Columbia University Press, 1992.
Steiner, A., 'St Jerome and the First Terzina of the *Divine Comedy*', *Modern Language Notes*, vol. 52, no. 4 (1937), pp. 259–60.
Strugatskii, A., and B. Strugatskii, *Zona*, New York, Adventa, 1983.
Tarkovskii, Ar., *Poems/Stikhi*, transl. P. Norman, London, Poets' & Painters' Press, 1998.
Taylor, R., ed. and transl., and I. Christie, ed., *The Film Factory: Russian and Soviet Cinema in Documents 1896–1939*, London, Routledge, 1988.
Todorov, T., *The Fantastic: A Structural Approach to a Literary Genre*, transl. R. Howard, Ithaca, NY, Cornell University Press, 1973.
Tolstoy, L., *The Death of Ivan Ilyich and Other Stories*, transl. R. Pevear and L. Volokhonsky, New York, Vintage, 2009.
Wachtel, M., *The Development of Russian Verse: Meter and its Meanings*, Cambridge, Cambridge University Press, 2006.
Williams, D. C., 'The Myth of Passage', *Journal of Philosophy*, vol. 48, no. 15 (1951), pp. 457–72.
Uspenskii, B., *Semiotika iskusstva*, Moscow, Iazyki russkoi kul'tury, 1995.
Zhegin, L. F., *Iazyk zhivopisnogo proizvedeniia (Uslovnost' drevnego iskusstva)*, Moscow, Iskusstvo, 1970.
Zubov, V. P., *Leonardo da Vinci*, transl. D. Kraus, Cambridge, MA, Harvard University Press, 1962.

INDEX

Abalov, Eduard, 15
Anselm of Havelberg, 152
Aristotle, 9
Artemiev, Eduard, 84, 142, 144
Auerbach, Erich, 136

Bach, Johann Sebastian, 84, 101, 193, 214, 245, 247
Bachelard, Gaston, 25, 39, 66, 102, 112, 114, 203
Bakhtin, Mikhail, 9, 40, 41, 78, 79
Balázs, Béla, 7
Barthes, Roland, 36
Baudrillard, Jean, 98
Bazin, André, 3, 8, 221, 223
Beckett, Samuel, 164, 166
Bely, Andrei, 103
Benjamin, Walter, 7, 171, 172, 175, 188, 189, 233, 234
Bergman, Ingmar, 100
Bergson, Henri-Louis, 10
Bible
  Ecclesiastes, 47, 53, 199
  First Corinthians, 47, 56–61
  Genesis, 174
  Isaiah, 47, 199
  John, 194, 199–202, 213, 215
  Luke, 147, 153–7
  Matthew, 47
  Revelation, 134, 141, 142, 147–56, 159, 166, 195, 199, 232, 237
Bloom, Harold, 204
Bogomolov, Vladimir, 15, 16, 75, 242
Borges, Jorge Luis, 5, 6, 159, 223
Bradley, Francis Herbert, 12

Brodsky, Joseph, 12, 133, 235
Bruegel, Pieter (the Elder), 48, 49, 85–8, 94, 101, 126

Carpaccio, Vittore, 48
Carroll, Lewis, 103
Castaneda, Carlos, 155, 232
Cervantes, Miguel de, 87–92, 134, 159
Chaadaev, Peter, 120
Chkalov, Valeri, 119
Chukhrai, Grigori, 107

Dante, 101, 134–9, 173
Deleuze, Gilles
  any-space-whatever, 11, 27, 28
  crystal-image, 4, 10, 105, 107, 111
  movement-image, 4, 10, 230
  time-image, 4, 10, 13, 132, 230
Della Francesca, Piero, 168
De Man, Paul, 233, 234
Derrida, Jacques, 153, 175, 186, 187, 188, 220, 234
Descartes, René, 11, 12, 224
Doane, Mary Ann, 68, 108
Doré, Gustave, 88
Dostoevsky, Fyodor, 142
Dürer, Albrecht, 30, 41

Eisenstein, Sergei, 3, 29, 222
Epstein, Jean, 12, 13, 220

Fellini, Federico, 100, 250
Florensky, Pavel, 17, 63, 64, 69
Foucault, Michel, 5, 39, 104
Freud, Sigmund, 17, 89, 235

Gorky, Maxim, 220
Guerra, Tonino, 168, 200, 235, 246, 250

Hegel, Georg Wilhelm Friedrich, 132
Heidegger, Martin, 86, 212, 229
Heraclitus, 1, 5, 12, 25, 50, 124
Hesse, Hermann, 102
Hoffmann, Ernst Theodor Amadeus, 234, 235
Hölderlin, Friedrich, 229

Jakobson, Roman, 171, 172, 234
Jameson, Fredric, 143
Jaspers, Karl, 218
Johnson, Barbara, 190

Kermode, Frank, 132, 205
Konchalovsky, Andron (Andrei), 42, 242, 243, 249
Kubrick, Stanley, 83

Lacan, Jacques, 91, 109, 229, 235
Lambert, Francis, 152
Laozi, 146, 147, 166, 231
Lawrence, David Herbert, 149
Lejeune, Philippe, 133
Lem, Stanisław, 75–81, 90, 96
Leonardo da Vinci, 101, 119, 193, 196–9, 206, 210, 215, 230
Lévi-Strauss, Claude, 203
Lumière, Auguste Marie Louis Nicolas and Louis Jean, 220
Luther, Martin, 151

McCall, Anthony, 223
McMullen, Ken, 220
Mandelstam, Osip, 1, 136
Marker, Chris, 69
Metz, Christian, 11, 103
Misharin, Alexander, 244, 249
Montaigne, Michel de, 1, 39
Montale, Eugenio, 17, 133

Nietzsche, Friedrich, 194, 218, 237

Pamuk, Orhan, 233
Pasolini, Pier Paolo, 189–90
Pergolesi, Giovanni Battista, 101, 119, 245
Plato, 11, 221
Proust, Marcel, 102, 109, 120
Purcell, Henry, 101, 245
Pushkin, Alexander, 103, 120, 121, 173

Quine, Willard Van Orman, 176, 189
Quinton, Anthony, 221

Rank, Otto, 235
Ravel, Joseph-Maurice, 161
Rembrandt, Harmenszoon van Rijn, 97, 149
Resnais, Alain, 100
Rohmer, Éric, 6
Rousseau, Jean-Jacques, 120

Sartre, Jean-Paul, 17, 19, 224
Schopenhauer, Arthur, 1, 19
Seneca, 237
Shakespeare, William, 5, 104, 113, 121, 156, 159, 202–5, 238
Sontag, Susan, 35, 83, 221
Stam, Robert, 11
Strugatsky, Boris and Arkadi, 140, 141, 200, 231, 232, 245

Tarkovsky, Andrei
  colour, 2, 6, 14, 69–73, 84, 93, 103, 113–15, 128, 130, 144, 147, 151, 162, 202, 207, 209, 220, 238, 239
  documentary chronicle, 3, 34, 35, 40, 100–2, 107, 118–26, 159, 230
  family, 100, 101, 108–18, 122, 126, 159, 168, 178, 215, 228, 229, 234
  films:
    Andrei Rublev, 7, 28, 42–75, 86, 199, 217, 225–7, 243
    Ivan's Childhood, 2, 11, 15–42, 44, 74, 75, 143, 186, 207, 215, 217, 224, 225, 242, 243
    The Killers, 224, 241
    Mirror, 7, 21, 93, 99–140, 143, 157, 159, 167, 217, 218, 228–31, 244, 245
    Nostalghia, 8, 21, 85, 142, 167–92, 231, 233–7, 246, 247
    Sacrifice, 8, 11, 21, 113, 142, 193–217, 231, 236–9, 247, 248
    Solaris, 7, 70, 71, 73–99, 126, 134, 143, 146, 210, 227, 228, 243, 244
    Stalker, 7, 134, 140–66, 195, 199, 209, 217, 218, 231–3, 245, 246
    Steamroller and Violin, 224, 242
    There Will Be No Leave Today, 224, 241
    Time of Travel, 224, 235, 246

Tarkovsky, Andrei *(cont.)*
  levitation, 16, 19, 40, 42–4, 49–51, 53, 77, 86–8, 119, 128, 183, 206, 226
  long take, 2, 3, 6–8, 24, 49, 103, 140, 141, 144, 149, 151, 152, 154–6, 164, 176, 177, 183, 184, 189–90, 193, 194, 198, 209–11, 215–19, 223
  miniature, 68, 111, 143, 144, 178, 203–5, 207, 231
  mirror reflection, 22, 24, 29, 74, 84, 85, 91, 93, 100–9, 111, 113–15, 118, 119, 126, 128, 139, 144, 156–9, 177, 179, 180, 189, 195, 200, 206, 207, 209, 224, 228, 229, 232–5
  montage, 3, 4, 13, 21, 29, 45, 103, 141, 190, 217, 222
  negative (photography), 31–6
  ruins, 22, 25–31, 35, 36, 40, 44, 63, 85, 96, 97, 140, 144, 146, 147, 161, 185–90, 197, 206, 212, 213, 235
  sculpting in time, 2–5, 8, 13, 14, 142, 223
  shot/reverse-shot, 36, 112, 128, 155, 156, 173, 174
  soundtrack, 13, 14, 16, 21–9, 32, 41, 50, 53, 62, 67, 71, 82, 84, 86. 94, 95, 101, 108, 113, 114, 108–19, 122–4, 129, 142, 143, 146, 147, 151, 152, 161, 174, 177, 178, 183, 195, 197, 206–13, 230, 234, 239
Tarkovsky, Arseni, 39, 85, 101, 108–19, 122–5, 128–30, 134, 137, 139, 159, 160, 172, 180–4, 190, 229, 244, 245
Tiutchev, Fedor, 162–4, 245
Todorov, Tzvetan, 93
Tolstoy, Lev, 173, 237
Trier, Lars von, 239
Tsvetkov, Alexei, 218

Uspensky, Boris, 69

Van Eyck, Jan, 152, 157, 233

Zeno, 9, 10
Žižek, Slavoj, 54, 81, 94, 126, 146, 213, 222, 236, 239, 255

www.ingramcontent.com/pod-product-compliance
Lightning Source LLC
Chambersburg PA
CBHW050344230426
43663CB00010B/1980